THROUGH A LENS DARKLY

HOW THE NEWS MEDIA
PERCEIVE AND PORTRAY EVANGELICALS

THROUGH A LENS DARKLY

HOW THE NEWS MEDIA
PERCEIVE AND PORTRAY EVANGELICALS

DAVID M. HASKELL

CLEMENTS ACADEMIC

TORONTO

THROUGH A LENS DARKLY
Copyright © 2009 David M. Haskell

Clements Academic is the scholarly imprint of
CLEMENTS PUBLISHING
6021 Yonge Street, Box 213
Toronto, Ontario M2M 3W2 Canada
www.clementspublishing.com

Author royalties from the sale of this book are donated to the charity Samaritan's Purse Canada.

Typeset by Make Design Company
Peterborough, Ontario
<www.makedesigncompany.com>

Cover: "Bruce Clemenger of the Evangelical Fellowship of Canada speaks to a scrum in the Supreme Court of Canada, October 2004" Image used by permission of the Evangelical Fellowship of Canada

Library and Archives Canada Cataloguing in Publication Data

Haskell, David M., 1968-
Through a lens darkly : how the news media perceive and portray evangelicals / David M. Haskell.

Includes bibliographical references.
ISBN 978-1-894667-92-0

1. Evangelicalism—Press coverage—Canada. 2. Mass media—Religious aspects—Christianity. 3. Religion and the press—Canada. 4. Mass media—Objectivity—Canada. 5. Journalism—Objectivity—Canada.
I. Title.

BV652.97.C3H38 2008   280'.40971   C2008-906164-0

To Jim and Lois Pepper
and the other leaders on the "Summer Team"
who gave me an example to follow

Acknowledgements

This book combines several studies I have conducted into a unified and thematic whole. The analysis of evangelicals in Canadian television news detailed in Chapters 5, 6, and 8 was published in a condensed form in the Spring 2007 issue of the *Journal of Communication and Religion* under the title, "Evangelical Christians in Canadian national television news, 1994–2004: A frame analysis." The study of non-evangelicals' reactions to news reports about evangelicals, which is highlighted in Chapter 9, is found in its entirety in the Fall 2007 issue of the *Journal of Media and Religion* under the title, "News media influence on nonevangelicals' perceptions of evangelical Christians: A case study." The study of how national newspapers covered evangelicals engaged in Canada's same-sex marriage debate, which is summarized in the Afterword of this book, was originally written for and presented at the "Sacred and Secular in a Global Canada" Conference held May 9 through 12, 2008 at the University of Western Ontario's Huron College. That study is also slated to appear as a chapter in a forthcoming book titled *Religion Unbound: Essays in Contemporary Religious Identity and Rights in Canada* edited by Dr. William Acres of Huron College. I gratefully acknowledge the editors of these publications for their granting of copyright permission on these respective works.

I am indebted to several friends for guiding and supporting me in this research. When I first undertook the task of researching evangelicals in the media, Dr. Augie Fleras of the University of Waterloo graciously became my personal guide (and sometimes translator) to the world of frame theory and social constructionism. I am grateful to Drs. Johannes Froneman and Lynnette Fourie of North-West University who advised me during my doctoral thesis and taught me to look deeper. I would like to thank the staff at Wilfrid Laurier University Press for organizing and overseeing the peer-review process for this book. A special word of thanks goes to Rob Clements of Clements Academic publishing who gets things done with speed, courtesy and integrity. Finally, I am most grateful to my wife, Maggie, who endures a man who "spends a lot of time in his head."

Contents

CHAPTER 4: NEWS AND NEWS FRAMING

CHAPTER 5: METHODOLOGY

CHAPTER 6: NEWS REPORTS ABOUT EVANGELICALS: THE GOOD, THE BAD, AND THE NEUTRAL

AFTERWORD: IMPORTANT FINDINGS ABOUT NEWSPAPERS

LIST OF FIGURES

LIST OF TABLES

Preface

Near the end of this book, I am going to suggest that journalists, in the interests of fair and balanced news coverage, disclose the personal beliefs or allegiances that might have coloured their reporting. It seems only fair that I should take my own advice and begin this book by doing the same.

I am a practicing Christian (the old joke is that I'm practicing because, as yet, I haven't gotten it right). I readily embrace most of the traditional beliefs and creeds of the early Church; however, many of my evangelical friends say I'm too liberal for their comfort. For example, while I think that sexual orientation is irrelevant to a person's Christianity, a great number of my evangelical brothers and sisters believe I am wrong. Interestingly, we all back up our opinions with verses from the same Bible. So it goes. We have amicably agreed to disagree. And while I do not always agree with evangelicals, I think most are very good people who do much to make this world better. Certainly, I think evangelicals should be free to publicly express their beliefs without interference or coercion.

I am also a former TV reporter who still makes occasional forays back into the industry. Many of my close friends are working journalists. I think that most people who take jobs in the news media are driven by a strong desire to protect the weak in society—there is no nobler aspiration. However, sometimes I think journalists (and I am speaking from experience) become opinionated and paternalistic. Unfortunately, the thoughts "I will be fair and balanced" and "I know what is right and I'm damn well going to do something about it" cannot mutually exist in the mind of a journalist on assignment. I think journalists should be free to promote the issues and causes that are near-and-dear to them—just not in their news coverage. Personal perspectives should be relegated to taverns, dinner tables and clearly designated opinion columns.

Having clarified my alliances and personal perspectives, I leave it to the reader to judge whether, over the course of this book, my treatment of evangelicals and members of news media is equitable.

This book is meant to inform. It is also meant to teach. The difference is subtle but it is real. To my mind, a work that informs adds to existing knowledge held by the reader—it assumes certain ideas and principles need no explanation. It throws the reader into the deep end of the pool. On the other hand, a book (or a person for that matter) that teaches institutes a step-by-step process whereby single, smaller ideas build upon one and other until a well-defined theoretical construct is formed. It shows the reader how to swim before requiring the deep-water plunge.

As a teaching vehicle, my objective is to make this work accessible to all readers. I have assumed my audience has little prior knowledge of the subjects that are covered. So, in the first half of this book evangelicals and evangelicalism are described at length. A synopsis of what previous researchers have discovered about the media's coverage of religion is presented. The role of the news media in a democracy is discussed as is the influence of media messages. Specific theories of mass communications are explored. Even social science research methodologies are given some explanation. All of these ideas lay the foundation for fully understanding the research findings, conclusions and recommendations presented in the book's second half.

A "teaching text" has a distinct advantage over texts meant simply to inform, in that it significantly broadens readers' knowledge in a variety of areas while simultaneously providing them with a depth of understanding related to one particular focus (in this case, the relationship between the Canadian news media and evangelicals). To a certain extent a "teaching text" affords readers a "fall back position" or a "plan B": even if they find the main thrust of book to be uninteresting (which I hope won't be the case) they finish with a certain satisfaction knowing that "something" has been learned.

Of course, some readers may be coming to this text with extensive knowledge of many of the peripheral subjects that are covered. Accordingly, they may choose to skip whole chapters and get right to the "meat" of this current research. Happily, I think such readers will find that the layout and style of this book allows them to easily begin *in medias res.*

Finally, a quick word about my use of gender-neutral language in this text. Where grammatically tasteful, my examples that involve humans use the plural forms *their, they* and *them* to avoid designating an abstract party as male or female (when discussing "readers" in the paragraphs above I followed this technique). However, when the plural forms compromise the grammatical integrity or flow of the writing I refer to my abstract human exemplars as either he or she. To avoid linguistically biasing the text in favour of males or females, these gender-specific descriptors are used in equal measure throughout the book. The only exception to this practice is in Chapter 7 where the journalists' responses to the survey questions are presented. There, I use the admittedly awkward he/she, him/her gender constructions to avoid any possibility of breaching participants' anonymity.

CHAPTER 1

Introduction

For now we see through a glass, darkly; but then face to face:
now I know in part; but then shall I know even as
also I am known. —1 Corinthians 13:12 (KJV)

THE PROBLEM

Canadian evangelicals have an image problem. Many non-evangelicals see them as "Fast-talking, money-hustling television preachers. Pushy, simplistic proselytizers. Dogmatic, narrow-minded know-it-alls. Straight-laced, thin-lipped killjoys."[1] Most recently, the attributes of "ignorant, right-wing, and—perhaps worst of all—American" have been added to the character sketch.[2] A recent survey quantified this negative perception others have of evangelicals. When asked about their feelings toward certain people in society, 31% of Canadians said they would be uneasy meeting someone who was an evangelical.[3, 4]

Why would almost one third of the population want to keep evangelicals at arms length? A number of factors seem to be at work.

Evangelicals themselves have long realized that their faith and lifestyle sets them apart from others. As Protestants who believe in the authority of scripture, they use the lessons and edicts of the Bible to gauge what is good and right for their own life and for society. Accordingly, their personal morals and social values tend to be more conservative and absolute than other Canadians (in fact, the moniker "conservative Protestants" is synonymous with the term evangelicals). Thus, on several issues, Canada's evangelicals find themselves at odds with majority opinion. Whereas evangelicals tend to be opposed to homosexual lifestyle and gay marriage, abortion, sexual promiscuity, pornography, gambling, and the use of illegal drugs, a majority of Canadians are untroubled by, or support, these issues.[5]

However, evangelicals do not think the negative perception others have of them results solely from ideological differences. They point out that other religious minorities with equally divergent value systems are viewed more favourably by the population-at-large than they are. For example, just 6.5% of Canadians say they would feel uncomfortable living next to a Muslim.[6] It would seem that federal sponsorship of multiculturalism since the 1960s and the enshrining of minority rights in the Canadian Charter in 1982 have led to a national sense of accommodation toward other minority faiths, but not for the 12% of the population who are evangelicals.

Many evangelicals will admit that the abhorrent behaviour and pronouncements of some prominent leaders within their faith community—particularly, elite members of the Christian right movement in the US—contributes to their negative public image. They know that when someone like televangelist Pat Robertson calls for the assassination of the president of Venezuela, or when former leader of the National Association of Evangelicals, Ted Haggard, buys drugs and has an affair with a gay prostitute, the reputation of evangelicals *everywhere* suffers. The Bible suggests "the sins of the father will be revisited upon the son".[7] In similar fashion, the sins of deviant evangelical leaders get transposed onto the entire faith community.

But Canadian evangelicals think their image problem goes beyond "a few bad apples spoiling the whole barrel." They argue that the dalliances of one or two of their elite southern cousins should not be enough to sully their collective reputation, especially since, as a community,

Canadian evangelicals volunteer more hours and give more money to charity than any other group in the country.[8] They reason that the pervasive altruism and philanthropy of the rank and file faithful—readily apparent to any who would care to look—should provide some sort of inoculation against guilt by association and character defamation.

So, when placing blame for their negative image, after looking inward, most evangelicals point a finger outside their own camp. If the balance of public opinion remains weighted against them, they believe it is because the news media are putting their "thumb on the scale."

In short, evangelicals in Canada think the media are biased against them. Nearly 70% feel their faith group is "rarely" or "never" fairly portrayed in the media.[9] When detailing how the media have trespassed against them, evangelicals cite sins of omission and commission. They say that journalists working for their country's major news organizations most often ignore issues and events that are evangelical-related. However, on the odd occasion when coverage is given, the ideas and opinions of the featured evangelicals are taken out of context or "spun" in a negative way. Even the most innocuous issue or event, they argue, is reported in such a way so as to appear deviant or sinister in some respect.

If asked to give evidence of their misrepresentation by the media, Canadian evangelicals trod out an established canon of "jaundiced journalism" which they believe proves, at least anecdotally, news men and women are out to get them.

VICE-PRESIDENTIAL CANDIDATE SARAH PALIN

It may seem somewhat ironic, but one of the latest examples that Canada's evangelicals present as proof that their nation's news media "have it in for them" involves a born-again *American* politician. Relatively unknown as the governor of the State of Alaska and former mayor of the City of Wasilla, at the end of August, 2008 Sarah Palin vaulted to instant celebrity when she was named Republican Vice-Presidential

Candidate by Presidential running-mate John McCain. In the first few days following her nomination, the American media generated a mountain of reports that tried to explain who she was, where she came from and what she stood for. The Canadian media followed suit. On both sides of the border, journalists devoted a great deal of ink and air time to the fact that Palin was a staunch evangelical Christian. However, it was the news content of one outlet, public broadcaster CBC television, that raised the ire of evangelicals in Canada. They argued that coverage by the CBC's flagship news program *The National*—in particular, reporting done by Washington correspondent Neil Macdonald—deliberately distorted facts in order to depict Palin's evangelical faith as crazy and dangerous.

While a few of Macdonald's stories were perceived to contain anti-evangelical innuendo, the piece he filed September 3rd, 2008, the night of Palin's acceptance speech at the Republican National Convention, was deemed to be outright defamation. At issue, as far as Canadian evangelicals were concerned, were two assertions Macdonald made in the report.

First, he suggested that Palin, inspired by her evangelical beliefs, used her powers as mayor of Wasilla to ban books she deemed morally offensive from her city's library. Specifically, he told his audience: ". . . Palin, an Evangelical Christian, once tried to ban books from a public library in Alaska and fired the librarian who resisted."[10]

It seems Macdonald relied on Internet "sources" for his information: the book-banning allegation was pervasively promoted on numerous websites—particularly those with ties to the Democratic Party. However, when the matter was actually investigated by American news outlets it was found to be without merit. For example, *USA Today* reported "that no books at the [Wasilla] library have ever been banned" and "that a list circulating on the Internet of books allegedly banned in Wasilla was actually a copy of books banned at one time or another in the United States."[11] Furthermore, regarding Palin's firing of the "librarian who resisted," the newspaper determined that Palin did "request that the city's department heads, including Emmons [the librarian], reapply for their positions" after she assumed the office of mayor (this was standard practice in that municipality), but the censorship issue was not raised and "the librarian kept her job until she resigned three years later."[12]

Of Canada's national television news programs, CBC's *The National* was the only one to include this unsubstantiated rumour in a report. To Canadian evangelicals, Macdonald's assertion that Palin would use her political clout to force her evangelical views on others revealed either a lack of research or a deliberate attempt to misrepresent her character. In light of other factors outlined below, the latter explanation appeared most likely.

Days before Macdonald's story, other international news organizations explored Palin's political record and discovered that when it came to executing her duties of office, her personal religious beliefs never trumped the will of the people. For example, on August 31th, 2008 the *London Times* praised Palin's open-mindedness saying, "[personally] she opposes same-sex marriage, but one of her first acts in office [as governor] was to veto a bill that would have blocked health benefits for gay lovers of public employees."[13] On various Web sites dedicated to conservative viewpoints, Canadian evangelicals questioned why Macdonald would highlight an unsubstantiated rumour that painted Palin as an intolerant theocrat, but not mention a verifiable example that showed her willingness to govern pluralistically.[14]

After claiming Palin's faith drove her to ban books, Macdonald ran a snippet from a speech she had delivered to a local church earlier that year. The interview clip was meant to convince viewers that, as an evangelical, Palin was dangerously jingoistic. It showed her telling those in the pews that she believed America's war against Iraq was endorsed by God Himself. The problem was Macdonald had edited off the beginning of the clip and in doing so had changed the meaning completely. A posting on YouTube where Palin's complete speech could be viewed allowed Canadian evangelicals to compare Macdonald's version to the real McCoy. The news of the discrepancy travelled quickly by word-of-mouth and individual email. Those who were enraged were only outnumbered by those who wondered why Macdonald would do such a thing.

The portion of interview that Macdonald included in his report began *in medias res* with Palin saying, "Our leaders, our national leaders are sending them out on a task that is from God."[15] However, what Palin had actually said was this:

> Pray for our military, he's [her oldest son] going to be deployed in September to Iraq. Pray for our military men and women who are striving to do what is right. Also for this country [pray] that our leaders, our national leaders are sending them out on a task that is from God. [16]

Someone watching or reading the full quote in its true context could plainly see that Palin was not raising a war cry, she was raising a question. A question steeped in humility with no hint of jingoism; she asked: "Is this war a task from God?" It is a question to which she does not have an answer and advises praying for divine guidance in the hope of finding the right path.

Personally, I find it somewhat puzzling that Macdonald resorted to the use of fictions and fabrications to pad his account of Sarah Palin's negative attributes. While governor, Palin had been party to her share of *verifiable* indiscretions (though none were as radical as banning books or saying "God wants the US fighting a war in Iraq").[17] That Macdonald felt compelled to "independently produce" additional examples of her shortcomings might suggest he has a personal perspective he is keen to promote.[18]

MAYOR DIANNE HASKETT

The canon of jaundiced journalism includes the news coverage that former mayor of London, Ontario, Dianne Haskett received during the late 1990s. In 1995, Haskett refused to declare a Gay Pride Day in her city. Though she never stated it outright, it was widely held that her evangelical faith influenced her decision. A local homosexual association laid a complaint against her with the Ontario Human Rights Commission, and in 1997 the Commission found her, and by extension the City of London, guilty of discrimination. It ordered the city to pay $10,000 to the homosexual association and to proclaim a Gay Pride Day if requested in the future. City officials were also required to meet with the homosexual association to promote good relations.

Haskett refused to comply with the decision of the Human Rights Commission. Instead, she placed a paid ad in the local paper, the *London Free Press*, stating:

> I will not bow down to the ruling of the Human Rights Commission and I am willing to bear any consequences of that. I will not offer any proclamations, either presently, or in the future. In fact, let me make it clear that I intend to cease from making any proclamations of any kind hereafter. As to the fine that the Human Rights Commission has imposed of $10,000 against me and the City, I want to contribute my share. I am going to be commencing, immediately, a three-week unpaid leave of absence and ask that the monies saved by the City be designated for this purpose.[19]

The timing of Haskett's departure from public life could not have been more dramatic. Her self-imposed exile took place exactly three weeks prior to the municipal election—a time when she should have been campaigning.

For the most part, coverage of the battle between Haskett and the homosexual community painted the former as villain and the latter as victim. Local and national columnists attacked Haskett for failing to perform what they saw as her "duty" as mayor. Of her actions, a columnist for the *Toronto Star* wrote:

> Dianne Haskett (the individual) is entitled to hold negative views about homosexuality and act upon them within the confines of the law. Mayor Dianne Haskett, however, has competing moral obligations. As an elected public official, Haskett must serve and represent everyone in her community equally - despite her opinions.[20]

The columnists from the hometown paper were far more caustic. Writing the day after Haskett's announcement, *Free Press* writer Morris Della Costa mocked her religious convictions, calling her a mystic in the tradition of "Merlin the Magician"—a man who ran away to the "Crystal Cave" to find himself.[21] Later, in the same column, he suggested Haskett was a religious extremist for staying true to her beliefs saying, "It is the act of a true zealot who allows her religious beliefs to rule above all."[22] In a follow-up column a few days later, Della Costa accused Haskett of being in league with the most extreme and intolerant factions of society. He supported his claim using two pieces of evidence. He noted that after his earlier column, he had received threatening calls from "gay bashers"—it was implied these anonymous callers were representative of Haskett's supporters. He also noted that Haskett's decision to stand up to the Human Rights Commission was praised on a Web site run by neo-Nazis.[23]

Free Press City Hall columnist, Chip Martin, went further than ridiculing Haskett's religious convictions. In a column titled, "Mayor acted oddly before last election" he managed to connect Haskett's faith with images of mental instability.[24] Borrowing quotes from a three-year-old interview with Haskett's bitter ex-business partner, Martin implied that the mayor was prone to cracking under pressure to the point of "hearing voices." To reinforce his theory, Martin pointed out that prior to her first foray into local politics Haskett had taken time to be alone. Upon returning to her day-to-day routines, she allegedly confided in her former associate that she had "received a calling from God to run for municipal office."[25] It was Martin's strong suggestion that anyone who feels divinely led toward a particular career choice is suffering from psychotic delusions. One supposes that Haskett took some comfort knowing that her psychosis was shared by a host of noble individuals. David Livingston, Martin Luther King Jr., Mother Teresa of Calcutta, and other world-changing personalities all claimed to have "received a calling from God."

Despite the negative comments she received from media personalities—and despite taking a leave of absence rather than waging a campaign for re-election—Haskett won the 1997 municipal contest by a greater margin than when she first came to office. Ironically, the media's treatment may have shorn up Haskett's support. It is quite likely that constituents who supported other candidates in the past saw Haskett as the embattled underdog and threw her their "sympathy vote." That may have been the case, but following the election the mayor was in no mood to thank the media. At her victory party, she expressed frustration over her treatment by the press saying, "The unrelenting assault by the media must stop and the mean-spirited attacks coming from many sectors of the community must cease."[26]

EVANGELICALS IN THE FEDERAL CONSERVATIVE PARTY

As demonstrated by the Palin Case, there are occasions when a single news report is so offensive to evangelical sensibilities that it alone becomes part of their canon of prejudicial proof texts. Such an article appeared on the front page of Canada's national newspaper, *The Globe and Mail*, under the headline: "Christian activists capturing Tory races: Some in party worry new riding nominees will reinforce notion of 'hidden agenda'."[27] The story, which ran in the spring of 2005, was about eight evangelical Christians who had won the federal Conservative nomination in their respective ridings. These successful nominees later ran in the national election in January, 2006.

The report was seen by evangelicals and their supporters as "A front page smear on Christians."[28] They outlined numerous problems with the piece. First, they took umbrage with the headline itself, pointing out that the evangelical candidates had won their nominations by democratic means—they had not "captured" them. By describing what was a fair-and-square victory as a "capture," the Globe was insinuating that the win was achieved by force or trickery. The Globe reporter was seen as trying to push the trickery angle later in the story when she suggested that the evangelical candidates exploited the naivety of immigrants to win their nominations. She wrote, they "persuaded parishioners, particularly new Canadians, to join the party and vote for recommended candidates."[29] Critics pointed out that her criticism was unfounded as it is standard practice for political candidates to petition their ethnic, cultural, or religious community for support. Furthermore, they noted that in the past, non-evangelical candidates from other parties had been commended for being "inclusive" when they encouraged newcomers to join in the processes of democracy.[30]

Some Christian writers noted that the piece was peppered with negatively suggestive terms like "hardline" religious right; "hidden agenda"; "single-issue" people; and "religious zealots" all of which implied the evangelical nominees were a threat to Canadian culture and society.[31] Context was also said to be missing: the religious background of candidates in Canada's 300 other federal ridings was never highlighted. What generated the most anger, though, was what many saw as the paper's double-standard when it came to evangelicals. One pro-evangelical commentator summed up the feeling saying: "Do you think The *Globe and Mail* would use headlines like 'Indo-Canadian activists capturing Liberal races,' or 'Muslim Activists forcing Liberals to shift position on Israel?'"[32]

STOCKWELL DAY AND THE 2000 FEDERAL ELECTION

Of all the examples of alleged media bias that have made their way into evangelicals' canon of jaundiced journalism, one single case gets cited more often then others. Most evangelicals feel that coverage of the 2000 federal election, featuring politician Stockwell Day, showed once-and-for-all that media folk just don't like their kind.

At the beginning of July 2000, Day, an outspoken evangelical, became the new leader of the Canadian Alliance Party—at the time, Canada's official opposition to the governing Liberal Party. In September, a win in a by-election gave Day a seat in the House of Commons where he assumed the position of Leader of the Opposition. One month later, Prime Minister Jean Chretien announced a federal election to be held at the end of November.

The federal election campaign of 2000 became more about religion than politics. Day's conviction not to perform public duties on a Sunday, his assertion that "Jesus is Lord of the whole universe," and especially his belief in creationism garnered an overwhelming amount of media attention.[33] Just after winning the leadership of his party, Canada's most established news magazine, *Macleans*, featured Day on its cover; under his picture was the caption: "How Scary?" The associated article focused on the effect Day's religious beliefs might have on his political policies.[34] Columns and editorials in The *Globe and Mail* seized on the same angle and accused Day of being "un-Canadian" because he admitted his faith influenced all the decisions he made in his life, including his political decisions.[35] The headline for one *Globe* article about Day declared: "God has no place on the ballot: Canada lacks the U.S. taste for—and protections from—the influence of religion in politics."[36]

In the middle of the election campaign, the country's national public broadcaster, CBC television, aired a documentary on the national news titled: *The Fundamental Day*.[37] Many felt the documentary purposely attacked Day's evangelical Christian beliefs in the hopes of proving him unfit to hold office.[38] In a press conference the day after the airing of the documentary, Day confirmed his beliefs, but said they were no more pertinent to his policy platform than a Roman Catholic's belief in the Virgin Mary or a Hindu's belief in Krishna's descent from heaven.[39] However, the media seemed to disagree; their rhetoric against Day's beliefs continued to escalate. Aghast at the media's hostility toward Day, a multi-faith consortium composed of Jewish, Muslim, and Christian leaders called on journalists to show religious tolerance and to recognize that "every faith contains fundamental statements of belief that espouse the truth"[40]. After his party's defeat, Day accused the media of an anti-evangelical bias, pointing out that other politicians were not subject to "the third degree" with regard to their religious beliefs.[41]

Interestingly, in the eyes of some politically-minded evangelicals a certain amount of good came out of the Stockwell Day imbroglio. His case became an abject lesson of what could go wrong if a devout politician was too forthcoming about his religious beliefs. With Day's experience in mind, new, self-imposed rules of order came into force for Canadian political contenders who also happened to be evangelicals. The unwritten policy is a twist on the adage, "If you can't say anything nice, don't say anything at all." As applied by today's evangelical politicians, the wisdom goes: "The news media won't say anything nice about your faith so, when it comes to your faith, don't say anything at all." This modus operandi is exemplified in the "understated" evangelical beliefs of Conservative Prime Minister Stephen Harper.

PROVING OR NEGATING EVANGELICALS' CLAIM OF BIAS

In charging the news media with bias, Day and most other evangelicals are not unique. Many other minority groups have made the same accusation.[42] In fact, research has shown that members of an ideologically cohesive group are predisposed to thinking that the media's coverage of their community is antagonistic, slanted, or outright wrong.[43] It seems that there is a grain of truth to the old newsroom saying "anyone who knows something about anything is likely to be unhappy with the way it is covered in the news media."[44]

However, what gives credibility to Canadian evangelicals' accusation of prejudice is the fact that other, non-evangelical Canadians, have noticed a bias as well. A survey conducted by Ipsos Reid showed that almost half of non-evangelicals (48%) agree that there is a general bias in Canadian society against those with evangelical viewpoints.[45] While participants were not specifically asked if they felt that *the news media* were biased against evangelicals, convention suggests that the survey respondents would have strongly associated society's view with that of the media's. To a certain extent, the media are the mirror in which a society is reflected.

For evangelicals to secure such a high rate of sympathetic agreement from those outside their community is significant. By way of comparison, just 28% of the general population agree that the media have a negative bias toward ethnic minorities.[46]

Of course, perceptions, even when shared by almost half the population and reinforced by a few colourful anecdotes of media mistreatment, do not equal reality. Until now, no attempt has been made to systematically and empirically test Canadian evangelicals' charge of chronic ill treatment by the media. Therefore, one of the goals of this book is to validate or negate the evangelicals' claim through a comprehensive and purposeful examination of news coverage. But this research also digs deeper. In addition to determining *how* the news media report on evangelicals, this book's second key objective is to determine *why* the news media report on evangelicals the way they do.

I discuss my methodology at length in Chapter 5, so at this point I will simply provide a brief overview of what my research entailed. First, I examined the portrayals of evangelicals and evangelicalism in the national, nightly news reports of Canada's largest television networks—CTV, Global and CBC—for the period from January 1994 to January 2005. To determine whether evangelicals were portrayed positively, neutrally, or negatively over this 11-year span, the language, context, and content of the reports was analyzed using the principles of frame theory (the details of frame theory are discussed in Chapter 4).

Second, I surveyed national television news personnel regarding their opinions on religion in general and evangelicals in particular. Full-time employees of CTV, Global, and CBC national news programs responsible for creating, revising, or overseeing *the written text* of news reports (that is, reporters, producers, writers) were eligible to participate. The survey was composed of probing, open-ended questions.

Third, I compared the results from the analysis of the news reports to the results of the survey, to determine if there are linkages between how national television journalists feel about evangelicals and how they portray evangelicals in the stories they produce.

In Canada, there has been very little research on the subject of religion and the news media and therefore, this book (and, for that matter, any forthcoming research) makes an essential contribution. When religion has been the focus of academic study in the past, Canadian researchers have tended to lump all faith groups together in order to explore religion coverage as a single variable.[47] By studying the media's interaction with one faith group—evangelicals—my hope is to gain a more accurate assessment of that particular relationship and to understand its potential effects.

However, for you the reader to fully understand the results (Chapters 6 and 7), discussion points (Chapters 8 and 9) and the conclusions (Chapter 10) of this research, certain background information must be presented and key concepts and terms must be explained. To that end, the next four chapters of this book lay a theoretical foundation. Chapter 2 introduces the reader to Canadian evangelicals and the social landscape in which they are situated. Similarly, Chapter 3 focuses on the news industry, its product and people, with a specific emphasis on what has been previously determined about the intersection of news, religion and evangelicals. Chapter 4 briefly outlines the ideas and concepts associated with news media framing and frame theory. Chapter 5, as stated previously, outlines the methodologies I used for this research.

CHAPTER 2

Evangelicals in Canada

Admittedly, numbers and statistics cannot convey the "spirit" of group. Even descriptions of beliefs and behaviours do not do justice to a group's ethos. Truly, if one wants to get a feeling for who evangelicals are and what they are all about one must "see them in action" in their churches, at their concerts or conferences, or in their mission work (that is, their volunteering and charitable pursuits). With that disclaimer in mind, I present the very sketchiest of character sketches for evangelicals in Canada.

EVANGELICALS BY THE NUMBERS

About three and half million Canadians, or 12% of the population, are evangelical Christians.[1] They are fairly evenly dispersed across Canada, with the exception of the province of Quebec where they are estimated to make up less than 1% of the population. Quebec's large Roman Catholic population (83%) and small Protestant population (4.7%), in addition to its people's significant embrace of secularism, may account for the province's lack of evangelicals.[2]

As with most faith groups, women outnumber the men. There are about five evangelical women for every four evangelical men. These men and women are more likely to be married than non-evangelical Canadians (64% married compared to 46%) and less likely to be divorced (16% divorced compared to 20%). A high number are seniors. Thirty-four percent are age 55 or over compared to 27% of the population-at-large. In terms of the household size, household income, and the highest level of education achieved, little difference exists between evangelicals and non-evangelicals in Canada.[3]

Despite their overarching moniker, evangelicals are not a coherent or unified religious group. About 8% of evangelicals attend churches that are defined by their conservative Protestant doctrine.[4] In Canada, these churches include the Adventist, Apostolic, Baptist, Brethren, Christian and Missionary Alliance, Christian Reformed, Church of God, Free Methodist, Lutheran Church–Canada, Mennonite, Nazarene, Pentecostal, Salvation Army, Vineyard, Wesleyan and a host of independent and nondenominational churches.[5] Furthermore, pockets of evangelicals make their spiritual home in Canada's four mainline denominations: the Anglican, Evangelical Lutheran, Presbyterian and United churches.[6] (Though they often find themselves at odds with their fellow parishioners and even clergy who are more theologically liberal then themselves). They are even found outside formal religious institutions for, indeed, it is what one believes, and not where one worships, that makes one an evangelical Christian.[7]

However, when deciding who is and who is not an evangelical an important differentiation must be made. Catholics, even when they hold similar tenets of faith, are not classified as evangelicals. Because Catholics accept and practice religious traditions that are not corroborated or directly sanctioned by scripture—these traditions being those that originated later in the life of the Christian community, after the canon of the New Testament was set—they are set apart from Protestants in general, and from evangelicals in particular. Protestants since the Reformation have insisted upon "Sola Scriptura"—the principle that the Bible alone is the source of God's revelation to humankind. In keeping with the founders of their faith, evangelicals stress the primacy of scripture. In fact, "biblicism"—the belief that the Bible is the true word of God and teaches all that is necessary for right living and salvation from sin—is their predominant defining characteristic. Given this key difference (and several others not mentioned), scholars prefer to use the label "conservative Catholics" or "charismatic Catholics" when referring to Catholics with evangelical-like beliefs.[8] This differentiation will also be made throughout this book.

RELIGIOUS BELIEFS OF CANADIAN EVANGELICALS

In addition to biblicism, evangelicals are defined by four other characteristics: conversionism, crucicentrism, activism, and a high tension eschatology (a belief that Jesus' second coming is near).[9] Each of these terms deserves detailed explanation, but first a few more words about biblicism.

It is incorrect to say that evangelicals take everything in the Bible literally—when one talks of evangelicals' biblicism, certain realities must be acknowledged. First, how much or which parts of scripture are taken literally depends on the level of conservatism within a specific evangelical faith community. For example, members of a Southern Baptist or a Fellowship Baptist Church characteristically have a more literal view of scripture than those from a Convention Baptist Church (if you are not familiar with all the varieties of Baptists don't be alarmed— most rank and file Baptists aren't either). As a rule, in most evangelical communities, scripture from the New Testament that reads as rules or edicts to believers is interpreted and followed literally. Similarly, the gospel accounts of Jesus' birth, life, death and resurrection are most often taken at face value. On the other hand, those scriptures in the Old Testament that follow a simple narrative structure—passages like the stories of Adam and Eve, Noah and the flood and Jonah and the whale—are sometimes interpreted more symbolically. Finally, evangelicals give ideas, rules or practices advocated in the New Testament precedence over contradictory ideas, rules or practices posited in the Old Testament.

Survey data show about 60% of Canadian evangelicals agree with the statement: "I feel the Bible is God's word and is to be taken literally word for word."[10] However, that percentage increases to 100% when the statement is less rigidly structured to read: "I believe the Bible to be the Word of God and is reliable and trustworthy."[11, 12]

How do evangelicals know that the Bible is the Word of God and is reliable and trustworthy? As with all their religious beliefs, evangelicals back up their assertion that the Bible is the divinely derived by citing "proof texts" from scripture. The passage of scripture that is most often referenced comes from 2 Timothy 3:16 and reads, "All Scripture is inspired by God and profitable for teaching, for reproof, for correction, for training in righteousness; that the man of God may be adequate, equipped for every good work." If you ask them in private, some evangelicals will concede that using verses from the Bible to prove that the Bible itself is divinely inspired has a certain odd circularity. In some ways, it is like having a hockey team call their own penalties.

Regarding the trait of conversionism, it refers to the evangelical belief that one must make a conscious decision to be a Christian and follow Christ.[13] Often referred to as "being saved"—that is, saved from death and hell—or "asking Jesus into your heart," the process requires that an individual acknowledge, either privately or publicly, that she is a sinner. Next, she asks for God's forgiveness and believes that it has been granted (along with eternal life) because of Jesus' sacrifice on the cross. (The importance of Jesus' crucifixion will be explored at length in the discussion of crucicentrism below).

Romans 10:9–10 is one passage of scripture that evangelicals use to justify their step-by-step process of conversion. It reads: "If you confess with your mouth, 'Jesus as Lord,' and believe in your heart that God raised him from the dead, you will be saved. For it is with your heart that you believe and are justified, and it is with your mouth that you confess and are saved."

For some, the experience of conversion (from one's sinful past to a new Christ-centred life) is dramatic and emotional, but for 65% of evangelicals their "day of decision" was a "natural consequence of religious socialization."[14] That is, they were brought up in the church and saw their public declaration of faith as a religious right of passage. About 20% of evangelicals cannot identify a specific conversion experience at all. Instead, they say their decision to follow Christ was "a gradual change over time."[15] The nature of their conversion aside, 99% of Canada's evangelicals agree that they have committed their lives to Christ.[16]

When an individual comes from outside the evangelical fold and the conversion experience is tied to a conscious decision made on a specific day, it is typically expected that the "converted" person will dramatically begin to exhibit more Christ-like behaviour.[17] For example, the convert might begin to do volunteer work as a tangible sign that he is putting the needs of others ahead of his own. Often, a converted person is said to be "born-again"—the term refers to the fact that one is no longer the same person but a new creature in Christ.[18] The term itself derives its origin from Jesus' words to Nicodemus the Pharisee found in the Gospel of John 3:3. Jesus says, "I tell you the truth, no one can see the kingdom of God unless he is born again." As noted in the previous chapter, if any term or statement could be "regarded as a litmus test for determining who is, or who is not, an evangelical" being born-again is such a test, for only evangelicals are truly comfortable with that label.[19]

To say evangelicals are "crucicentric" is to say that the crucifixion of Christ is the very centre, or heart, of their faith. While belief in Christ's death and resurrection is common to most Christian believers, evangelicals view the crucifixion (and its associated elements) as the single most important part of Jesus' legacy. For example, it is more important than anything he taught. For most, it is the base upon which the foundation of their own Christianity rests. The crucifixion is crucial to evangelicals because they hold that the blood Christ shed while on the cross supernaturally expunges believers' sin. By extension, having one's sin expunged is a necessary precondition for acceptance into heaven. That Jesus rose again is of the utmost importance to evangelicals, as well, because it is seen as proof positive that Jesus was (and is) empowered by God and therefore has the authority to reward his believers with eternal life. Jesus' crucifixion and subsequent resurrection are the primary focus of most religious talk inside and outside evangelical churches. It is spoken of with a sense of awe—believers are confounded by the miraculous nature of the event, the enormity of the love required for such a sacrifice and the promise of eternal life.[20]

The survey data show that 98% of Canadian evangelicals believe that Jesus was crucified and raised from the dead. When asked to respond to the statement "I believe that through the life, death, and resurrection of Jesus, God provided a way for the forgiveness of my sins," 100% of evangelical respondents agreed.[21]

The trait of activism relates to evangelicals' desire to promote their Christian faith through their words and deeds.[22] Evangelicals dedicate a significant amount of time and money to programs within their own churches, but even with their church-related activities excluded, evangelicals still devote more time to volunteer organizations and more money to charities than other Canadians.[23] No doubt, this behaviour finds its impetus in Jesus' command in Matthew 7:12 to "do unto others." In addition to their works, evangelicals feel compelled to tell others about Jesus. As most evangelicals are convinced that those who do not accept Christ as their Saviour will be doomed to hell (Jesus says in the Gospel of John 14:6, "No one comes to the Father [gets to be with God in heaven] except by me") one understands why they place such importance on sharing the Gospel with others whenever possible. Eighty-six percent of Canadian evangelicals think it is important to act on their belief and encourage non-Christians to become Christians.[24]

Finally, evangelicals—more so than any other Christian faith group—possess a high tension eschatology. They believe that Christ will return to the earth and his arrival will be sooner (many believe the next 100 years) as opposed to later.[25] All four gospels report Jesus saying he will return; this is followed by a warning to his followers to be ready for that day. Some of the Apostle Paul's letters—for example, 1 and 2 Thessalonians—echo that same theme.

Thanks in large part to popular books like *The Late Great Planet Earth* and the *Left Behind* series of novels which have enjoyed massive readership, many evangelicals in North America have adopted a decidedly pre-millennial outlook believing that Christ's second coming will be preceded by two events: the rapture and the tribulation.[26] The rapture is defined as God's instantaneous removal of all true Christians from the earth into heaven. While the true believers are taken up into bliss, those left behind are forced to go through a final world war fought between the new followers of Christ (those who became Christians after the rapture) and the armies of Satan (composed of those who still refuse to believe in Jesus as the messiah). This time of war between God and Satan's forces is commonly referred to as the tribulation. The tribulation ends with a final battle known as Armageddon when Jesus physically returns, "coming in the clouds." Using supernatural power, he defeats the forces of Satan. Seventy-seven percent of evangelicals in Canada believe there will be a literal rapture.[27]

Other scripture-derived tenets of faith that evangelicals hold include the belief that God exists as a Trinity, consisting of the Father, Son (Jesus) and Holy Spirit—three persons within a single entity. They believe that God is a personal force more akin to a supernatural Father than an impersonal cosmic energy, and that Satan is a real entity dedicated to enacting evil in the world. Most believe in miracles, angels, visions or messages from God, demons, demon possession and exorcism. Most believe that heaven exists as a place of beauty and perpetual happiness where committed Christians go when they die, and that hell exists as a place of torment where the unsaved go after death.[28] To varying degrees, evangelicals are critical of the theory of evolution. A minority reject it outright as completely false. However, most hold a more nuanced position, believing that the process occurred but was ordained and guided by God. For those in the majority, the creation story found in the Book of Genesis need not be interpreted as a point for point account of the world's beginning.[29]

In addition to the beliefs listed above, the religious practices of evangelicals also distinguish them from the rest of the population. Evangelicals tend to be more fervent in their church attendance, reading of the Bible and dedication to prayer.[30] For example, 68% of Canadian evangelicals attended church once a week or more compared to 8% attendance for other Canadians.[31] Evangelicals are also more likely than other Christians or the population-at-large to attend religious meetings like Bible studies, prayer groups, and spiritual retreats and seminars.[32] Other religious practices like regularly watching faith-oriented TV programs and listening to contemporary Christian music are activities that are virtually exclusive to evangelicals.[33]

When non-evangelicals think of evangelical religious practice, Bible-studies and listening to contemporary Christian music seldom come to mind. Instead, they picture a boisterous worship service—hand clapping and raising of hands in church, shouts of "Amen" and "Hallelujah"—and ecstatic religious behaviours such as speaking in tongues, prophesizing, faith healing and other miracles. While some evangelical groups and denominations enjoy these elements of religious practice, many do not. In Canada, ecstatic or charismatic religious expression is most often found in Pentecostal, Vineyard, Apostolic and other non-denominational or "Full Gospel" churches.[34]

SOCIAL VALUES OF CANADIAN EVANGELICALS

As mentioned in Chapter 1, evangelicals use the lessons and edicts of the Bible to gauge what is good and right for their own life and for society and, as such, their personal morals and social values tend to be more conservative and absolute than those of most Canadians. For evangelicals, fidelity in relationships, honesty, and charity are categorical imperatives and not situational options. While these personal virtues are generally esteemed by the rest of society, Canada's evangelicals find themselves ostracized by the general population for the social views they hold. Most non-evangelical Canadians show at least soft support for gay marriage and homosexuality, abortion, pre-marital sexual activity, pornography, gambling and the use of recreational drugs.[35] On the other hand, evangelicals in Canada tend to oppose those practices.[36] In addition, some evangelical communities are opposed to women taking on the highest leadership roles in the church; others go farther and say that women should be the submissive partner in a married relationship.[37] Conversely, very few non-evangelical Canadians support the notion that the man should be the head of the household.[38]

As with their religious beliefs, evangelicals justify each of their social views with appeals to specific passages of scripture. For example, to support their stand against homosexual lifestyles they cite Leviticus 18:22 which reads, "Do not lie with a man as one lies with a woman; that is detestable" and 1 Corinthians 6:9–11 which states, "Neither the sexually immoral nor idolaters nor adulterers nor male prostitutes nor homosexual offenders nor thieves nor the greedy nor drunkards nor slanderers nor swindlers will inherit the kingdom of God."

To support their position against abortion, evangelicals cite Psalm 139:13–14: "For you created my inmost being; you knit me together in my mother's womb. I praise you because I am fearfully and wonderfully made" and the commandment "You shall not murder" found in the Book of Exodus 20:13. Jesus' instruction to care for the vulnerable in society as reflected in his parable of the sheep and the goats (Matthew 25:31–46) and his overarching declaration to "Do unto others as you would have them do unto you" (Matthew 7:12) are also viewed as calls to protect children in the womb.

Evangelicals see their values as medicine for a society suffering from various social ills and, in their opinion, to deny society the benefits of that medicine would be negligent. Again, it is adherence to specific scripture—like Jesus' great commissioning to "go into all the world and preach his gospel to every nation" (Matthew 28:19)—that results in this attitude and its associated behaviours.

Since the mid-1980s evangelicals have focused their social activism on two broad targets: sexual morality and church-state matters (though these battlefields sometimes overlap). In their war on sexual morality, battles have been fought against abortion, extramarital sex and homosexuality. In their war against the state, battles have been waged for government funding of faith-based schools, inclusion of prayer, religious education and religious activities in public schools and greater use of Christian symbols, references and practices in the buildings and processes of government. Battles have been fought against school curriculum that runs contrary to scripture (for example, that which promote premarital sex or homosexual lifestyles) and government interference in the operation of faith-based schools.

In their attempts to advance God's Kingdom, evangelicals have employed such worldly measures as demonstrations, petitions, political lobbying and the courts. However, much to their chagrin, they have very little to show for their efforts. In fact, in recent decades Canadian culture has steadily become less compatible with evangelical beliefs and values.

THE SECULARIZATION OF CANADA

To understand evangelicals most completely, it is important to situate them within their cultural context. Just as the idea of light is more readily understood when it can be contrasted against darkness, to have a full appreciation of Canadian evangelicals one needs to compare them to the population-at-large. As highlighted in the section above, evangelicals' engagement in the public square tends to reactive. In this section, the root cause of this reactionary ethos is explored.

In the last 25 years or so, Canada has experienced a tremendous shift toward secularism. Janet Epp-Buckingham, former Director of Religious Liberty for the Evangelical Fellowship of Canada, thinks Canada's progression toward secularization (and, in turn, its retreat from traditional Christianity) began in earnest with the introduction of country's Charter of Rights and Freedoms in 1982. She notes that the Charter's guarantee that all faiths are equal under the law opened the door for minority groups to legally challenge any government institution, legislation or practice that afforded Christianity privileged status.[39]

The very first Charter cases were relatively innocuous and seemed to be more a rejection of Christian-based traditions than outright hostility toward the faith—the cases were not even brought forth by religious groups. Storeowners, hoping to operate on Sundays, "claimed that laws enforcing the Christian Sabbath offended the religious freedom of those who were not Christian. The Supreme Court agreed with that assessment and in 1985 Sunday shopping became a reality in Canada."[40]

However, the next cases *were* brought by religious groups. In 1988, Muslims and Jews challenged the use of the Lord's Prayer in public schools as part of opening exercises. The Ontario court of appeal ruled in their favour and struck down the prayer's use. Two years later, non-Christians in Ontario's Elgin County challenged the way religious education was taught in public schools, arguing that it was too Christian-focused. The courts agreed and set out new guidelines for religious education, insisting that all the world's major faiths be covered equally—regardless of the religious demographic of the student population. At the time, 96% of the students in Elgin Country, where this case originated, were Christian.[41]

Epp-Buckingham believes these cases and others like them had a terrific influence on Canadian society. She says members of the government, the media and the population-at-large were taught that it is right for Christianity to be banned from the public sphere. It was a lesson, she says, that they learned only too well. Now, even when Christian symbols, traditions or practices are not forbidden by law—the collective response is to have them removed anyway.[42]

Numerous instances support Epp-Buckingham's observation that Christianity, especially in its more traditional manifestations, has become a faith *non grata* in terms of public discourse and practice. For example, in September 1998, a memorial service was held at Peggy's Cove, Nova Scotia, for 229 people who died in the Swissair Flight 111 crash. Before the start of the service, a federal official—reportedly from the Prime Minister's Office—told the Protestant minister and the Catholic priest that they would not be allowed to utter the name of Jesus Christ, nor refer to the Bible. A rabbi was allowed to read from the Torah, a Muslim from the Koran, and a native Canadian was allowed to speak of the Great Spirit; only the Christian clergy were censored.[43] Similarly, in 2001, following the September 11 attacks on New York and the Pentagon in Washington D.C., Canada's federal government held a public memorial service on Parliament Hill in Ottawa. Though it is typical on such occasions to cite Biblical texts or to speak of God, no religious references were made throughout the ceremony.[44] At the 2003 swearing-in ceremony of Canada's twenty-first Prime Minister, Paul Martin, the religious dimension was provided by a native elder conducting a cleansing ceremony for Martin, fanning sage smoke over the incoming prime minister with an eagle feather. Martin professes to be a devout Catholic and does not practice native spirituality.[45] However, no other religious officials, Catholic or otherwise, took part in the inauguration.

There are examples of government agencies, municipal governments and even businesses excluding Christianity and its symbols from the public square. When handing out licenses to TV and radio stations, it has been observed that Canada's broadcast regulator—the Canadian Radio-television and Telecommunications Commission (CRTC)—has historically denied stations dedicated to Christian-only programming the right to operate while willingly expediting the approval of stations with overtly sexual content. In the early 1980s the CRTC received applications from the Playboy Channel (a station dedicated to adult issues and "soft" pornography) and several Christian-faith stations. The Playboy channel was approved but none of the Christian stations. Twenty years, and multiple applications later, some of the Christian stations have received approval to broadcast, though not as part of the regular cable line-up. Instead, they are relegated to the status of specialty channels (that is, channels that cable customers must order specifically and pay for separately).[46]

Professor of Law at Carleton University, Margaret Ogilvie, argues that when it comes to Christianity, Canada's courts and human rights tribunals are also guilty of the duplicitous behaviour. She explains that where challenges for accommodation in the workplace have been made by members of non-Christian faiths, the courts and tribunals "have always acceded to their requests," but when devout Christians have asked for accommodation on religious grounds the judicial decisions have almost always gone against them.[47]

Specific cases illustrate Ogilvie's point. Since the early 1990s all employers have been made to accommodate the holy days of Jewish and Muslim employees. Likewise, construction companies have been told that Sikh employees must be permitted to wear turbans even if safety helmets might be more advisable. Hospitals and schools, too, have been instructed that kirpans (the ornamental knives worn by Sikh men) must be allowed in their weapon-free environments.[48] Evangelicals, on the other hand have been told that their beliefs must be kept out of the workplace.

Printer Scott Brockie was fined $5,000 in 2000 by the Ontario Human Rights Commission because he refused to print letterhead and envelopes for the Canadian Lesbian and Gay Archives. Brockie insisted that he was happy to do work for individual homosexuals; in fact, he had printed materials for individual homosexual clients in the past. However, he refused to print materials for the Archives because he believed the institution actively promoted greater homosexual activity in society, which he said was contrary to his beliefs as a born-again Christian. The adjudicator in the case decided that Brockie's "rights as a Christian were subordinate to the rights of homosexuals not to be discriminated against," and that "he must restrict the practice of Christianity to his home and church, and not take it with him into the public marketplace."[49] Brockie was ordered to provide printing services "to lesbians and gays and to organizations in existence for their benefit."[50]

A human rights tribunal in Prince Edward Island ordered bed and breakfast owners Dagmar and Arnost Cepica to accept homosexual clients. Rather than "be forced to condone homosexual acts under their own roof" the devout Christian couple shut down their business in 2001.[51] In 2004, the British Columbia College of Teachers suspended evangelical Chris Kempling, a high school guidance counselor, from his job because "he wrote letters to his local paper outlining his views on the nature of homosexuality."[52] He was suspended despite the fact that he had never disparaged homosexual rights or homosexual lifestyles while performing his duties at his school.[53]

Some of the efforts to purge traditional Christian symbols and beliefs from the public sphere have bordered on humorous. For instance, in December of 2002, over the Christmas holiday season, municipal officials of Canada's biggest city, Toronto, issued press releases indicating that the 50-foot evergreen tree set up outside city hall was to be referred to as a "holiday tree" and not as a Christmas tree. That same December the Royal Canadian Mint ran commercials that changed the old holiday standard the *Twelve Days of Christmas* to the *Twelve Days of Giving* while Gap Clothing stores insisted their staff wish customers "Happy Holidays" instead of "Merry Christmas."[54] Interestingly, it is these trivial, odd-ball "slights" against Christianity that get the most play in the media and generate the most letters to the editor.

In addition to infiltrating the practices and policies of government, courts, and business, a rejection of religious tradition can be found at the grassroots level of Canadian society. While it is beyond the purview of this book to judge whether this rejection is attributable to an institutional agenda "trickling down," the fact remains that nationwide a growing number of citizens nationwide are embracing secularism as a defining element of their national identity—adding it to the established characteristics of liberalism, pluralism and tolerance. While an outright abandonment of faith is far from underway, the gap between believers and non-believers expands each year.[55] The effect on the nation's churches has, in some cases, been dramatic.

Today, about 12.8 million Canadians, or 43% of the population, are Roman Catholic and 8.7 million, or 29% of the population, are Protestant. In the last decade there has been a steady downward trend in the number of Canadians who belong to these two overarching faith communities. Roman Catholics, as a percentage of the total population, have dropped by 2% since 1991 and Protestants have dropped by 6%.[56]

The significant decline of Protestantism in Canada is tied to losses in the mainline denominations. In Anglican, Evangelical Lutheran, Presbyterian and United churches across the country, older members are dying and few young people are taking their place. As expressed earlier in this chapter, mainline denominations are more liberal in their religious beliefs than conservative Protestant denominations. For members of mainline churches, "properly understanding words in the Bible requires an examination of their context within the Bible itself and a sensitivity to the meaning they had for their original audience."[57] They "accept and embrace biblical interpretation and higher criticism" and, as such, much of scripture is taken as metaphorical and allegorical.[58] For example, some members of mainline churches would discount the virgin birth of Jesus as an historical event. They would say its inclusion in the Gospels of Luke and Matthew was a literary device used by the writers of the texts to symbolically communicate the importance of Christ's birth. Some mainliners chalk up the divinity of Jesus and his resurrection to metaphor. In fact, in the mid-1990s, the moderator (leader) of the United Church of Canada, the Reverend Bill Phipps, caused considerable controversy inside and outside his denomination when he publicly declared that Jesus was not God and in terms of "the scientific fact" his resurrection was not believable.[59]

Since 1991, the United, Anglican, Presbyterian, and Lutheran churches have declined by 8%, 7%, 36%, and 5%, respectively.[60] The latest figures of Statistics Canada report the United Church has about 2.8 million members, the Anglican Church 2 million, Presbyterian 410 thousand and Lutheran 607 thousand.[61] However, other independent demographic studies suggest that these figures are highly inflated.[62]

While mainline Protestant denominations are in decline, conservative Protestant denominations (that is, those specifically associated with evangelicals and evangelical doctrine) have grown by about 1% a year since the 1950s. Such growth, though seemingly small, has allowed those attending conservative Protestant Churches to consistently comprise about 8% of the overall Canadian population since the late 1800s.[63] Some observers have attributed the success of conservative Protestant churches to their ability to hold onto their own. That is, "they appear to do a very effective job of retaining their children, as well as their [current members] as they move from place to place—two problematic areas for mainline Protestants in particular."[64] However, others have posited a more complex hypothesis as to why mainline churches are dying while their evangelical cousins are vibrant and healthy.

Sociologist Rodney Stark suggests that mainline denominations with their laissez-faire doctrine—that is, doctrine that is fairly permissive when it comes to what members *have* to believe and what behaviours they *have* to follow—are far more likely to die out than faiths that take a harder line with members. He explains that, on the whole, people join and stay with a faith group only if they are convinced that that faith group *alone* offers the solution to their spiritual needs.[65] It is Stark's suggestion that when a mainline church—in keeping with its liberal, pluralistic ethos—proclaims that it is *just one path* among many that a spiritual seeker might choose to wander down, it is shooting itself in the foot. It is akin to the makers of one product saying in their advertisements "Go ahead and buy our competitor's model. It is just as good."

In contrast, conservative Protestant churches claim to have "the Truth" and "the way of salvation." While joining such a congregation may come at a high cost—members might be asked to abandon elements of their lifestyle that they really enjoy or be required to believe doctrines that cannot be verified empirically—adherents feel they are getting a bargain. For them, membership includes the reward of a transformed life in the present and the promise of eternal life in the future.[66]

In addition, Stark says religious bodies that are more demanding and exclusive are at an advantage because they tend to screen out members whose participation and commitment would be low. They are left with a core of motivated individuals who are willing to show up to church regularly, give their time and money to the denomination, and actively recruit new members. The commitment of members of hard line faith groups is further strengthened by a feeling of not belonging to the rest of society. Because their values and norms are at odds with the population at large, members of the faith group become more active in the micro-community of their church where they feel welcomed and accepted.[67]

If Stark is correct, by closely aligning themselves with societal trends and dominant culture, mainline churches are actually causing their current members to be less committed to their denomination. Ultimately, less committed members just stop showing up. Similarly, they are also hampering their ability to recruit committed new members because its "admission standards" are too easy to meet. The notion that "we're more likely to prize something we have to work for" also rings true for religion. I guess in some ways Groucho Marx's comment that "he wouldn't want to join a club that would be willing to have him as a member" fits too.

Yes, conservative churches in Canada are vibrant and healthy but so is the group of Canadians reporting "no religion." As stated earlier, the gap between believers and non-believers expands each year. In 2006, 19% percent of the population claimed no religious faith, up from 15% in 1995.[68] And more bad news may be on the horizon for religion in Canada.

Despite the vibrancy demonstrated by Canada's conservative Protestant churches, pollster and president of Environics Research Group, Michael Adams, is convinced that religion is not on the "come-back trail." He bases his opinion on recent polls and extensive surveys his company has conducted across Canada. He says if one wants a quick snapshot of the state of religion in Canada one need only look at the figures for church attendance. In the last 50 years weekly church attendance has dropped more than a third—down to a record low of 20% in 2000.[69]

However, Canada's foremost sociologist of religion, Reginald Bibby staunchly disagrees with Adam's assertion that religion has reached its zenith in Canada and, in ironic fashion, cites religious attendance polls himself to prove his point. Bibby states that his most recent Project Canada survey, completed in late 2005, found:

> . . . that weekly attendance now stands at 25%—a modest increase
> but nonetheless an increase over what was expected by most to be

a decline from 22% five years earlier. This is the first time since we began tracking national trends that the numbers have gone up.[70]

In addition to his own research, Bibby notes three other recent studies, including a 2004 Gallup Poll, found weekly religious attendance to be between 27 and 37%—levels not seen since the early 1980s.[71] These numbers, along with other survey data showing that most Canadians still profess belief in traditional Christian doctrine (for example, Jesus is the Son of God), lead Bibby to conclude that Canada is on the cusp of a religious renaissance.[72]

While Adams and Bibby disagree in their predictions about the future of religion in Canada, they share a similar opinion about the state of religion in the present. Both acknowledge that for a majority of Canadians alive today, religion and religious belief is unimportant in their lives on a day-to-day basis.[73]

The fact that religion plays a diminished role in the lives of most Canadians today, combined with the other factors discussed in this chapter, does much to explain why evangelicals have adopted a reactionary position in their civic engagement. What was once theirs is slipping away and their *reaction* is to try to get it back. There is little doubt that, given the choice, Canada's evangelicals would prefer not be in a state of perpetual reaction and retrenchment. Be that as it may, the case could be made that their feelings of assailment are good for them.

Arguing in a similar manner to Stark, sociologist Lewis Coser argues that conflict has a group-binding function that mobilizes the energies of a group and increases its cohesion. By emphasizing the enemy without, a group develops greater togetherness while reaffirming and solidifying its identity.[74] While it sounds odd, Canadian society becoming less evangelical has probably led evangelicals in this country to become more evangelical. The survey data bear this out. Indeed, as the population-at-large has become more secular over the last 25 years, the country's evangelicals have become increasingly more conservative in their morals and values.[75] In fact, in many ways Canadian evangelicals now have more in common with evangelicals in the U.S. than they do with most of their fellow Canadians.

COMPARING CANADIAN AND AMERICAN EVANGELICALS

Using international survey data and face-to-face in-depth interviews with Americans and Canadians belonging to conservative Protestant denominations, sociologist Sam Reimer determined that "in the main, [American and Canadian evangelicals have] only minor regional and national differences in their central religious beliefs, religious experience, orthodoxy, or orthopraxy."[76] However, he found Canadian evangelicals are more moderate than their American counterparts in regard to biblicism, activism, religious expression, tolerance of others, and political involvement.[77]

For example, when asked which single belief or practice should be the most important to Christians, American evangelicals said that following the Bible and doing what it says ranks above all else. Canadians evangelicals, on the other hand, did not dwell on biblical correctness but instead said, "what is most important for Christians is to be close to God, to spend time praying, worshiping and experiencing [His] great love."[78] The relaxed attitude toward scripture is part of a larger evangelical tradition in Canada where minor concerns over points of theology are ignored in order to accomplish a greater good. The best example of this tradition in action is the formation of the United Church of Canada. In 1925, the Methodist and Congregational churches, along with a third of Presbyterian churches, joined to form a single religious body with an evangelical ethos (of course, as discussed, things have changed dramatically since this inception).[79] They saw themselves as "heirs to a common revivalist tradition, which fostered a pragmatic approach to religion, emphasizing the importance of Christian life and service over doctrinal niceties."[80] A modern example of this inclination toward cooperation is the Evangelical Fellowship of Canada. Formed in 1964, this pan-denominational organization is dedicated to providing a voice to the political and social concerns of all the nation's evangelicals.[81]

Historically, American evangelicals have been less willing to compromise when it comes to scriptural interpretation and matters of doctrine. By way of comparison, in the 1920s—when Canada's evangelicals were coming together to form the United Church—evangelicals in the U.S. were embroiled in the modernist-fundamentalist conflict that saw many evangelicals "split from their denominations to form independent bodies."[82]

Canadian evangelicals are also less predisposed to activism than American. As previously mentioned, 86% feel it is important to encourage non-Christians to become Christians.[83] This figure is nearly 10% lower than in the U.S.[84] Reimer attributes Canadians' hesitation to aggressively proselytize to a "religious climate where church groups are not to compete but are to service their own."[85]

Some suggest that the hesitancy of Canadian churches to solicit new members is linked to the governmental support which they received during the 1800s and early 1900s. Because most of Canada's denominations, even those with evangelical leanings, could count on governmental funds to aid in their operations, they had little motivation to expand their base of participation.[86] Conversely, in America, from the beginning, church and state have been radically separated and in that pluralist environment the different religious traditions have been forced to compete with each other for members. This competition for members among churches has been compared to the competition for customers that businesses undertake in a free-market economy.[87] In both cases, the organization with the "goods"—be it a church or a business—must purposefully pursue their target market and convince them that their "product" is better than that of their competitor. As with businesses, competition among churches leads to innovation among the competitors and greater commitment among the "consumers" (congregants) who have deliberately chosen one "brand" (denomination) over another.

Reimer also suggests that the hesitation Canadian evangelicals show toward actively sharing their faith is part of a larger national culture of tolerance and politeness.[88] Tolerance of others' beliefs and ideals is a highly prized trait among Canadians because it, more than anything else, distinguishes them from Americans.[89] The desire to be seen as other than American is strong in Canada. Because Canadians look, dress, eat and, for the most part, talk like Americans, they have come to define their national identity not so much by what they are, but by what they are not. To be sure, the "we-are-different-from-Americans sentiment is a mainstay of Canadian national identity."[90]

Reimer states that "regardless of whether one looks at racial, political, religious, or moral tolerance, Canadian evangelicals are more tolerant."[91] In his research, tolerance (also termed irenicism) was defined as "attitudes toward other individuals or groups that are not sectarian, partisan, prejudiced, or patriarchal."[92] For example, Reimer states that 82.5% of evangelicals in Canada agreed they would be pleased to have a person of another race live next door to them, while only 75% of American evangelicals agreed. Similarly, when asked if they would vote for a Muslim political leader, 65% of Canadian evangelicals agreed but just 45% of American.[93]

Michael Adams says that in Canada, tolerance of diversity has been institutionalized through state-sponsored programs that promote multiculturalism, and through a national Charter of Rights and Freedoms that outlaws discrimination on the grounds of religion, sex, race, ethnicity or sexual orientation. Government support for multiculturalism since the 1960s and the enactment of the Charter in 1982 has, in turn, precipitated other modern Canadian trends such as acceptance of women's and gay's rights.[94]

Other commentators are more general in their assessment and suggest that a history punctuated by compromise and respect for diversity has given rise to the culture of accommodation in Canada that now permeates almost all social groups, including evangelicals.[95] Conversely, the intolerance that sometimes manifests itself with American evangelicalism is thought to find its roots in the American historical tendency toward individualism, revolution and dissent.[96]

In addition to the ubiquitous spirit of accommodation that now permeates all Canada, the demure nature of Canadian evangelicalism is also due in large part to an increased British influence following the war of 1812.[97] Before the War of 1812 (1812–1814), over half of Canada's English-speaking population was of American origin. These transplanted Americans were Protestant, and many were "radical" evangelicals—men and woman who had experienced a dramatic conversion experience and practiced an exuberant, participatory style of worship.[98]

However, when the war ended, immigration from United States dried up and so too did the "ready-made" supply of radical evangelical clergy and parishioners. Instead, a wave of immigrants from the British Isles rushed to fill the void. They swelled the population and turned a country, once predominantly American in origin, into a country that was overwhelmingly British. For the most part, the new immigrants joined the established denominations of Anglican, Methodist, Presbyterian and Baptist. They rejected American-style radical evangelicalism and encouraged a new moderate, "British-style" evangelicalism.[99] This new evangelicalism was marked by "more conventional piety, restraint of emotional excesses, better educated clergy, political conservatism, and stricter church discipline."[100] The desire to be un-American that has made Canadian evangelicals more moderate and tolerant has also influenced how this faith group engages political activity. It is because they fear being ridiculed as "too American" that, up to now, many Canadian evangelicals have abstained from mixing religion directly with politics. Lobbying politicians has been fair game but, traditionally, evangelicals have forgone targeted involvement in political parties.[101]

In the United States politics and religion are inextricably linked. Evangelical politicians, from the lowest public official to the leader of the nation, openly profess their faith and make references to God and scripture in their speeches.[102] Once, during a presidential candidates' debate, self-declared evangelical George W. Bush told a journalist that

Jesus Christ was the philosopher who had most greatly influenced his life.[103] According to popular convention, in Canada such public confessions of faith are not acceptable; for Canadian public officials the only acceptable religious conviction is an unobtrusive one.[104] Certainly, many of Canada's top elected officials hold this to be true—including former Prime Ministers Jean Chretien and Paul Martin. Both have stated that it is incumbent upon elected officials to divorce their private beliefs from public policy.[105] Canada's former Minister of Culture and Deputy Prime Minister, Sheila Copps, added that politicians should also "refrain from invoking the Judeo-Christian God to avoid offending others in Canada's multi-ethnic society."[106]

Politicians with strong religious convictions who do not abandon their beliefs at the door of the legislature risk being labeled "too American" or "un-Canadian."[107] They also risk their political career, as was discovered by Stockwell Day, the erstwhile leader of Canada's official opposition. The media called Day's mix of politics and faith an "import from the American Christian Right," and "decidedly un-Canadian in its ugliness."[108] Jeffrey Simpson of Canada's national newspaper the *Globe and Mail* summarized the opinion of his colleagues in the media saying, "That Mr. Day has strong religious beliefs is fine; that he brings them into the public domain is not. At least not in this secular country . . ."[109]

As noted in the Introduction of this book, the hard ride Canada's national journalists gave Stockwell Day seems to have influenced the media relations strategy of Conservative Prime Minister Stephen Harper—an evangelical himself. When journalists come calling, his faith is off limits. Furthermore, Harper has insisted that the evangelical MPs in his party uphold a vow of silence when it comes to voicing their religious perspectives.

On occasion, Harper's concerns over a faith-related media "bushwhack" have unintentionally resulted in comical situations. For instance, during the federal election campaign of 2006 Harper appeared at a rally for Harold Albrecht, the Conservative candidate for Kitchener-Conestoga. Albrecht, a pastor for an evangelical church, was known for his opposition to same-sex marriage. According to a report in the *Globe and Mail*, "when reporters tried to question Mr. Albrecht about his views after the rally, Conservative handlers blocked them from getting close. Mr. Albrecht was hustled into a kitchen where he stood alone as the news media were told he was too busy to speak with them."[110]

Some journalists, like veteran religion reporter Douglas Todd, while not supportive of Harper's tight-lipped stance, appear to understand his motivation. In a 2007 profile focussing on Harper's faith, Todd remarked:

> Harper, the 48-year-old leader of a minority Conservative govern-
> ment, virtually never talks publicly about his Christian beliefs . . .
> Some political observers say Harper—who has been criticized for
> muzzling his cabinet and his many evangelical MPs—could suffer
> politically if he were more open about his form of Christianity in a
> diverse, multicultural country such as Canada.[111]

Recent polling data confirms that public officials will "suffer politically" if they speak openly about their faith. Leading up to the 2008 federal election, Angus Reid Strategies conducted a national survey and found "two-thirds of Canadians (66%) believe it is inappropriate for political candidates to talk about their religious beliefs as part of their campaigns, while one-in-four (25%) considers these actions as appropriate"[112]

In addition to a fear of public scorn, historically two other factors have also kept Canadian evangelicals from mobilizing and putting their agenda forward politically: lack of finances and lack of media support.[113] That is to say, Canadian evangelicals have neither the money nor the means to get their message out. Unlike in the U.S., evangelicalism in Canada has "produced few wealthy businesspersons and no large foundations to underwrite major projects."[114]

Finally, the political inactivity of Canadian evangelicals is due in some measure to the fact that no political party has seemed to align with their specific interests. In the U.S., most evangelicals actively support the Republican Party because of its conservative stand on social and economic issues.[115] In Canada, however, up to the late 1980s evangelicals tended to divide their support among all parties because no single party identified itself with hardcore social conservatism.[116]

That political void changed somewhat in 1987 when Preston Manning, a devout evangelical and son of a former provincial premier, formed the federal Reform Party. As the party has grown and expanded, its leader has changed, as has its name: from Reform, to the Canadian Alliance, to simply the Conservative Party. But throughout its many incarnations it has held fast to its commitment to fiscal and social conservatism.[117] However, its attachment to fiscal conservatism may be its Achilles' heel when it comes to appealing to Canadian evangelicals.

It is undeniable that conservative Protestant support for Canada's Conservative Party grows with each federal election. In the 2006 federal election, Stephen Harper's Conservatives garnered 62.5% of the evangelical vote.[118] However, in America, evangelicals still show more uniform support of their "party on the right"—the Republicans—than do Canadian evangelicals.[119] The difference lies in the fact that many of Canada's evangelicals do not meld their social conservatism with economic conservatism as is done in the U.S.; instead, many evangelicals north of the 49th parallel have a leftist bent. They want more government spending on social programs like healthcare and low-income housing for the poor, not less. Canadian evangelicals proclivity for socialism is attributed, in large part, to Canadian evangelicals' historical associations with left-leaning political organizations like the Social Credit Party lead by evangelical radio preacher "Bible Bill" Aberhart, and the Cooperative Commonwealth Federation Party, led by Baptist clergyman Tommy Douglas.[120]

That Canadian evangelicals have, in the last decade, begun connecting religion and politics is seen as part of a larger trend toward the Americanization of their faith. Today most of the evangelical books, magazines, radio and TV shows that Canadians access are produced in America and have a decidedly American outlook. Many of Canada's evangelical clergy have received some or all of their training in the U.S. and about 20% are Americans who moved north.[121]

Finally, in terms of religious practice, Canadian evangelicals have more in common with American evangelicals than with the other Canadians. Canadian evangelicals are just slightly more fervent about weekly church attendance and daily Bible reading, while evangelicals in America are more dedicated to weekly Bible studies and slightly more diligent about praying daily. However, in most cases the difference in the rates of religious practice between the two groups is less than five percentage points.[122]

CHAPTER 3

Evangelicals and the News Media: A Review of Past Research

When it comes to the media's *coverage of religion* in Canada, past research tells us little. Past research tells us even less about the media's *coverage of evangelicals*. Over the last 25 years, a handful of Canadian studies have examined religion coverage in Canada. Typically, all religions are lumped together to be analyzed and only occasionally do the researchers make observations related to how specific faith groups are treated. For the most part, Canadian research from the past is little more than numerical assessments of which religion received coverage and how much.

Most of the in-depth research pertaining to the news media's coverage of religion has been conducted in the United States. Several multi-year studies have explored the history, content and tone of religion coverage in the American context. Some of those looked specifically at the coverage of evangelicals as part of their examination. Additionally, three recent studies in the U.S. were dedicated to examining the news media's portrayal of fundamentalists Christians—a subgroup of evangelical Christians characterized by their strict biblical literalism, militancy and tendency to be separatistic.

I will begin the discussion of what we know about the media's coverage of religion in general, and evangelicals in particular, by focusing on American research. As demonstrated in the previous chapter, close affinity exists between evangelicals in the two countries; near the end of this chapter we will see that American journalists share a close attitudinal profile with Canadian news personnel. Given these similarities, it is reasonable to assume that the broad trends reflected in the findings of the U.S. research are, at least in part, applicable to Canada. This chapter will conclude with a discussion of the extant Canadian studies.

AMERICAN STUDIES

Up until the early 1970s, religion coverage in the U.S. was on the decline. But midway through the decade it began to enjoy a renaissance—increasing 30% by the mid-1980s. However, the nature of the coverage was markedly different from that in ages past. Mainstream religious institutions no longer dominated coverage (traditionally half of religion coverage was dedicated directly or indirectly to mainline Protestant denominations). Instead, religion stories began to explore counterculture religious ideas and movements. Cults and the born-again, or Jesus People, movement of evangelical Protestantism, also came into the spotlight.[1]

In particular, the evangelical beliefs of American president Jimmy Carter, and the rise of Christian fundamentalist and leader of the Moral Majority, Jerry Falwell, dominated U.S. headlines in the late 1970s and early 1980s. Religion stories remained prominent in the late 1980s and early 1990s with the televangelist scandals of Jim and Tammy Bakker and Jimmy Swaggart, the pedophile scandals of the Catholic Church, and the Presidential campaigns of Reverend Jesse Jackson and Christian talk show host Pat Robinson.[2] Battles over homosexual rights, gay marriage, cloning, stem cell research, along with more sexual abuse scandals within the Catholic Church, ensured that the Christian faith received extensive coverage through the 1990s and into the twenty-first century.[3] No study has explored whether coverage of religious issues is growing in Canada. However, it seems probable that similar to the situation in the U.S., coverage has increased since the 1970s, especially given the ample attention Canada's media have paid to evangelicals engaged in the political process over the last two decades, and their more recent fixation on radical Islam.

Sarah Orwig's doctoral study of four American newspapers (the *New York Times*, the *Atlanta Journal Constitution*, the *Los Angeles Times* and the *Chicago Tribune*) tracked the news media's shift away from covering the spiritual and theological dimension of stories was over a 105-year period (1893 to 1998)[4]. The study catalogued four distinct periods of religion coverage. It showed that between 1893 and the 1920s references to theology and doctrine were the mainstay of religion stories. Also, daily devotionals and sermon reviews were considered important parts of the newspaper. In the mid-1920s, critical "judgments about faith entered into the discourse."[5] Much of the criticism was directed at fundamentalist Christians who were engaged in a national public debate over the teaching of evolution in public schools. Orwig hypothesizes that the fierceness of the debate may have contributed to a nationwide wariness toward the discussion of beliefs.[6] She found that by 1955, religion coverage "had nothing to do with beliefs" and instead focused on the external outcomes of belief—predominantly the "good works" of religious people.[7] By 1998, the emphasis on external outcomes of religion was so complete that "religion in contemporary newspapers tends to be understood and valued for its relevance to social, political and economic interests" and not for its "connection to an other worldly perspective."[8]

The most thorough study of religion coverage in America to date was conducted by media researchers S. Robert Lichter, Linda Lichter, and Dan Amundson. They examined a 10% random sample of 2,365 religion stories that appeared from 1969 through 1998 in *The New York Times, Washington Post, Time, Newsweek* and *US News & World*

Report, and on the evening newscasts of ABC, CBS and NBC. Only news items dealing with religion in the U.S., and only those that included religion as a major component—comprising one third of the story or more—were included in the study.[9]

Their study found that religion coverage in newspapers, news magazines and on TV had grown steadily through the 1970s and 1980s, and then doubled between 1990 and 1998. From 1969 to 1998, Protestants and Catholics received about two-thirds of the coverage, followed by Judaism (12%) and Islam (3%). While still dominant in the 1990s, the proportion of news items devoted to Catholics and mainline Protestants declined significantly, while coverage of Judaism remained stable and coverage of Islam increased. Also on the rise was coverage of new religious movements and Eastern religions. By the 1990s, one quarter of all religion stories were about these non-mainstream faiths.[10]

The researchers also noted a striking incongruity. Despite the fact that all of the stories featured religious men and women engaged in religiously inspired pursuits, most stories contained little information about theology or spirituality (a finding that had been likewise noted by Orwig). In fact, only 7% referenced any religious beliefs or doctrines. Furthermore, when theological references *were made* they were most often in relation to non-Christian religions.[11]

While the stories seldom addressed the spiritual dimension of a religious issue, whenever possible they did exploit an issue's political dimension. In fact, by the 1990s more religion stories were about Church-State conflicts than any other topic. For example, evangelicals fighting for prayer and scripture study in public schools generated heavy coverage.[12]

After stories on Church-State conflicts, stories featuring churches or clergy involved in crimes or scandal (generally of a sexual or financial nature) increased the most. Combined, stories about Church-State conflicts and church/clergy scandals made up 20% of all religion stories in the 1990s. Lichter and colleagues suggest that the dramatic turn toward conflict and controversy and away from issues such as church governance represents the single most important trend in the coverage of religion.[13]

Regarding whose opinions are privileged and whose are muted, the researchers determined that the American news media, in their coverage of controversial issues such as abortion, homosexuality and the separation between church and state, tended to give more prominence to opinions featuring traditional religious values rather than to opinions featuring liberal or secular values.[14] However, on the topic of women's involvement in church leadership, liberal opinions advocating more inclusive church policies outnumbered conservative opinions advocating that women's roles be limited.[15]

The last portion of the study focused solely on the American news media's coverage of evangelicals. The goal was to determine whether the coverage that evangelicals received was markedly different from the coverage of other faiths. It was found that between 1970 and 1998, just 6% of all religion stories focused on evangelical Christians.[16] This percentage was proportionately low, considering evangelicals at the time comprised between a quarter and a third of America's population.[17]

While evangelicals received proportionally less coverage, they were significantly overrepresented in stories of a negative nature. Specifically, 16% of all stories related to sexual scandal featured evangelicals, 24% of stories debating extramarital sex featured evangelicals and 15% of stories criticizing homosexuals featured evangelicals.[18] The researchers noted that only one faith group—Catholics—surpassed evangelicals in coverage defined by conflict and controversy. Specifically, Catholics accounted for over 70% of coverage on controversies surrounding reproductive issues and 60% of coverage dedicated to debates over sexual morality, yet overall, Catholics accounted for just 28% of religion coverage.[19]

Other research has shown that conservative Catholics and conservative Protestants are theologically very compatible—in fact, in terms of traditional religious beliefs and practices, evangelicals often have more in common with devout Catholics than with other Protestants from mainline denominations.[20] It is not surprising then that Catholics and evangelical Protestants share a similar media profile.

Like the Lichter, Lichter and Amundson study, a 2004 study of national television news coverage on the ABC, CBS and NBC networks by Tim Graham of the Media Research Center found that religion coverage since the 1990s has doubled.[21] He also determined that religion stories that feature conflict or controversy received the most airtime. For example, he noted that if the topic of the story was a message from the Pope it was delivered as a 20 or 30-second anchor brief; but if the topic was sexual abuse by a Catholic priest, or the installation of a gay Episcopalian bishop, the story was delivered as a two or three-minute reporter-based news package.[22] Graham noted the Catholic Church received the most airtime among faiths, due to widespread and persistant reports related to Catholic clergy sexual abuse.[23]

Similar to Lichter and colleagues, Graham determined that very few religion stories explored a spiritual or theological dimension; instead, "stories were approached from a secular and political perspective."[24] However, unlike Lichter and colleagues, Graham found that news reports about religion most often did not highlight the opinions of conservative religious believers. Conversely, he found that when choosing experts to interview for stories "[t]he networks heavily favored "religious" scholars and journalists who strongly question orthodox religion and accuracy of the Gospels."[25] Furthermore, he noted that when sources holding conservative Christian beliefs were given voice, they were subjected to prejudicial treatment. Specifically, those interviewees who expressed a high view of scripture where labeled "conservative," "ultra-conservative," or "fundamentalist" (either in the audio of the report or in a video graphic on screen) 11% of the time. Conversely, interviewees who expressed secular views or opposed Christian orthodoxy were almost never referred to as "liberals or secularists."[26] Finally, Graham noted conservative Christians' beliefs tended to be portrayed as "self-interested assertion[s] that should be viewed as factually questionable," while liberal or secular ideologies were depicted as modern, sensible and destined to prevail.[27]

A similar study of national television news on CNN, PBS, CBS, NBC and ABC, conducted a decade earlier by Graham and his Media Research Center colleague Steve Kaminski, also found religion coverage to be biased against people of traditional religious beliefs.[28] Like the 2004 Graham study, it noted that the "secular" side of an issue was always given voice, while religious concerns and religiously-informed opinion were given less time or were ignored completely. It also found that, while respectful of all others, reporters often described people of conservative religious faith using pejorative terms.[29]

In 2000, the Garrett Evangelical Theological Seminary of Northwestern University joined with the university's Medill School of Journalism to publish the results of a content analysis of religion news content. A sample of reports was drawn from newspapers (the *New York Times, USA Today,* and two Chicago daily newspapers), magazines (*Time, Newsweek,* and *U.S. News & World Report*) and from television news (the national news programs of CBS, NBC, ABC and the local Chicago affiliates of these networks) over a six-month period.[30] Researchers found that between 11% and 20% of all stories from daily newspapers, weekly newsmagazines, or TV newscasts referenced religion, spirituality or values. However, very few of those stories had religion, spirituality or values as their primary focus. In stories where religion did figure predominantly, the reporting often lacked theological or historical context.[31] (Lichter and colleagues and Graham made a similar observation). In terms of providing context, the study judged that daily newspapers did a better job than television news and, in contrast to Graham's and Graham & Kaminski's findings, the Garrett-Medill study detected only a slight bias against religious practitioners.[32] However, it must be noted that the Garrett-Medill study examined the media's treatment of religious practitioners of all degrees (nominal to devout) and of all faiths. Other research has determined that the media's coverage of adherents of mainline Protestant, Eastern, and new religious movements tends to be positive and favourable.[33] As such, a study examining the treatment of all faith groups collectively would be skewed toward the positive.

In an earlier study, Judith Buddenbaum examined sample newscasts from ABC, CBS, and NBC from the years 1976, 1981 and 1986. She determined that 6% to 11% of all news reports contained some kind of religious content.[34] While these figures seem low when compared to the 11% to 20% figures of the Garrett-Medill study, they are in keeping with the trends identified by Lichter and colleagues and Graham. It must be remembered, it was not until the 1990s that religion coverage doubled. Similar to the Garrett-Medill study, Buddenbaum's analysis also determined that the overall treatment of religion in the news was fair.[35] However, all religions were analyzed as a monolith potentially skewing the findings toward the positive—the media's treatment of individual faith groups was not examined.

Three of the most recent studies of religion coverage in the U.S. focused solely on the news media's portrayal of fundamentalist Christians. Because fundamentalists are a prominent sub-group of evangelical Christians—marked by their staunch conservatism—the findings of these American studies provide an important bridge to my own research into the Canadian media's depiction of evangelicals. The studies also share a similarity to the research conducted specifically for this book in that they employed *frame analysis*, as opposed to straight *content analysis*, as their methodology. (Frame analysis and frame theory will be discussed at length in the next chapter.)

Peter Kerr and Patricia Moy from the University of Washington examined newspaper coverage of fundamentalist Christians between 1980 and 2000. A total of 2,689 articles from newspapers across America was compiled using the Lexis-Nexis database and the search words "Fundamentalist" or "Fundamentalism" in combination with the term "Christians." The study found that over the specified two decades, the number of newspaper stories mentioning fundamentalist Christians rose steadily, and on average they portrayed fundamentalists in a slightly negative fashion.[36] In particular, the fundamentalists were depicted as somewhat intolerant, somewhat criminal-minded, a little unintelligent and irresponsible, a little pushy and unpatriotic, a little violent and a little prone to dangerous behaviours. Stories that showed fundamentalists as politically involved tended to portray them in a neutral or balanced fashion.[37]

Independent of Moy, Kerr conducted a nearly identical study to determine how fundamentalist Christians were depicted on national television network news between 1980 to 2000. The evening news reports of ABC, CBS, NBC, FOX and CNN were analyzed and it was determined that over the 20-year period, television news portrayed fundamentalist Christians in a slightly negative manner but not so negatively as newspapers.[38] While still depicting fundamentalists as somewhat intolerant, somewhat criminal-minded and a little irresponsible, in relation to intelligence and tendency toward aggression, television news portrayed members of this faith group neutrally. When the focus of a TV news report was political involvement or patriotism, fundamentalists tended to be portrayed positively.[39] Regarding specific topics of coverage, political issues brought fundamentalists into the spotlight most often; education was the second most frequent topic.[40]

We now come to the final American study to be discussed. While pursuing his doctorate at the University of Texas at Austin, Kyle Huckins examined how the *New York Times, Los Angeles Times and Washington Post* differed in their presentation of the two religious figures: Christian fundamentalist and social activist, Reverend Jerry Falwell, and liberal theologian and social activist, Reverend William Sloane Coffin. The time period for the study was 1980 to 1989.[41] Huckins found the coverage of all three newspapers was slightly negative in tone toward Falwell while, on average, it remained balanced or positive toward mainline Christian Coffin. Huckins concluded that "the media will marginalize (either through negativity or lack of attention) social movements perceived as outside mainstream politics."[42]

CANADIAN STUDIES

Larry Cornies' study of religion content in the province of Ontario's daily newspapers was the first of its kind in Canada. For his Masters thesis at the University of Western Ontario, Cornies examined coverage in three of Ontario's daily newspapers—the nationally circulated *Globe and Mail*, the mid-sized *London Free Press*, and the smaller circulation paper the *Sault Star*—between the years 1981 and 1986. Only stories in which religion, religious individuals or religious institutions played a key role were analyzed.[43]

He determined that about 55% of religion coverage examined Canadian faith issues. With regard to which faith groups get coverage and how much, he found that Roman Catholics, who comprised 35.6% of the population of Ontario in 1981, garnered 38% of the religion coverage. Protestants at 51.8% of the provincial population got 20% of the coverage with the Anglican Church receiving 8% and all other protestant groups sharing the remaining 12%. Jews at 1.7% of the population got 14% of the coverage and Muslims at 0.6% of the population got 7%.[44] What Cornies thought was most notable about the statistics was the paucity of coverage afforded mainline Protestant groups in Ontario. The largest Protestant denomination in the country, the United Church, was featured less often than the smaller evangelical denomination, the Pentecostal Church (Cornies did not provide specific figures).[45]

In relation to topic, Cornies found that 59% of all religion coverage in the daily press related to the political and social action of religious bodies. Stories in this category focused primarily on church groups fighting for or against issues of public and social policy.[46] This corresponds to Lichter and colleagues's in the U.S. who found that during the 1980s stories related to church-state conflict had become most common.[47] However, Cornies' findings differed significantly from several of the U.S. studies, in that he found a significant portion of Canadian stories, 24%, contained information about theology or spirituality. His second largest category, these stories focused on debate over theological issues, such as the contest between evolution and creationism. Seven percent of stories dealt with church celebrations and worship; 2% dealt with charitable work of religious organization.[48]

It is notable that Cornies did not feel a category for crimes and scandal was warranted. Of course, the most likely reason for this relates to the time period in which his study was conducted. It was not until the late 1980s and early 1990s that the televangelist scandals of Jim and Tammy Bakker and Jimmy Swaggart, and the pedophile scandals of the Catholic Church became big news in North America.

The next study of religion in Canadian news was conducted nine years later. By this time scandal was a dominant part of the reportage. The study, conducted by Ian Barrier as part of his graduate work at Carleton University, was a qualitative analysis of news coverage of court proceedings involving members of a Catholic religious order, the Brothers of the Christians Schools. The Brothers were found to have sexually abused boys under their care at reform schools in both Alfred and Uxbridge, Ontario in the 1970s. In 1990, arrests were made and charges laid when former students of the school went to police with their stories. The study examined *Canadian Press* newswire coverage of the scandal from 1990, when the story broke, to 1993, when many of the Brothers were sentenced.[49] The major finding was that secular media outlets, when they cover religious issues or groups, purposely avoid the spiritual dimension of the story. Church scandals are treated as typical crime or court stories relegating "religious questions and implications . . . to a lesser status."[50] The study concluded that while it may be easier for a reporter to ignore "questions of theology, faith and morality" and cover stories about believers "from a civic rather than religious dimension," journalism of that nature does a disservice to the majority of Canadians for whom religion is important.[51]

A year after Barrier's study, Susan Wilson Murray, while working as a researcher for Simon Fraser University's Newswatch Canada Project, conducted a content analysis of religion reporting from the *Globe and Mail*. The stories that were analyzed appeared over a four-month period in 1995. Only those that focused on long-standing religious denominations were examined—letters to the editor were also excluded. A sample of 78 stories was generated. Just over half of the stories were specifically related to religion in Canada, while about 10% were specific to the U.S., and the rest were generic in nature or focused on religious events and communities in countries around the world.[52]

The largest number of stories, 22, featured Roman Catholics. Eighteen stories featured Muslims. Very few stories were written specifically about Protestants as a collective; instead, Protestants were covered according to their specific denomination. Of 26 stories featuring Protestants, 6 referenced evangelicals and 10 referenced fundamentalists Christians.[53]

Of the 78 stories, 52% were deemed to contain negative content, while 19% had positive content and 29% had neutral. Negative content was defined as featuring unwelcome change, violent or abuse behaviours and practices, or illegal or immoral activities. Conversely, content was considered positive if it reflected a welcome change, a pleasant, hopeful or encouraging experience. The tone of the articles was analyzed for positive, negative and neutral attributes as well. While most of the articles, 43%, were neutral in their tone toward religion and religious individuals, 37% were deemed to be negative, and just 20% positive. Tone was determined by examining how reporters and sources described the actions of people, the practices of religious groups, or the events in each article.[54] The study did not discuss the content and tone as it related to specific faith groups.

A study released that same year by Canada's Fraser Institute analyzed the religion content of TV news stories from the CBC's and CTV's prime time news shows airing over the course of 1994. Ninety-five reports, 52 from CBC and 43 from CTV, featured people of faith or focused on religious issues. Stories about non-Christian faith groups comprised 65% of the CBC's stories and 48% of CTV's reports. In contrast, just 17% of the CBC's stories were about Roman Catholics and only 18% featured Protestant denominations. At 32%, CTV afforded more coverage to Roman Catholics, but at 20% it was almost equal to the CBC in its coverage of Protestants. At the time of the study Catholics made up 45% of Canada's population, while Protestants accounted for 35%. Researchers noted that if percentage of Canada's population was a guide to the amount of coverage a faith group received, Christian faith groups, particularly Protestants, were greatly under-represented while others were over-represented. Researchers also noted that stories featuring Christian faith groups tended to be shorter than those reports featuring non-Christian religious groups—except when the Christian groups were involved in conflict.[55] This observation echoes the findings of Graham and Graham and Kaminski in the U.S.

Finally, Ryerson University Professor Joyce Smith's study of religion coverage in Canada examined 20 newspapers—small, mid, and large circulation dailies—from across the country during three, seven day periods in early 1999. She determined that the newspapers with the largest circulation also tended to have the most religion coverage.[56] Regarding who gets coverage, Smith found out of all stories with religious content, 14.5% referenced Protestantism or a specific Protestant denomination while 13.5% featured Catholics or Catholicism. Judaism was referenced in 9.5% of stories, Islam in 6.5%, followed by Buddhism and Hinduism at 1.5% each. When Protestantism was broken down denominationally it was found that the United Church was featured in 4% of all religion stories, followed by the Anglican Church in 3.5% of stories and Presbyterians in 1%. Evangelical denominations, when taken collectively, were featured in about 6% of all religion stories.[57] Smith's figure mirrors the percentage of coverage that Lichter and colleagues determined evangelicals received in the American press.[58]

WHY THE NEWS MEDIA COVER
EVANGELICALS THE WAY THEY DO

Reviewing the empirical data makes it clear that certain qualities characterize the news media's coverage of religion in general, and evangelicals in particular. As relayed above, coverage of this latter faith group has been found to avoid the spiritual or theological side of issues; instead, the political, social or economic dimension of stories is highlighted. Coverage tends to be sparse, it also tends to be negative in content (that is, stories focus primarily on negative situations rife with conflict) and negative in tone (that is, stories are pejorative in their description/depiction of conservative believers like evangelicals).

71

Having identified these characteristics it is important to consider why they manifest in the first place. I will now discuss some current theories as to why members of the news media cover religion and evangelicals the way they do.

WHY NO THEOLOGY?

There are several opinions as to why theological or doctrinal content is absent from stories about evangelicals, and for that matter, stories about religion in general. Lack of education and formal training has been cited as a cause. Few journalists in the U.S. are trained to cover the complicated topic of religion. In Canada, no textbook on reporting contains references, let alone a chapter, on reporting religion or the religion beat. Furthermore, no school of journalism at a Canadian community college or university offers a course in reporting religion.

Without academic training to produce qualified religion reporters, their numbers are few. However, it seems that even if qualified religion reporters were available, the demand for such professionals would be limited. Those in charge of news outlets do not value religion stories highly enough to dedicate staff to that beat. It has been observed that "the media seldom hire journalists who specialize in religion reporting."[59] At most newspapers in America the ratio of people working on the sports beat to those on the religion beat is 10 to one or worse.[60] With no designated personnel, stories with a strong faith angle tend to be covered by general assignment reporters with little experience or expertise in the field of religion. In Canada, there are no designated religion reporters working for national television news programs. Daily newspapers in Canada employ about a half-dozen full-time religion reporters, though some of these journalists are asked to "double-up" and cover other beats as well.

Instead of blaming lack of training, others have suggested that it is journalists' staunch dedication to "the facts" that hampers their ability to cover the spiritual side of an issue. That is, because "journalism is empirical in nature," news people are not practiced in the language of the "subjective, intuitive, and unverifiable."[61] Researcher Stewart Hoover agrees that it is journalists' aversion to the subjective that makes them pursue the political, economic, social, or criminal dimension of religion stories. He concludes it is in the realm of the tangible and material that the news media feel most comfortable; conversely, "religion makes claims that often are not verifiable in the conventional sense, and this makes journalists, and particularly editors, nervous."[62]

WHY SPARSE, NEGATIVE CONTENT?

We should not be surprised that television news stories about religion and evangelicals tend to focus on negative situations rife with conflict, given that most news stories, regardless of who is featured in them, focus on these elements as well. Journalistic convention holds that certain types of events and issues are simply more worthy of coverage than others. Four decades ago, Johan Galtung and M. Holmboe Ruge determined that the presence of certain elements, or specific criteria in a news event, cause journalists to deem one situation more worthy of coverage than another. They determined that, among other factors, events that are negative, easy to grasp, unexpected, involve elite personalities or significant numbers, and that can be depicted as a battle between individuals, are far more likely to receive coverage.[63]

Paraphrasing the findings of Galtung and Ruge's and setting them in a decidedly Christian context, theorist Mike Maus explains:

> Millions worship each week . . . proclaim the Gospel and serve
> humanity by feeding the hungry . . . These are not the kinds of
> events journalists define as news. It is news, though when a popular
> minister gets caught in greed or lust. The secular media report
> the unusual; they seldom deal with the usual, and the more usual
> something is, the less attention it gets.[64]

By taking Maus' reasoning one step further, one is able to provide a possible explanation as to why evangelicals experience a paucity of coverage. If evangelicals are covered infrequently, it could very well be because they behave *too well*. That is to say, most of the activities and events evangelicals are involved in are positive and in keeping with Christian ideals of charity and goodwill, and therefore garner little media attention. Whether evangelicals' good behaviour diminishes the amount of news coverage they receive requires empirical study to be confirmed. However, a recent television news report gives some anecdotal support to that assertion. In 2005, a group of Canadian evangelical Christians demonstrated in Ottawa on Parliament Hill. They were voicing their concerns over impending same-sex marriage legislation. The reporter described the demonstration saying: "They didn't shout slogans, they didn't carry signs or banners. Instead, this group of Evangelical Christians gathered on Parliament Hill for an Easter Sunrise service and proclaimed their message with prayers and hymns."[65] The reporter also noted: ". . . we [Global News] were the only media organization that came out to listen."[66]

To a certain extent, the news media's penchant for, and promotion of, stories featuring conflict and controversy is driven by a financial imperative. Media outlets exist to inform but also to make money and money is made by selling advertising. Because advertising rates are tied to market penetration, the more people watching or reading a company's news product, the more that company can charge for advertising. To ensure the greatest audience, news content is adjusted accordingly. Media professionals know that easy to understand, sensational, negative news has greater mass appeal than complicated or positive news and thus it is more profitable.[67] For example, experience suggests to them that a story about evangelicals protesting pro-gay kindergarten textbooks will sell more newspapers or engage more viewers than a story about Evangelicals raising funds to buy books for needy children.

Media critics Neil Postman and Steve Powers observe that of all the news media, television news gives most attention to stories featuring conflict and controversy.[68] Richard Ericson suggests that television preoccupation with this one story type is due to the constraints of its format. He notes that:

[a] newspaper can build its readership by appealing to an aggregate
of minorities, each of whom will select and read only particular sections and items from the total volume available in the
newspaper. Television must do the selecting of items for its audience
and hold its attention throughout the newscast. Therefore television
includes material that is attractive to the widest range of people,
which means an appeal to the lowest-common-denominator mass
audience.[69]

Ian Barrier says more simply "[t]he complexity of religion just does
not translate well to television newscasts. Television, even more than
newspapers, loves the bizarre, the weird and the scandalous because
television newscasts are not structured to deal with difficult concepts."[70]
Of the news in general, he concedes that editors and reporters have to
select stories of interest to their readers and viewers if they hope to
achieve higher circulation and better ratings to stay profitable. And
he realizes that scandals are legitimate news and the media cannot
be faulted for reporting controversies related to religious leaders or
religious organizations. However, he says that the media can be faulted
because "in the media's rush to find the next aberrant story, the deep
reading, more abstract and ethereal stories of people and their search
for faith are often neglected."[71]

In addition to supplanting deeper stories of peoples' search for faith,
theorist Mark Silk argues that coverage of evangelicals that focuses
primarily on negative situations is problematic for yet another reason.
He states that the aura of negativity surrounding such situations is
transferred onto the antagonists of the story; ultimately, all evangelicals are viewed as discordant individuals because of the issues with
which they are associated.[72]

WHY NEGATIVE TONE? (OR, THE ATTITUDES OF JOURNALISTS AFFECT COVERAGE)

Most media scholars take it for granted that the values and beliefs
journalists hold influence the news stories they construct. (As we will
see next chapter, this idea is one of the foundational precepts of frame

theory.) By that reasoning, if news reports are pejorative in their presentation of evangelicals and evangelicalism, it is likely because journalists personally disagree with many of the beliefs and values espoused by this faith group. Up to this point, no research has specifically examined news personnel's view of evangelicals. However, results of past attitudinal surveys of American and Canadian journalists suggest that they have very little in common with conservative Christians. In fact, the existing data show it would be difficult to find two communities that are so similar in look, language, and dress but think so differently.

In the 2007 book *The American Journalist in the 21st Century*, Indiana University journalism professor David H. Weaver along with several colleagues details the results of a comprehensive survey of journalists. Among other findings, the researchers determined that 40% of media personnel characterized themselves as politically left-leaning while 25% positioned themselves on the right.[73] On social issues they were more liberal than the population-at-large. For example, almost 40% felt "abortion should be legal under any circumstances as compared with 25% of the general public."[74] In relation to religious beliefs, journalists were found to be out-of-step with average Americans; the researchers remarked, "the percentage of journalists rating religion or religious belief as "very important" was significantly lower (36%) than in the overall U.S. population (61%)."[75] Furthermore, 44% of journalists said they had nothing to do with mainstream U.S. religions or practiced no religion at all compared to 20% of the public. Also of interest, the researchers identified "a notable drop in the percentage of journalists coming from a Protestant background." In fact, "journalists from a Protestant background were underrepresented, Catholic and Jews were somewhat overrepresented in journalism compared with the overall population."[76] Surprisingly, fewer journalists identified themselves as Evangelicals Christians (5%) than those who identified themselves as Jewish (6.2%).[77]

In 2005, an American survey commissioned by the Annenberg Public Policy Center at the University of Pennsylvania polled journalists from newspapers, broadcast and cable networks, top-market and other local television stations, Web sites, national radio networks, wire services, top-50-market local radio stations and magazines. The journalists' responses to questions about personal beliefs and values seldom shared commonality with the beliefs and values of evangelicals. For example, nearly three in five journalists (59%) favoured laws allowing "two men or two women to marry each other." A third (34%) said they attended worship services only "a few times a year" and almost a quarter (23%) said they "never" attended. Just over a quarter (27%) said they attend either "every week" or "almost every week." In terms of governing ideology, 31% of journalists described themselves as "very liberal" or "liberal" compared to just 9% who identified themselves as "very conservative" or "conservative." Forty-nine percent maintained they were "moderate."[78]

A year earlier, the Pew Research Centre for the People and the Press commissioned a similar survey of journalists and media executives at local and national-level media outlets. At a rate of five to one, national journalists identify themselves as "liberal" (34%) versus "conservative" (7%). Liberals also outnumber conservatives in local newsrooms: 23% of the local journalists said they were liberals while 12% called themselves conservative.[79]

One of the first studies of news personal attitudes, and certainly the most famous, was conducted over 20 years ago by S. Robert Lichter, then with George Washington University, and Stanley Rothman of Smith College. Lichter and Rothman interviewed 240 news professionals working for the *New York Times, Washington Post, Wall Street Journal, Time, Newsweek, US News & World Report*, ABC, CBS, NBC and PBS. Their data demonstrated that journalists, more so than the population at large, hold liberal positions on a wide range of social, political and religious issues (of course, compared to conservative Christians the attitudinal differences would have been even greater).[80] The study was fleshed out more fully and presented in Lichter and Rothman's subsequent book, *The Media Elite*. Some of the specific findings were: over half of elite media personnel did not regard adultery as wrong; 90% percent agreed that a woman has the right to an abortion with 79%

strongly agreeing; three-quarters were at ease with homosexuality.[81] When it came to attending religious services only 8% of the media elite said they attended services regularly, "88 percent seldom or never attended," and "exactly half eschew any religious affiliation."[82] The irreligious nature of journalists was so striking that the researchers noted "a distinctive characteristic of the media elite is its secular outlook."[83]

Almost two decades after his pioneering work with Lichter, Rothman and colleague Amy Black conducted a similar survey as a follow-up to his earlier study of media elites. This time, two hundred and forty-two news personnel from *USA* Today, Los Angeles Times, Associated Press, and CNN were queried.[84] In some respects, journalists had become more socially permissive. For example, Rothman and Black found nearly all of the media elite (97%) agreed that "it is a woman's right to decide whether or not to have an abortion," and five out of six (84%) agreed strongly.[85] On the issue of homosexuality, approval became more firm. Three-quarters of journalists (73%) agreed that "homosexuality is as acceptable a lifestyle as heterosexuality," and 40% agreed strongly.[86] With regard to religion, the researchers noted a shift toward faith. This time, 30% of the journalists said they attended religious service at least monthly (just 10% lower than average Americans) and only 22% reported no religious affiliation (compared to 10% nationally).[87] It is Rothman's opinion that his findings show journalists at elite media organizations have become more religious since 1980.[88] However, there is reason to be critical of Rothman's assertion. First, his sample is drawn from significantly fewer media outlets overall, and second, almost all of the New York City-based media outlets (for example, the New York Times, Wall Street Journal, Time, Newsweek, US News & World Report, ABC, CBS, NBC) were eliminated from the newer study. It is the opinion of many academics and industry personnel alike, that New York journalists, and the media outlets for which they work, are the most liberal and secular in all America.[89] By excluding the most secular of journalists from his study, Rothman may have skewed his findings toward the religious side of the scale.

Up to now, no study has specifically explored Canadian journalists' attitudes toward evangelicals and evangelicals' beliefs. However, as in the U.S., a few studies have more broadly determined where journalists in this country stand on a variety of social, political, economic and religious issues. From the Canadian studies, it becomes clear that many of the values and causes Canadian journalists hold and support run counter to those held by evangelicals.

Quite recently, Marsha Barber and Ann Rauhala's from Ryerson University explored the demographic and political leanings of Canada's television news directors. The researchers found that Canadian news directors, whom they describe as the people "with the most direct responsibility for programming the news on any given day," to be more secular than the rest of the population.[90] Nearly a quarter indicated they had no religious affiliation compared to just 16.2% of the public. They were about half as likely as other Canadians to attend religious services weekly, "almost half (47.8%) of news directors attend a place of worship either once a year or not at all."[91] Among the news directors, those working for Canada's public broadcaster, the Canadian Broadcasting Corporation (CBC), stood out for their lack of religious commitment. The researchers stated that, "CBC news directors are more secular. A third (34.8%) said they never go to a place of worship. This is twice the number (15.9%) of those in the private sector who made the same claim."[92]

Politically, the researchers found that as a group, television news directors were slightly more left-leaning than the population-at-large. When asked which federal party they would vote for if they went to the polls tomorrow, 56% of responding news directors said they would vote for a party of the left or moderate left (10.4% NDP; Liberal 45.8%) while a quarter (25%) said they would vote for a party on the right or moderate right (Canadian Alliance, 10.4%; Progressive Conservative 14.6%). (As suggested by these answers, the survey was conducted before the Canadian Alliance Party and Progressive Conservative Party had merged to form the Conservative Party.) Almost 17% said they would not vote for any of the major political parties. Conversely, the population at large showed slightly greater support for the political right. Using an average of several polls conducted in 2002 (again, before the merging of the Canadian Alliance and Progressive Conservatives), Barber and Rauhala determined that one third of Canadians (32.5%) planned to vote either for the Progressive Conservatives (16.5%) or the Canadian Alliance (16%). Popular support for the Liberals was about 43% and 14.5% for the NDP.[93]

Broken down by network affiliation, one group of news directors— those employed by the CBC—stood out for their left-leaning political outlook. The researchers found CBC employees were far more likely to vote for the New Democratic Party (NDP) than private sector employees with rates of 13% and 4.5%, respectively. Furthermore, no CBC news directors were supportive of the Canadian Alliance, at the time the most socially conservative of the national parties. Conversely, 11.4% of private sector news directors said they would vote for the Alliance if the opportunity arose.[94]

That Canadian journalists are ideologically more liberal than con- servative was first proven empirically more than a decade ago by David Pritchard and Florian Sauvageau, who surveyed over 550 journalists working in different media across the nation.[95] Regarding TV journal- ists, the researchers found that most felt that the news organizations they worked for were "slightly left of centre" when it came to political outlook while they themselves were ideologically more left-leaning than their employers.[96]

The most extensive cataloguing of Canadian journalists' attitudes was performed by Lydia Miljan, now at the University of Windsor, and Barry Cooper at the University of Calgary. Using a standard set of questions related to social, political and religious issues, the research- ers compared journalists' responses with those of the Canadian public. A sample of more than 600 English and French-speaking Canadians from the general population were interviewed by phone, along with 123 English-speaking journalists from major English-language news outlets including the *Globe and Mail*, the *Toronto Star*, the *Financial Post*, selected Southam and Sun chain newpapers, as well as the news-divisions of CBC radio and television, CTV, and Baton Broadcasting. Fifty-five French-speaking journalists from major news outlets in the province of Quebec such as, *Le Devoir, Le Soleil, Le Journal de Quebec*, and the television and radio services of Radio-Canada were also interviewed. The respondents were a mix of management staff and "frontline" reporters.[97]

Because their survey used quantitative measures, the small sample size of the French-language journalists proved problematic for the researchers when it came time to draw conclusions from their data. However, the data regarding Canada's English-speaking journalists had strong reliability and validity and thus the study was not significantly weakened.[98] While the French-language media are influential within the province of Quebec, they hold little sway in the rest of the country. The inverse cannot be said of Canada's English-language media—it is influential across the nation and in Quebec.[99]

Based on the survey responses, Miljan and Cooper determined that more so than the public-at-large, Canada's English-speaking journalists support increased rights for gays and lesbians and a woman's right to an abortion.[100] Conversely, journalists register disdain for those groups that lobby against gay rights or abortion access.[101] When asked whether "the rights of homosexuals receive too much, somewhat much, or too little attention," only 4% of English-speaking journalists thought too much attention was given, compared with 52% of the general public. Twenty-nine percent of journalists thought that the rights of gays and lesbians received too little attention, compared with 16% of the public.[102] When asked whether a woman has both a moral and legal right to terminate her pregnancy, 53% of journalists "highly agreed," while 36% of the general population "highly agreed." At the other end of the scale, 14% of the public strongly disagreed with the statement, compared to just 3% of journalists.[103]

Using a sliding scale anchored on the left by the statement "The group does not deserve more respect than it receives today" and on the right by "The group deserves a lot more respect than it receives today" Canadian journalists were asked about the level of respect

Real Women—a group composed primarily of conservative Christian women who oppose abortion and endorse policies favouring traditional families—should be afforded. Sixty-three percent positioned their response on the "no more respect than today" side of the scale, 16% were neutral and 18% positioned on the "a lot more respect than today" side.[104] When pro-life organizations were the focus of respect, 76% of journalists' ratings fell on the "no more respect than today" side of the scale, 11% were neutral, and 13% fell closer to the "a lot more respect than today" anchor.[105]

In terms of religious belief, Miljan and Cooper determined that Canadian journalists working for the largest and most influential newspapers and broadcasters tend to be significantly cooler toward religion than the public-at-large. (By extension, we might conclude that they are far cooler toward religion than evangelicals). They found found that 32% of English-speaking Canadian journalists said they definitely believe in God compared with 66% of the general population; 14% of them said they definitely did not believe in God compared with 5% of the general population. Fifteen percent of the journalists said they attended a religious worship service regularly, compared with 23% of the general public.[106]

Equally interesting is what the researchers did not find. Of those journalists surveyed, none reported belonging to a conservative Protestant denomination. By way of comparison, 56% of journalists surveyed gave Roman Catholic as their religious affiliation, 23% reported belonging to mainline Protestant denominations and 6% reported Judaism to be their religion.[107] It would seem evangelical journalists are either very shy about disclosing their faith or they are severely under-represented in the news media. It is probably both. In the early 1990s, researcher Wesley Pippert estimated fewer than 50 journalists working at mainstream media outlets in the United States were evangelical Christians.[108] Furthermore, sociologist John Schmalzbauer's study of conservative Christian journalists working for elite media in the U.S. showed that evangelical reporters are afraid to disclose their faith. He found that 10% of evangelicals contacted refused to take part in his study because they felt it would harm their professional credibility if their colleagues knew they were devout Christians.[108] Schmalzbauer hypothesizes that progressive views dominate the culture within newsrooms and, therefore, someone expressing more conservative, religious views would be stigmatized.[110]

Regarding political orientation, Miljan and Cooper found "Canadian journalists place themselves to the left of their audiences."[111] When it came to which federal party they supported in the last federal election, "eight percent of the public indicated that they voted NDP; 20 percent of journalists claimed this to be their choice."[112] Apart from their broad support for the NDP, the voting patterns of journalists were not strikingly different from those of other Canadians.

Economically, the data showed that "journalists did not differ significantly from the public on economic questions. Both groups tended to support a middle-of-the-road position on economics, neither fully capitalist nor statist.[113]

In terms of attitudinal differences between news organizations, Miljan and Cooper, like Barber and Rauhala, observed that journalists working for the public broadcaster, the CBC, were the most left-leaning (socially, economically and politically) of all Canadian news personnel.[114]

In addition to being the most comprehensive chronicling of Canadian journalists attitudes to date, Miljan and Cooper's study is exemplary for another reason. As a second level of analysis, the study compared the responses the journalists gave to the survey questions about politics, social issues and the economy to stories that they had written about those subjects.[115] This was the first study in Canada to perform such a comparison. Miljan and Cooper's combined assessment was particularly significant because it allowed the researchers to determine if the values journalists hold make their way into the news items they create.

The news stories that were analyzed came from the *Globe and Mail, Calgary Herald* and *Le Devoir* newspapers and from CBC's *The National, CTV Evening News, and Le Telejournal* telecasts.[116] Based on their content analysis of the news coverage, the researchers concluded that the causes and ideals Canadian journalists personally support are championed in the stories they report. For example, in coverage of court cases where the rights of homosexuals were the focus, Miljan and Cooper found media personnel slanted their stories in favour of gays and lesbians; conversely, the position and opinions of opposing groups were subjected to criticism or excluded completely.[117]

While Miljan and Cooper determined that Canada's elite journalists are some of the strongest supporters of a woman's right to abortion they did not content analyze coverage of the abortion issue to see if that personal view colours their coverage. However, around the same time they were performing their content analysis, researchers at Simon Fraser University working on behalf of *Newswatch Canada* were conducting their own study of abortion coverage. Examining articles in *The Globe and Mail, Winnipeg Free Press, and Victoria Times-Colonist,* the study found 46% of opinions expressed in the stories were pro-choice, 19% were pro-life, and 35% were neutral.[118] The findings appear to reinforce Miljan and Cooper's overall argument.

As mentioned previously, Miljan and Cooper's survey questions touched on religious belief. However, the few questions that did focus on religion were of a quantitative nature meant to elicit succinct numerical or "yes/no" responses. In no way did they measure, let alone probe, the journalists' attitudes toward evangelicals. Further, during the second stage of their study—the content analysis—the researchers did not examine news coverage related to religious issues. This current research, therefore, has the distinction of being the first study to explore whether Canadian journalists' attitudes toward evangelicals affect their coverage of that faith community; to my knowledge, it is but the second to explore linkages between Canadian reporters' values and their coverage. Because the survey instrument used in my study employed a qualitative methodology, namely open-ended questions, the responses I gathered were lengthy, personal, and highly nuanced, thus affording a profoundly intimate look into the inner-workings of journalists' minds.

CHAPTER 4

News and News Framing

THE NEWS MEDIA

The news media have been given a nearly impossible mandate. In a democratic society, they are expected to provide a forum for public discussion and debate so that citizens can know their options—be they politically, socially, economically, or even religiously oriented—and make the best choices. In addition to their role as conduit to a marketplace of ideas, the news media are also to act as an auditor or watchdog over society, sounding an alarm when an institution, group, or individual veers from accepted legal and ethical practices or behaviours.

Again, society *expects* the news media to produce and transmit cultural knowledge and also *expects* them to wield influence. How ironic it is that for the very tasks we expect them to perform, the news media are often vilified. It would seem that the problem is one of degrees. Most times we will accept the media functioning like dogs on the hunt drawing our attention to this issue, and then to the next. In fact, we are usually pleased to have the media focus our attention on particular issues. After all, they have superior access to the "halls of power" and the "gutters of the underworld" and thus, are in a better position to know the important things that are transpiring. However, once the media have brought the issue to our attention we want them to leave us alone. We do not want newsgatherers influencing our opinion; we do not want reporters telling us how to think.

Gauging when the news media have crossed over the line from social responsibility to undue influence is a difficult task. In this chapter, I will present some ideas and theories that help clarify when the boundary between these two solitudes has been breached. I will begin by discussing what the news is popularly perceived to be and then move to what the news really is.

NEWS AS OBJECTIVITY

In Chapter 1, I said a key goal of this study is to determine if the news media mistreat evangelicals. That such a task can be executed implies that there is a right way, and a wrong way, for media professionals to perform their duties. That is, if journalists can be found "guilty" of mistreating or misrepresenting the people featured in their stories, then there must exist some rule or guideline that conveys how journalists *should treat* those they are reporting on.

The guideline to which I am alluding is, of course, objectivity. In Western Society it is taken for granted that "good journalism" is "objective journalism."[1] As we shall see in a moment, there is a significant disconnect between the ideal of journalistic objectivity and its practice, but for now, let's concentrate on defining the ideal.

Many people are surprised to learn that up to the late 1800s, it was expected that journalists would incorporate a definite editorial slant into their coverage. Indeed, newspapers, the dominant mass medium of the day, openly acknowledged their political leanings marketing themselves as conservative (Tory) or liberal (Reformer/Grit) publications. However, by the 1890s the notion that reporting of the news should be objective arose and by the early 1900s had taken hold.[2] Media historian, David Mindich suggests that "the 'objective' ethic that emerged in the last part of the nineteenth century paralleled a rising sense of journalism as a profession."[3] In an effort to raise their status to that of doctors and lawyers, news men and women established a set of ethical standards that could distinguish professional journalists from the unprofessional—objectivity was the mark of a professional.

To be considered objective, a story had to be written in a detached fashion—that is, the reporter writing the story had to let the facts speak for themselves and keep her personal opinions on the matter to herself. Objectivity was also said to be enhanced if the reporter offered "both sides" of the story in a non-partisan way, used eyewitness accounts of events when possible and corroborated her facts with multiple sources.[4]

Newspapers (and later radio and then television news shows) realized that objectivity could be profitable. By remaining neutral on issues related to politics, economics, or social issues, news organizations were more likely to appeal to a diverse cross section of the population. Put another way, by taking no observable stand they were less likely to offend, and thereby lose, portions of their audience.[5] Objective reporting even spurred sales. In the minds' of the public, objectivity was associated with truthfulness and citizens sought out the most truthful news. Ultimately, the reputation, and by extension, the profitability of a newspaper, radio, or TV newscast was directly tied to its perceived objectivity/factualness.[6]

Told for decades that news reports are written by professional journalists dedicated to the principal of objectivity, people (at least a large portion of them) have come to see the news as a value-free presentations of "the facts." In short, it is now conventional wisdom that the news is, for the most part, True. But the conventional wisdom is wrong—at least that is the opinion of most communications researchers today (of which I am one).

NEWS AS SOCIAL CONSTRUCTION

Despite what journalists might say, news is not an objective presentation of the facts, it is a socially constructed product influenced by the subjective views and opinions of its creators.[7] To call news socially constructed is to highlight its true nature and origins: it is *made* by humans and is therefore subject to limitations, manipulations and biases. The social constructionist position (the formal theory associated with the view that social phenomenon, including news, is "human-made") broadly argues that concepts or practices in a society which are repeated and reproduced over an extended period of time take on the appearance of being natural and immutable. The fact that they are an invention of a particular culture is forgotten or goes unnoticed. This theoretical premise was first popularized in the mid-1960s by Peter Berger and Thomas Luckmann. Establishing the parameters for future discussion, these researchers said that at its heart, the constructionist position assumes that: (1) reality in and of itself is ultimately unknowable; and (2) what we call "reality" is not *a priori* "fact," but the constantly shifting product of *cultural consensus*. Hence, "reality," to the extent that it can be said to exist, is multi-layered, mutable, and sensitive to specific cultural contexts and orientations.[8]

Regarding the media, the social constructionist position reminds us that news reports do not spring forth fully formed from the ground where a news event occurs; what gets transported to our television screen or newspaper page is not the original entity, but a very modified and condensed version of the original. Canadian media theorists Rowland Lorimer and Mike Gasher use this example to elucidate the constructionist position as it applies to news:

> News reports, while based on actual events and real people, never simply 'mirror' reality, as some journalists would contend. A mirror, after all, shows us only what is placed before it, nothing more and nothing less . . . The mirror metaphor and the associated notion of 'reflection' do not adequately describe the role of journalists as content producers. If news media were mirrors, new reports of an event would be virtually identical to one another [which they are not].[9]

According to the constructionist perspective, it is impossible for journalists to reproduce events and issues for the public without first filtering them through a host of internal sociocultural influences. To be sure, the observations a journalist makes when creating a news item are influenced and tempered by "the cultural air we breathe, the whole ideological atmosphere of society, which tells us that some things can be said and others had best not be said."[10] Understanding that news is socially constructed wakes us to the notion that news reports are not value-free packages of facts and it allows us to inoculate ourselves against the media's influence. We can remind ourselves that an event depicted in the news "as common sense" or the "way things are" may represent the wishful thinking of the reporter and not the reality of the situation.

The social constructionist position also forces us to ask a critical question. Given that complete objectivity is impossible, would it be more tenable and genuine to insist that journalists abandon all pretext of objective reporting? In light of how journalism is *currently* understood by the public and practised by reporters, the answer to that question is "no."[11] It is obvious that such a free-for-all approach—were it to be employed without the implementation of a new systemic and structural framework—would not alleviate the problem of biased news coverage but would, instead, make it significantly worse. British Prime Minister, Winston Churchill, is reported to have said, "Democracy is the worst form of government except for all those other forms that have been tried from time to time." A similar assertion could be made about journalistic objectivity. At present, it is the most effective model Western-based journalism has to offer—despite its flaws. Until a new paradigm arises to replace the old, the best the news-consuming public can hope for is that the journalists who bring them their information will act in accordance with the *ideal* of objectivity and thereby endeavour to keep their personal biases in check when covering news events. While human nature makes objective reporting a sisyphusian pursuit, "good" journalism, as it is popularly defined and understood today, consciously pursues it nonetheless. In fact, it is because journalists and the public alike subscribe to the notion that news coverage should endeavour to be objective, that the task set out in this book is legitimate. That is, it is valid to explore whether Canadian journalists succeed or fail in their attempts to report on evangelicals objectively because it remains the normative convention that they should strive to do so.

AGENDA SETTING AND THE NEWS

From the 1970s into the 1980s the tenets of the social constructionist position were increasingly used to explore the production and dissemination of news. However, during this same period another theoretical approach—agenda-setting theory—was being applied to the study of news.

By the mid-1960s media scholars had clarified, for the most part, why journalists gave some events and issues news coverage but not others. There was a strong chance that a situation would "make the news" if it possessed certain elements referred to as "news values." These elements made the event or issue more interesting or exciting for an audience (as noted previously: conflict, the unexpected, and celebrity, are some typical news values). In the end, a situation that contained the most, or the purist, news values had the greatest chance of making the front page or the top of the newscast. (Although, as we shall see later in this section, in addition to a proliferation of news values, a few other factors can also influence whether a news outlet picks up an issue).

Having determined why some issues and events get selected for news coverage, scholars turned their attention to the affect that those selected items (collectively described as the media's agenda) had on people's perceptions (the public's agenda).

When most of us pick up a newspaper or turn on a TV news program, we come with the question, "What's the news today?" It is seldom, if ever the case, that we come asking, "Do *I* think *this* [whatever you are reading or watching] is *news* today?" Agenda-setting theory, on the other hand, would have us ask just that. It requires us to acknowledge, and then examine, the news media's ability to raise the importance of an issue in the public's mind through repeated coverage.

Professors Everett Rogers and James Dearing defined agenda-setting as "a process through which the mass media communicate the relative importance of various issues and events to the public."[12] This idea, that the media can influence the public's agenda, or what people deem to be *important issues*, is neatly expressed in a famous quote by theorist Bernard Cohen. He wrote that the press "may not be successful much of the time in telling people what to think, but it is stunningly successful in telling its readers what to think about."[13]

Although Cohen was writing about the concept of agenda-setting and the media in the early 1960s, it was not until the early 1970s that Maxwell McCombs and Donald Shaw provided the first empirical proof of the mass media's agenda-setting function. Studying the American presidential election of 1968, McCombs and Shaw hypothesized that the news media influenced which issues Americans thought were the most the important in the campaign. To test their hypothesis the researchers selected and interviewed a group of 100 undecided voters, and simultaneously conducted a content analysis of the news media to which those voters had access.[14] Respondents were asked to list the major problems in the country and when their answers were compared to the results of the content analysis, a correlation was found between the respondents' and the media's lists of most important issues. The researchers attributed the near perfect correlation they found between the media's and the respondents' lists to the media's agenda-setting function. However, they admitted that correlation did not prove causation. They noted it could have been the case that the media had simply "tapped into" and reflected concerns that the public already possessed; that is, the media may have been simply mirroring the agenda already set by the public.[15]

Several studies that followed McCombs and Shaw's seminal work empirically established that that the public agenda trails the media agenda. To be exact, they showed that the public's priorities about particular issues form *after* the media have commenced reporting on those issues.[16] A groundbreaking study by Shanto Iyengar, Mark Peters, and Donald Kinder dramatically showed the causal influence the media has on the public agenda. The researchers divided a pool of university age participants into three groups. Each group watched different, specially edited TV newscasts. Group one's newscasts always had lead stories of an environmental nature, two's lead stories focused on national defense, and three's focused on economic inflation. When surveyed about their personal concerns regarding the world—members of each group elevated the lead issue from their newscasts to the top of their individual list of concerns.[17]

Over the last two decades, while conducting their studies of agenda-setting, researchers have noticed that as they examine the news media's agenda—that is, the stories deemed worthy of publication or broadcast—other factors besides a profusion of "news values" can have a bearing on which stories media outlets afford prominence. For example, it has been determined that high profile politicians, like Presidents and Prime Ministers, can influence the media's agenda. One study showed that after the U.S. federal government's declaration of "war on drugs," newspaper coverage of the drug war increased dramatically.[18] Other U.S. studies have likewise shown that the U.S. President or other government officials set the agenda for most important issues nationally.[19] Still other studies have determined that special interest and advocacy groups are able to influence the news media's agenda through the sending of media releases or the staging of events.[20] Similarly, research has shown public relations professionals employed by government, corporations, institutions and organizations can be highly effective at "persuading" the media to pick-up an issue. Key to the success of public relation campaigns is the tool known as the information subsidy. Information subsidies can be as simple as a press release or a meeting notice, but they may also be as refined and complex as a full magazine or a ready-to-air video. When public relations professionals provide information subsidies to journalists, the journalists need not research that information themselves. As such, they are able to produce a story in little time and with little effort.

Several studies have sought to measure the degree to which information subsidies supplied by public relations professionals have influenced the media's agenda. Some have shown that half of the content in elite national newspapers in the U.S. comes from media releases and press conferences.[21] One study in particular conducted by Leon Sigal found more than half of front-page stories for the *New York Times* and the *Washington Post* traced their origins back to press releases and special issue advocates.[22] Other research has determined that local and network television newscast rely on press conferences, press releases, and official proceedings for more than 70% of stories.[23]

In addition to government, interest groups, and public relations professionals influencing the media's agenda, it appears that elite media outlets can set the agenda for smaller outlets. The logic appears to be: "If the 'big boys' think it is important enough to cover, then we do too." Two independent studies concluded that the *New York Times* set the agenda for other national, regional, and local media.[24] Other research has more broadly determined that elite national news outlets in the U.S. set the news agenda for smaller news outlets in the rest of the country.[25] Those studying Canadian news suggest that a similar situation exists in this country.[26]

Studies of agenda-setting throughout the 1970s and 1980s were able to quantify the level of media attention an issue was given; they were also able to show that news stories can, and do, influence "what we think about." However, they were less successful at determining if news stories influence *how* the public thinks about issues. Hoping to remedy these deficiencies, researchers began looking for a new theoretical model to analyze the news.

FRAME ANALYSIS AND NEWS FRAMING

In the late 1980s and early 1990s a convergence of techniques for analysis of news coverage emerged. Elements of social constructionism with its emphasis on cultural influence and journalistic agency combined with the ideas and methods of agenda-setting theory and its associated research to create a new approach to media exploration: frame analysis. Like agenda-setting theory, frame theory (as it is applied to news) takes as its foundational premise that news stories provide their audiences with important subjects to think about. However, it goes a step further and insists that news stories also provide "contextual cues or frames in which to evaluate those subjects."[27] Finally, it maintains that media personnel are able to promote specific interpretations for the events and issues they cover and, in doing so, influence public opinion.[28]

The idea that news reports tell us both *what* issues to think about and *how* to think about them did not originate with frame theory; it had evolved and solidified. As early as the 1920s people working in the news media observed that the product they created had the power to convey meaning and emphasis through inclusion, exclusion and other storytelling conventions.[29] The idea of framing itself was on the scene in the 1970s. Erving Goffman, a sociologist, began the discussion of framing as a concept, writing that frames are a means of "actively classify[ing] and organis[ing] our life experience to make sense of them."[30] Late in that same decade, sociologist Gaye Tuchman applied the concept of framing to the news media writing, "news is a window on the world. Through its frame . . . the news aims to tell us what we want to know, need to know, and should know."[31] In this sense, we can see that news is not a depiction of what "is" but instead is a transmission of selected ideas that have been constructed with specific goals in mind. Following Tuchman's lead, sociologist Todd Gitlin described framing in relation to the news, observing that "[m]edia frames, largely unspoken and unacknowledged, organize the world both for journalists who report it and, in some important degree, for us who rely on their reports."[32]

Though the definition of frames and framing in relation to news has grown considerably clearer, there is still some difference of interpretation among scholars. Some see it as a second level of agenda-setting. Maxwell McCombs and George Estrada, for instance, state that framing is a second level of agenda setting that elevates the importance of certain features or aspects of a particular event or issue. They write:

> When we consider the key term of this theoretical metaphor—
> the agenda—in totally abstract terms, the potential for expanding
> beyond an agenda of issues becomes clear. In the majority of the
> studies to date the unit of analysis on each agenda is an object, a
> public issue. Beyond the agenda of objects, there is also another
> dimension to consider. Each of these objects has numerous attri-
> butes—those characteristics and properties that fill in and animate
> the picture of each object. Just as objects vary in salience, so do the
> attributes of each object.[33]

However, others disagree, arguing that framing should be viewed as a concept separate from agenda-setting. Those opposed to con-flating the two concepts point out that frame theory—like social constructionism—emphasizes greater agency and responsibility on the part of news media professionals. Robert Entman, in his widely-cited and well-respected definition of framing stated that frames take a perceived reality and "promote a particular problem definition, causal interpretation, moral evaluation and/or treatment recommendation for the item described."[34] In his definition, the participatory role played by the journalist—acting as the agent who *promotes* a particular problem definition and *makes* a moral evaluation—is easily discerned. Theorist Jim Kuypers articulating the "purist's view" of framing, explains that framing "moves beyond second-level agenda-setting in that it posits that the media not only focus attention on particular attributes of an issue, making some portions more salient than others, it does so in such a manner that a particular political agenda is advanced."[35] Similarly, media scholar Gerald Kosicki draws attention to the agency of media personnel writing, "Media gatekeepers do not merely keep watch over information, shuffling it here and there. Instead, they engage in active construction of the messages, emphasizing certain aspects of an issue and not others."[36]

The headlines from two of Canada's competing national newspapers provide a vivid example of how the perspective of media personnel can affect the framing of a story. In the fall of 1997, female employees working public sector jobs in nursing homes, day-care centres and social-service organizations took the government of Ontario to court. They were fighting for pay equity. The court decided in favour of the female employees. The day after the verdict, the left-leaning, pro-worker *Toronto Star* ran the following headline on their frontpage: "Women win on pay equity."[37] Conversely, the pro-business, fiscally conservative *Globe and Mail* ran this frontpage headline: "Ontario loses pay-equity fight."[38] The cultural ethos of each news outlets was reflected in the respective frames they chose to employ.[39]

As the example above illustrates, at its most basic level news media framing is a process of information selection and emphasis. When they create a news story, journalists must use interpretive judgment selecting and emphasizing some facts and leaving others out. Entman in his definition further explains that frames (the end result of the process of framing) "select some aspects of a perceived reality and make them more salient in a communicating text."[40] To say an aspect of perceived reality is more salient in a communicating text means some elements of an event or issue have been made more prominent, meaningful, significant or memorable within the context of a news report.[41]

Others have expanded on Entman's idea of inclusion and omission of information, applying it to journalists' selection of sources. A report that uses "elite" media sources, such as institutional experts, business owners, and government officials will frame an issue or event very differently from one which uses "people on the street" or unofficial stakeholders as sources.[42] Certainly, police interviewed for a story about violence in the city's core will have a different slant on the issue than those who are living in the core neighbourhoods. Some media critics suggest that journalists sometimes promote their own interpretation of an issue by searching out interview subjects who will exemplify *their* take on a situation or by finding "experts" who will say what *they* would like to say.[43]

Obviously, when information is included in a news report, it becomes more salient, for that which is left out remains unknown to the audience. However, the language of a news report also increases the saliency of certain facts. When creating the frame for their report, journalists can use metaphors, exemplars, stereotypes, catchphrases and other audio and visual symbols as a shortcut to relay a complex idea quickly.[44] Simply put, some words come "loaded" with pre-existing meaning. For example, saying that someone "came across like a used car salesman" calls up a multitude of negative images of a sleezy, sycophantic conman. Even the connotations of individual words can influence how an audience feels about the issue or event.[45] For instance, a news report about the Para-Olympics could refer to athletes as a people with disabilities or as a handicapped people. While seeming to be similar, the former term focuses on the people, whereas the latter term draws attention to their disabilities.[46] Similarly, a news story could refer to a woman as a hooker, a prostitute, or a sex-trade worker; however, the third moniker affords greater status and legitimacy to the woman than the two preceding descriptors.

Similarly, the quotes/sound bites from sources (interviewees) that are chosen by the reporter and inserted into a news piece contribute to the news frame as well. In his research, Steven Clayman identified three reasons why journalists select the quotes and sound bites that they do. They were: narrative relevance, conspicuousness, and extractability. Narrative relevance relates to a quote's ability to meld with the story-telling function of a news report; the quote must contribute to the unity of the story. Conspicuousness refers to a quote's sensational nature; the more sensational or dramatic a quote, the more likely it will be chosen. Extractability refers to the simplicity with which a quote can be taken from a longer interview and "dropped in" to a news report; quotes requiring a significant amount of contextualization are seldom chosen.[47]

Regarding the selection of quotes from sources, other researchers posit that the extent to which a journalist agrees with the ideology of a group can be discerned by examining the quotes that he puts into his

news report. Those groups with whom the reporter shares similar ideologies will most often have their words reproduced verbatim; that is,
the reporter will quote those sources directly and extensively. In letting
the sources "speak" in their own words, the journalist imbues those
words with factual authority; hence, they are taken more seriously by
the news audience. Conversely, those sources with whom the reporter
does not share sympathies, will have their message filtered through
the paraphrased narration of the report. That is, they will tend not to
be quoted directly.[48] Paraphrased ideas are taken less seriously by the
audience "if only because it is recognized that the original account
was recast and may have been tampered with—inadvertently or
deliberately."[49]

Despite a news frame's vulnerability to conscious and unconscious
manipulation by journalists, it is important to point out that framing
is necessary to the production and consumption of news. When a
reporter covers an event that lasts hours or even days, it is impossible
for her to convey everything that happened in a two-minute television
news story or a 500-word print article. Similarly, when a reporter covers
an issue that pits several individuals or groups against each other, it is
impossible for her to give voice to every point each stakeholder raised.
As news-consumers, we want journalists to go to events, as our proxy,
and tell us "just the important information" from that experience. We
do not have the desire or the time to hear every detail—we want the
"irrelevant information" left out—frames allow this to happen.

Frames are also useful in that they can provide easy-to-comprehend
templates for journalists and audiences alike. If a specific frame has
been used repeatedly in relation to a particular issue or situation, it
becomes "recognizable" (that is, news audiences are familiar with its
characters and plotline). Accordingly, a journalist can use that frame
to process a large amount of information quickly. He simply "attaches"
new bits of information to the "ready-made" frame. Similarly, a well-es-
tablished frame allows the audience to quickly grasp the gist of a piece
without much effort; they can rely on held knowledge and past experiences to fill in the gaps.[50] One of the most recognizable story templates

is the "horse-race" frame that is often applied to elections. As opposed to detailing the platforms upon which the candidates are running, this frame focuses on the polling numbers of competing contestants, highlights a few of their most outrageous and election-damaging gaffs, and draws a conclusion about who is in the lead. Journalists and audience find this frame expedient, if not particular insightful.

Regarding established frames, Entman concurs that the influence of a particular frame increases through "repetition, placement, and reinforcing [cultural] associations."[51] Certainly, the more often a frame appears, the greater its resonance with the culture. Conversely, frames that promote a different perspective and appear less often are less likely to resonate with the broader culture because their ideas and language seem foreign and unfamiliar.[52] Researchers have examined why some frames become "favourites" and enjoy the normative status that familiarity affords. Celeste Condit at the University of Georgia suggests that successful frames (those that get used again and again to the point of becoming naturalized) are:

> Derived from widely based political and moral authorities who represent the experiences and interests of all members of the community. In contrast, illegitimate frames—those likely to be subject to effective argumentative challenge—feature the 'teachings' of only one partisan group in the community (thereby getting us to act in their interests by passing off 'their heritage' as 'ours').[53]

Other research has found frames that resonate most with the population-at-large have these common elements: generalizability, an appearance of common sense, and the application of concrete facts coupled with emotional rhetoric or endorsement by official sources.[54] Furthermore, if a frame's sponsor possesses great economic, political and cultural resources, and has an understanding of and access to media organizations, it is also more like to become normative.[55]

In addition to repetition, the influence of a frame is also increased when it goes unopposed by another frame with a competing message; that is, when it enjoys what I call exclusivity. Entman notes "receivers' [audiences'] responses are clearly affected if they perceive and possess information about one interpretation and possess little incommensurable data about alternatives."[56] In so far as a news frame presents one version of events, the more often it is used exclusively in relation to a specific situation, the more natural or normal its version of reality becomes. When used repeatedly to the exclusion of all others it teaches the audience the "one way" to think about an issue.

Elucidating the idea of how some frames become normative, communications scholar Dietram Scheufele divides the framing process into four increasingly influential stages. "Frame building" occurs as journalists construct stories; next, "frame setting" takes place when those frames are "set" upon the public by mass dissemination. These frames become part of our thinking in a stage called "individual-level effects framing," which results in a final stage where frames are engrained on society and become "societal frames." Once engrained on society, the journalists themselves are influenced by the dominant frames and begin to incorporate them into new stories at the original "frame building stage."[57]

The final stage of Scheufele's model is interesting because it reminds us that journalists are also consumers of their own product and subject to its effects. It also suggests why certain news events get covered so similarly by different media outlets: one journalist sees a colleague's story expressing a complicated concept in a catchy, easy-to-understand way and then, for expediency, frames his/her own story similarly.[58]

Interestingly, the "societal frames" found in the last stage of Scheufele's process corresponds to what cultural studies theorists call a discursive formation. A brief explanation of the latter provides a deeper understanding of the former. The discursive formation, like the societal frame, forms as a result of a process of reflexivity. The discourse (or in Scheufele's model, the frame) travels through the media to the public and back again—time and again—purifying and solidifying itself, accepting fewer and fewer interpretations until it becomes the "normal" or "natural" way of thinking.[59]

To be sure, as a key organizing tool that supplies a context for collection, presentation, and interpretation of the news, frames are very useful. However, reporters run into trouble with regard to framing when they allow their personal biases to skew what should be their neutral relaying of an event or issue.

THE NEUTRAL FRAME

As discussed at the beginning of this chapter, we expect our journalists to be as objective as possible when relaying information so that we might come to our own opinions and decisions about events taking place around us. In cases where a hard-news reporter (as opposed to a designated opinion writer or columnist) radically interprets an issue through his own personal worldview—deliberately framing it in such a way so as to accentuate its negative (or positive) characteristics—he takes away the audience's right to decide how they feel about the information. This need not be so. Events and issues can be framed neutrally. A neutral or objective frame relays to the audience the ideas that the subjects (that is, the people the story is about) are putting forward, as *they intend* those ideas to be understood. The ideas of the subjects are not interpreted or filtered by the reporter according to his personal worldview. This is not to say that the reporter must be uncritical of what his interview subject is presenting as fact. If the subject's information is wrong or misleading and the reporter can prove it by producing objective, empirical data to the contrary, he should do so. Showing that an interview subject is incorrect or purposely twisting the truth is not negative framing, it is simply thorough reporting.

To continue, a neutral news frame will place events in perspective by providing relevant background and will allow those who are criticized in the body of the report to respond fully to the accusations of their critics. Finally, in cases where opinion, and not fact, is relayed, a neutral frame clearly distinguish it as opinion.[60]

I feel obliged to hammer home this one crucial point about neutral and non-neutral frames. Reporting on a negative situation is not the same thing as framing a situation negatively. People do terrible things—they kill, steal, lie, and make offensive comments. Journalists are required to report on these terrible events and can do so neutrally. As long as the journalist at the event lets the facts and the human subjects involved speak for themselves, she is not "guilty" of negative framing. A journalist is only "guilty" of non-neutral framing (be it negative or positive) when her selection of information and language usage is affected by her personal worldview and thus, her report exhibits tangible signs of promoting one side or perspective over another. Doris Graber at Columbia University refers to this breach as moving from "ordinary agenda-setting activities" to "deliberate agenda-building."[61]

I am stressing this "rule" of frame analysis—the method of analysis my study employs—because other studies examining fairness in Canadian news have been harshly berated for what critics considered their arbitrary and flawed categorization of negative reporting. In particular, I am thinking of former CBC News Chief Tony Berman's reaction to a study by the Fraser Institute that found stories on his network's national news to be "anti-American." In a lengthy opinion piece in the *National Post*, he complained that it was not legitimate for researchers to ascribe bias to his network's news simply because some of its reports about Americans described them negatively. He argued, "Using this dubious methodology, the "study" [of anti-Americanism] implies that the very act of reporting these statements displays a bias, which is patently false . . ."[62] As outlined above, frame analysis acknowledges that negative content does not necessarily equal negative framing. Thus, critics must find other reasons to condemn the conclusions drawn using this method.

EXTERNAL FRAMING FORCES

The majority of communication scholars are content with frame theory's overriding logic that journalists' feelings can affect frames. However, theorists arguing from a hegemonic perspective (which is rooted in Marxism) believe it is more than personal preferences that lead journalists away from neutral frames. They insist that journalists intentionally abandon neutral frames in order to promote the interests of society's cultural, political and economic elites. This position is not without some support. Working from a media hegemonic perspective, some researchers have found close parallels between dominant news frames and official government positions. In the U.S., parallels have been noticed for such issues as: air strikes on enemy aircraft, dissident social movements, labour disputes, and the Persian Gulf War.[63] In fact, some studies have shown journalists will promote the views of official sources, even when non-official sources are available to provide alternative frames.[64] It has also been determined that when journalists do include non-official frames, they tend to privilege official frames by making them "the starting point for discussing an issue."[65]

Some evangelicals in Canada have viewed their recent battle to preserve Canada's traditional definition of marriage (defined as the union of one man and one woman) through a hegemonic lens. They argue that gay and lesbian rights groups over the last decade have received extensive financial and legislative backing from consecutive Liberal governments and as such, they have been able to dominant the media's agenda. Ultimately, the tenacity of the pro-same-sex message has been able to persuade a significant number of Canadians that the definition of marriage can be expanded to include the union of two men or two women. Conversely, evangelicals argue, their perspective on the issue has been diminished, disregarded or ridiculed by media.[66]

While the media hegemonic thesis has some empirical support, most theorists feel that it oversimplifies the relationship between news and ideology and they point to evidence that mitigates the central tenets of the position. Kevin Carragee at Suffolk University, for example, found that hegemonic frames were more prevalent when an issue was tied to the well-being of the nation; however, those issues deemed peripheral to national interests were given more ideological latitude.[67] David Altheide at Arizona State cites several examples, including the Watergate scandal and Vietnam War, to show that journalists are not unthinkingly predisposed to support governing power elites.[68] Theorists Werner Severin and James Tankard remain agnostic on the matter:

> The idea of media hegemony is a difficult one to test with research. Although suggesting a powerful influence, it is somewhat vague in its actual implications. If it is true, it is describing such a pervasive phenomenon that it becomes difficult to study because is nearly impossible to set up a control group that is not subject to the effect being researched.[69]

As an alternative to the Marxist-influenced theories, a preponderance of researchers hold the less deterministic position that journalists, when they abandon neutral frames, tend to do so in order to promote society's dominant values or *what they believe* society's dominant values should be.[70] As discussed in the previous chapter, mainstream journalists, for the most part, believe liberal values are best. As such, they are inclined to promote those values and ideals in the news coverage they produce. Conversely, when an individual or group comes along and challenges established liberal conventions or norms, journalists tend to depict them in an unflattering fashion as a means to minimize their influence on society.[71]

Referring specifically to religious groups, reporter-turned-academic Mark Silk theorizes that mainline churches, with their more liberal articles of faith, will be portrayed favourably in news coverage because journalists are "wedded to the values of tolerance and inclusion that conventional churches preach."[72] Conversely, he suggests conservative churches will be depicted negatively because they are unwilling to accommodate certain social behaviours not sanctioned by the Bible.[73]

Silk's observations about the negative coverage of conservative Christians reflects themes other researchers have noted when studying various "outsider" communities. In his study of media framing of the Vietnam anti-war movement of the 1960s, Todd Gitlin found that the black and student peace movements were framed primarily as "civil disturbances"—a depiction Gitlin contends led to public support for the government rather than the protestors.[74] Similarly, William

Gamson at Boston College found that news frames emphasize class distinctions in adversarial and ideological ways. In his study of news frames of anti-nuclear activists' occupation of a nuclear reactor site he found that the mainstream media trivialized the goals of the protestors by framing student activists as "indulgent children of the affluent who have everything they need."[75]

In relation to journalists "adjusting" the content of their news report to promote the norms and values of larger society, theorist Daniel Hallin found that reporters feel justified in vacating their journalistic obligations to fairness and accuracy when covering groups or individuals that they positioned in the "zone of deviance." Groups located outside the mainstream "can be ridiculed, marginalized, or trivialized without giving a hearing to 'both sides' because reporters instinctively realize that [these groups] are beyond the pale."[76]

Given the criteria necessary to achieve success, the marginalized in society seldom triumph in contests of framing. However, some media scholars suggest that social "out-groups" occasionally have opportunities to frame their own positions in the national media. For example, researcher Bernadette Barker-Plummer, after analyzing the strategies employed by the women's movement over the course of its history, determined that groups outside the mainstream culture can "potentially at least, learn about news organizations' routines, practices and discursive logics, and take part in framing themselves."[77]

While in some cases the news media's privileging of one group's message over another's may be done intentionally, in others the muting is systemic in origin. That is, in some cases the normal functions of the news media—its processes, rules, and outputs—actually constitute barriers to full and equal participation in society's discourse. For example, television news reports typically have a very short turnaround time. That is, the time from which a TV reporter is assigned his story, to the time that story makes it to air, is very short; often no more than eight hours. A reporter working on a report about youth violence in the inner-city may want to interview gang members from the area to get "their side of the story" but is unable to track them down during

105

his shift because most live a nocturnal existence and sleep during the day. So, instead, the reporter schedules interviews with those he can reach: typically, the police, social workers and other "officials" who work regular hours.

Even the "packaging" of news reports affects which groups will be heard and how. A 90-second story on television or a 500-word piece in a newspaper leaves little room for a rich mix of opinions; the presentation of one pro and one con position on any particular issue is usually what conventional time or space allows. Similarly, Lorimer and Gasher add that everyday news organizations are presented with an overwhelming number of story options and choices must be made. Simply, no newscast is long enough and no newspaper has enough pages to accommodate all the potential stories that *could* be covered; therefore, some must be ignored.[78]

THE POWER OF FRAMES—SOME CLASSIC EXAMPLES

By presenting a few illustrative examples, the clearest understanding of framing can be gained. Several studies have shown the dramatic impact that the most subtle framing selections and emphases have on human perceptions. In one study, respondents were asked about a new government fee that was to be instituted. Researchers found that when the fee was referred to as a "tax," it was more negatively viewed than when it was called a "charge."[79] In another study researchers asked a random sample of physicians to choose between two options for dealing with a rare Asian disease. When an option was framed in terms of *lives saved*, nearly three-quarters of the respondents selected this course of action. Yet, when the same option was framed in terms of *lives lost* only 22% of subjects chose it.[80] Similarly, in a third study, medical patients and physicians were shown to be significantly less attracted to cancer surgery as a means to a cure when risk was framed in terms of mortality instead of survival rates.[81]

A study from the late 1990s is of particular interest because of its affinity to this current research. Conducted by Thomas Nelson, Rosalee

Clawson, and Zoe Oxley it focused on a group who—like evangelicals in Canada—hold views and values that are at odds with majority opinion. Specifically, the researchers conducted an experiment to examine the effect news frames had on people's tolerance for the Ku Klux Klan (KKK).[82] Participants in the experiment were put into one of two groups and then asked to watch a videotape of a half-hour newscast. Tapes for both groups began with the same generic news stories but ended with a different report about a KKK march. Regarding the basic points of information—who, what, and where—the news reports were identical. However, regarding why and how the march took place was different. By emphasizing certain facts and choosing interview clips from the marchers pertaining to the rights of individuals one of the reports framed the rally as a free speech issue. Conversely, by emphasizing other facts and choosing other interview clips the second report framed the event as a disruption of public order.[83] The researchers found that "participants who viewed the free speech story expressed more tolerance for the Klan than those participants who watched the public order story."[84] As a second stage of investigation, Nelson and colleagues conducted another similar experiment. To exert greater control over the information, the researchers created two print news stories and placed them on a bogus Internet news site. These "faked" stories focused on a request from the KKK to hold a speech and rally on a university campus. Similar to the TV news reports used in experiment one, the first story was constructed around a free speech frame and the second around a public order frame. Those participants who read the free-speech-framed-story expressed more tolerance for the Klan than those who read the public-order-framed story.[85]

MEASURING THE AFFECT OF JOURNALISTS' ATTITUDES ON COVERAGE

In relation to news coverage of social, economic and political issues, hundreds of studies have shown *how* journalists frame certain stories and *how* those frames affect audiences. A sample of those studies have been discussed above and many more can be found in academic journals. However, relatively few studies have demonstrated empircally that the pre-existing attitudes of journalists influence the frames they construct. The dearth of studies on this topic is actually quite surprising, given how important the link between reporter worldview and reporter coverage is to the credibility of frame theory. In Canada, up to now, only Lydia Miljan and Barry Cooper's study, which was discussed at length in the previous chapter, has ever used direct comparison of survey data and news report content to empirically establish the link between reporter ideology and coverage. This study is the second. Let us now turn to the methodology used to study the relationship between reporter ideology and coverage.

CHAPTER 5

Methodology

A s discussed briefly in Chapter 1, this study of evangelicals in
the news media involved two major research components. First,
television news reports about evangelical Christians were analyzed
with special attention paid to the frames used in the reports. Second,
an in-depth survey asking national television journalists about their
attitudes toward religion and evangelicals was conducted. Finally,
the results of the survey and the frame analysis were compared to
determine if there are linkages between how national television
journalists feel about evangelicals and how they portray them in the
stories they produce.

The frame analysis for this study employed a quantitative method of
data collection and analysis and the survey used a qualitative methodology. Combining quantitative and qualitative methods of data collection and analysis, as this study does, allows for multiple perspectives
and therefore controls for systematic errors that may be inherent in any
single technique.[1]

FRAME ANALYSIS

This component of the study investigated how evangelical Christians were framed in the nightly, national television news coverage
of Canada's three largest networks, CBC TV, CTV and Global TV,

THROUGH A LENS DARKLY

between January 1, 1994 and January 1, 2005.[2] Researchers agree that multi-year explorations are preferred over static cross-sectional designs because measurements over time reduce the influence of anomalous historical and social events.[3]

National nightly news from these three networks was chosen because it is the most influential. In combination, privately held CTV and Global and publicly funded CBC TV have over 60% of the market share.[4] Over three-quarters (77%) of Canadians regularly watch nightly national news programs on CBC, CTV or Global to keep abreast of current events, compared to 70% who read a daily newspaper, 58% who listen to radio news, and 27% who regularly look to the Internet for news.[5] Of the news shows available to Canadians, those that air nationally on CBC TV, CTV, and Global TV reach the largest audiences, with ratings averaging between 700,000 and 1 million viewers per night.[6] Conversely, news programs on other smaller Canadian networks such as CityTV, A-Channel, and the CH affiliation of stations—which tend to focuses on local and regional issues—glean significantly smaller audiences.[7]

It is not sheer audience size alone that makes the national newscasts of CBC, CTV and Global influential. Researchers have determined that elite national news outlets set the news agenda (both what will be covered and how it will be covered) for smaller news outlets in the rest of the country. According to Wheaton College Professor of Communication Em Griffin, when an elite outlet "features an issue, the rest of the nation's media tend to pick up the story."[8]

Lydia Miljan and Barry Cooper agree with Griffin, but go further arguing that national television news, specifically, sets the agenda that other *national media* will follow. Citing examples from business and politics, they explain that individuals or organizations who secure TV coverage for their cause "are more likely to obtain the outcome they desire because television attention is usually followed by newspaper, radio and magazine play."[9]

DATA POOL

Full-text print transcripts of the television news reports were the artifacts examined for this study. The transcripts from CTV's news reports were obtained through the Proquest CBCA Current Events Database. Full-text transcripts from Global and CBC TV were obtained from the news archivists-librarians at those networks.[10]

To be selected for inclusion in this study, the script of a news report had to contain one of the following key words (or its close variant): evangelical, fundamentalist Christian, conservative Christian, Christian right, Baptist, Pentecostal, or born-again. Christian fundamentalist and its variants were searched because, as noted previously, fundamentalist Christians are a subgroup of evangelicals. The Baptist and Pentecostal denominations house the country's largest number of evangelical members.[11] Conservative Christian, Christian right and born-again were searched because all are commonly used to describe evangelical Christians. However, if a report described an individual or group as Conservative Christian, Christian right, or born-again and also as Catholic that script was not included in the sample.

VALIDITY AND RELIABILITY OF THE FRAME ANALYSIS

It has been argued that the validity of research is an essential aspect in accepting the outcome of the research. In this regard, "validity designates that quality of research results which leads one to accept indisputable facts."[12] In order to ensure the validity of the frame analysis portion of this study, the entire population of scripts was analyzed by two coders (trained individuals charged with examining textual material and identifying, or coding, the presence of specified phenomenon). The coders trained over two days for about six hours, following the method proposed by Matthew Lombard, Jennifer Snyder-Duc and Cheryl Bracken (2002).[13]

Reliable research seeks to produce similar results over and over again. "Reliable data, by definition, are data that remain constant throughout variations in measuring process."[14] To establish reliability for the frame analysis portion of the study, the first day was dedicated to operationally defining terms and studying, discussing and adapting the coding instrument. The reliability of the coding instrument itself was informally assessed using a sample of 20 "trial" TV news scripts. The scripts were not part of the sample to be analyzed for the study; instead, they were randomly selected news reports that aired before January 1994 or after January 2005. To refine the coding instrument, the coders would first code one of the "trial" scripts and then compare their findings. Where inconsistencies occurred, the disconnect was discussed and, if needed, the descriptions and definitions on the coding instrument were fine-tuned.

On the second day, the reliability of the coding instrument was formally assessed using a pilot test with the coders working independently. A high level of agreement between coders was achieved. When performing the actual analysis, the coders again worked independently without consultation. Intercoder reliability was .88 using Holsti's formula. Inconsistencies between coders were resolved through discussion, yielding one set of data.

CODING CATEGORIES—NOMINAL VARIABLES

The examination of the reports used two levels of analysis: 1) the overall news report and, 2) the individual news frames. All of the news reports were coded for several nominal variables at the first stage of analysis (for a full description of these categories see the Coder's Guidebook, Appendix 1). This manifest content included: the date the report aired, the network that aired it, the number of words in the news report, its format, the number of theological references it contained, and the overall topic or main focus of the news report as it related to evangelicals.

Regarding the format of the news reports, the stories were placed into one of four categories. They were:

1. Anchor Read—shorter stories that are read live by the anchor during the newscast to the viewing audience (the anchor is seen and heard).

2. Anchor Read to a Clip—similar to the Anchor Read in that the story is read live by the anchor. However, at one point in the story (it can be right at the beginning, in the middle or at the end) the anchor's lines are interrupted/replaced by a pre-recorded interview clip from someone else. The clip is generally a 10 to 15-second quote from someone who was interviewed in the field/on the scene.

3. Reporter's Pre-Recorded Package—these are reporter-based stories introduced by the anchor but "told" by the reporter. They are generally the longest type of news story. They feature narration by the reporter and clips (quotes) from several different sources. A reporter's pre-recorded report is easily identified because the anchor always names the reporter who is "bringing us the story".

4. Live Interview/Live Commentary—the live interview is easily identifiable because it appears in question and answer format. Generally, it involves the anchor asking questions of an in-studio guest or of someone linked to the news station electronically. The live commentary involves a single speaker, most often the anchor or someone else from the network, delivering a prepared speech on an issue.

About the coding of theological references: American studies of religious news coverage have noted that very little theology makes its way into television news reports.[15] I felt that it was important to explore whether this was also the case in Canada. To that end, the number of times a theological statement was mentioned, as well as the nature of the theological reference itself, was coded. Also noted was who made the theological reference; be it an evangelical source, non-evangelical source, or the reporter.

Specifically, if a scripture verse(s) was quoted (or paraphrased) by a source or by a reporter it was counted as a theological reference. A theological reference was also deemed to have been made if the quote of a source or reporter included one of the following syntactic structures: "I/we/they believe . . ." (in reference to religion); "God/Jesus/Christ says . . ."; "the Bible/scripture says . . .". To capture the nature of the theological reference, the sentence or two in which it appeared was transcribed verbatim on the code sheet.

When a section of the news report mentioned several different theological points/religious beliefs in an unbroken sequence it was counted as just one theological reference. For a second theological reference to be counted, it had to be separated from the first reference in the script by non-theological information.

Coders determined a source's religious leanings or affiliation—evangelical or non-evangelical—by how they were described in the body of the report. Sources were coded as evangelical when they were shown actively supporting evangelical religious beliefs and causes, were called an evangelical (or a similar religious descriptor), and/or were said to belong to an evangelical group. Conversely, sources were coded as non-evangelical when they showed no signs of evangelical belief or behaviour, were described in terms unrelated to evangelical faith, and/or were said to belong to a non-evangelical organization (for example academic institutions, businesses, government agencies, community service organizations). See Appendices 1 (coding sheet), and 2 (code book with definitions) for details.

Regarding the topic of news reports, prior studies have found that religion coverage in general, and of evangelicals specifically, tends to focus on a handful of subject areas.[16] By adapting and combining the ideas of other researchers a list of possible topics was created. They were:

1. Evangelicals involved in religious observance/theological discussion

2. Evangelicals involved in internal church business/church governance (not involving doctrine or theology)

3. Evangelicals involved in charity work/volunteer work/mission work

4. Evangelicals involved in proselytizing/ "witnessing"

5. Evangelicals involved in social actions/protest (but not in the courts, not related to education and not with an overtly political focus)

6. Evangelicals involved in political action/issues (but not related to education and not enacted through the courts)

7. Evangelicals involved in legal actions/issues (but not related to criminal activity and not related to education)

8. Evangelicals involved in educational actions/issues

9. Evangelicals involved in criminal or immoral actions/issues

10. The life or exploits of a famous evangelical (i.e., TV evangelist, entertainer or big business owner)

If a coder felt that none of the topics on the list applied to his/her story, a final category, "other," could have been chosen.

CODING CATEGORIES—FRAMES

The second stage of analysis focused on news frames, using frames as the unit of analysis. It has been observed that the weakness of many framing studies is that they do not explain "which mechanisms were used to arrive at particular frames and, how [the frames] have been measured empirically."[17] To combat the charge of imprecise or capricious identification of frames, it has been suggested that coders be presented with a list of identifiable frame attributes which serve as "manifest indicators for the identification of frames."[18]

To combat the charge of ill-defined measurement, it has been suggested that researchers employ a rating scale to evaluate the negative, neutral or positive qualities of those frames that are identified.[19] In Peter Kerr and Patricia Moy's study of fundamentalist Christians in newspapers, and in Kerr's study of fundamentalist Christians in TV news, a rating scale and an inventory of potential frames were employed. High intercoder reliabilities in their studies suggests that this method is reliable.[20] With a mind to achieving similar success, the frame analysis portion of this study was modeled on the coding instruments used by these two American researchers. Specifically, coders for this study were given a pre-made list that categorized the numerous ways evangelicals *could be* framed in a news report. The coders' guidebook outlined in detail the keywords, situations and various other devices that could indicate the presence of specific frames. To gauge the emotive quality of an identified frame, coders used the model/criteria of the neutral frame as the control or measuring stick (see Chapter 4, The Neutral Frame, for details). That is to say, while analyzing the reports they remained ever conscious that a neutral frame is one that: puts forward the ideas of the news subjects as they *intend* those ideas to be understood; places events in perspective by providing relevant background; allows those who are criticized in the body of the report to respond to the accusations of their critics; and clearly delineates when opinion, and not fact, is relayed. Those frames that breached the neutral frame's criteria were deemed positive or negative according to the supporting textual elements.

Frame theorist James Tankard states that a list of frames with their attributes may be derived ahead of time based on theoretical or research literature about a topic.[21] The frames in this study's list were arrived at based on historical analysis, similar academic exploration done in the U.S., sociological research done in Canada, interviews with prominent Canadian evangelicals and a pilot study done on Canadian news reports.[22]

Twenty-four frames were presented in 12 pairs as opposites. Specifically, coders were to determine if a news report framed evangelicals as:

1. Intolerant, Neutral or Tolerant. To identify frames from this category, coders looked for evangelicals being portrayed as able to accommodate (or not) beliefs or values contrary to their own.

2. Insincere, Neutral or Sincere. For this category, coders analyzed portrayals of evangelicals involved in preaching, decorous or controlled worship, proselytizing, charity work or community outreach paying particular attention to the implicit and explicit references made regarding the motivation behind the evangelicals' words and deeds.

3. Unintelligent, Neutral or Intelligent. Coders looked for evangelicals being portrayed in terms of their intellectual ability or education level.

4. Neglectful, Neutral or Responsible. Coders looked for evangelicals being portrayed in terms of their obligations or duties to themselves, their jobs, their families and society.

5. Pushy with Social Views, Neutral or Respectfully Advocating Social Views. Coders looked for evangelicals being portrayed as activists (e.g. involved in marches, petitions, protests) with the goal of advancing their own social views and values.

6. Threatening Politically, Neutral or Reassuring Politically. Coders analyzed portrayals of evangelicals involved in politics or politicians who were evangelicals.

7. Criminally-Minded, Neutral or Law Abiding. Coders analyzed portrayals of evangelicals involved in ethical dilemmas, courts, criminal activities or situations where the law or legal matters were the focus.

8. Superstitious, Neutral or Spiritual. Coders analyzed portrayals of evangelicals involved in, or talking about, the supernatural (e.g. ecstatic or boisterous worship, prayer, spontaneous healings, speaking in tongues, prophecy or being "slain in the spirit").

9. Vengeful, Neutral or Forgiving. Coders looked for situations where evangelicals were wronged or perceived that they had been wronged and analyzed how the evangelicals were portrayed as responding to the offending party.

10. Un-Canadian, Neutral or Canadian. Coders looked for evangelicals being portrayed as "fitting in" or "not fitting in" with the rest of Canadian society. In particular, they looked for Canadian evangelicals being portrayed as more culturally "American" than Canadian.

11. Deserving of Media and Societal Bias, Neutral or Undeserving of Media and Societal Bias. Coders analyzed situations where evangelicals were portrayed as being subjected to societal or media bias (specific references to societal or media bias would be made).

12. Holding Outdated Values and Beliefs, Neutral or Holding Contemporary Values and Beliefs. For this category, coders looked for evangelicals being portrayed in terms of the current relevance of their values and beliefs.

(For a full description of these categories see the Coder's Guidebook, Appendix 1.)

A brief example illustrates how theoretical material could translate into a frame on a list. Researchers have observed that Canadian evangelicals—in the past and the present—have been characterized by the media, mainline churches, or by the population-at-large as being "too American."[23] Specifically, it is Canadian evangelicals' open (and sometimes boisterous) proclamation of their faith, and their willingness to let their faith inform their social and political activism, that is viewed as distinctly un-Canadian behaviour. (As detailed earlier, it is popular convention among most Canadians—the nominally religious, the irreligious, and the anti-religious—that faith is best when quiet, decorous and left out of the public square.) Based on the observations of these previous researchers, the "Un-Canadian/Canadian" frame designation was included on the coders' list of possible frames.

To facilitate measurement, each pair of frames was placed on an ordinal scale. The frame from the pair that expressed the negative quality (for example, intolerant) was stationed on the left of the scale where it was subdivided into its very negative and somewhat negative manifestations (very intolerant; somewhat intolerant). Similarly, the frame that expressed the positive quality was stationed on the right side of the scale and subdivided into its somewhat positive and very positive manifestations (somewhat tolerant; very tolerant). A rating of balanced/neutral was positioned at mid-scale. Each position on the scale was given a value starting at 1 on the far left and moving through to 5 on the right. For example, the opposites Intolerant and Tolerant appeared on the code sheet as:

Very Intolerant	Somewhat Intolerant	Balanced/ Neutral	Somewhat Tolerant	Very Tolerant	DID NOT MENTION
1	2	3	4	5	

To increase the validity of their ratings choice, coders were required to justify their decisions by providing textual evidence and, when necessary, explanatory notes.

SURVEY

This part of the study employed a questionnaire administered by e-mail or telephone to national newsroom personnel at CBC, CTV and Global television networks. The survey's goal was to investigate the journalists' attitudes toward religion in general, and evangelicals specifically.

VALIDITY AND RELIABILITY OF THE SURVEY

In order to develop a valid survey instrument, a first draft was prepared and distributed to a panel of experts for review and modification. The panel included scholars in the field of communication studies and social science research methods, executives from the Evangelical Fellowship of Canada and select news media personnel. This panel of experts helped to refine the questionnaire in regard to clarity, design, length and appropriateness for the purpose of this study.

Unlike most surveys which consist of close-ended questions that require the respondents to provide answers of just one or two words, this study's survey included probing, open-ended questions that allowed the respondents to answer in essay style. I want to stress the advantage that open-ended questions have over those that are close-ended: open-ended questions stimulate free responses and bring latent information to the surface and this is crucial when attempting to gauge the attitudes of a sample population. Survey experts George Gray and Neil Guppy note that because open-ended questions let respondents answer in their own words, using as few or as many words as they like, they allow them to stress what they feel is important and prevent the researcher's assumptions from inhibiting the answers.[24] Regarding the quality of data gathered from open-ended responses, a number of researchers have reported that respondents write lengthier and more self-disclosing comments on e-mail open-ended questionnaires than they do on mail survey questionnaires.[25]

When using a survey consisting of open-ended questions, reliability is a measure of the consistency of the questions' results. Consistency is defined as the ability of the respondents to understand the true meaning of the questions as they are stated. Random error is the most common cause for diminished questionnaire reliability; it occurs when questions are poorly worded, or when they are presented in a confusing fashion (for example, an earlier question unintentionally negates a later one). Therefore, to determine reliability a "pilot test" with the proposed questionnaire should be conducted on a sample group. The consistency of the measurement is tested by having the sample group take the survey twice (test, retest). If the results are consistent, then the instrument may be considered reliable.[26] The survey instrument for this study was tested and retested on a small group of local journalists and results showed the instrument to be reliable.

Regarding the format of this survey, Gray and Guppy note that surveys administered by e-mail or phone "may have lower rates of measurement error" because the distance between researcher and respondent "eliminates many of the non-verbal cues associated with personal interviews (where interviewer appearance and gesture have influences)."[27]

PARTICIPANTS

While national television reporters for CBC, CTV and Global networks were the prime targets for this survey, producers, writers, and managers (that is, anyone with a role in the creation or revising of the *written* content of the national news reports) were also asked to participate. Ninety-seven potential candidates were identified and each was sent an information letter on June 16, 2006, via e-mail. The letter outlined the study and asked for their participation (see Appendix 3).

Journalists interested in participating in the study were asked to reply, via e-mail, to the information letter; they were to specify whether they wanted to be e-mailed the survey questionnaire (to be completed on their computer and returned via e-mail) or whether they wanted to be contacted by phone to complete the questionnaire verbally.

The e-mail and telephone survey instruments contained identical open-ended questions (see Appendix 4 and 5).

I was solely responsible for conducting the survey. The last completed form was returned via e-mail in July, 2006. In total, 21 journalists participated in the survey; 20 through e-mail and 1 by telephone. This survey's response rate of 21.6% is within the normal range for e-mail surveys taking place since 2000. In her study of e-mail survey response rates, Kim Sheehan noted that over the last 15 years the average response rate has been decreasing; by 2000 it had dropped to 24%.[28] In 2003, researcher Thomas Johnson used e-mail to survey American journalists about news ethics and noted a continuing downward trend; he received a response rate of just 20.5% for his study.[29]

While higher response rates are always to be wished for, Gray and Guppy point out that the quality of a survey's results are not necessarily compromised by lower rates. It is only when those who did not participate in the survey are characteristically different from those who did participate that quality is compromised; that is, "only if nonrespondents are distinctive in comparison to respondents does their exclusion from the survey actually lead to bias or distortion in survey results"[30] As the respondents and nonrespondents of this survey were Canadian, national, television journalists they shared high uniformity.

Further, high response rates are less important when the data is qualitative and thus "content rich." Unlike quantitative data which relies on the ebb and flow of extensive numerical patterns to draw inferences, qualitative data does not need large samples to be valuable because it allows a researcher to produce significant insights by unwrapping the layers of meaning contained in even the briefest discourse. Other researchers studying Canadian journalists have prized qualitative data for its ability to capture and relay the innermost thoughts of media personnel and for its corresponding ability to facilitate a more accurate assessment of subjects' manifest behaviours. To determine Canadian journalists' attitudes toward public opinion, Anne Marie Gringras and Jean-Pierre Carrier of Laval University used semi-structured interviews to gather qualitative data from 26 reporters.[31] Over the last decade, Gringras and Carrier's work has remained the definitive work on the subject, thanks in large part to the penetrating findings their qualitative data allowed them to bring to the fore.

SURVEY QUESTIONS

Nine questions were included on the questionnaire. The questions are listed below along with the rationale for asking them:

1. What position do you hold/what job do you perform for your national news program?

Question 1 allowed me to verify that the respondent was in someway responsible for the creation or revision of the written content of television news reports. Whereas the opinion of reporters, writers, line-up editors and other such journalistic staff was being sought, the opinion of camera operators, floor directors and other more technical staff was not.

2. Do you consider yourself a practicing member of any religion? If yes, please briefly explain which religion you practice and if possible identify the specific denomination, branch, division, sect or subgroup to which you adhere.

3. Does your religious belief lead you to perform rituals or routines such as prayer, meditation, study of sacred texts or attending religious services? If yes, please briefly explain what they are and how often you participate in them.

A journalist's attitudes toward evangelicals may be influenced by his/her larger perception of religion in general; therefore, Questions 2 and 3 asked about the role religion played in the life of each news person. These questions allowed me to explore whether certain religious beliefs and practices (or lack of them) portended the amount of affinity a journalist felt for evangelicals. Question 2 was particularly important because it allowed me to determine if any of the national television journalists were evangelicals themselves.

4. Briefly state what you see as the main beliefs, characteristics and attitudes of evangelical Christians (for clarification, evangelical Christians are also known as conservative Protestants).

Question 4 explored what journalists perceived to be evangelicals' dominant traits; in particular, it sought to determine whether evangelicals are primarily associated with certain religious beliefs or specific social issues.

5. In terms of religious beliefs, how are you most similar to evangelical Christians?

6. In term of religious beliefs, how are you most at odds with evangelical Christians?

Questions 5 and 6 sought to determine which evangelical religious beliefs journalists are most comfortable with and which they are least comfortable with.

7. On which social issues do you find yourself in agreement or mostly in agreement with evangelical Christians?

8. On which social issues do you find yourself most at odds with evangelical Christians?

Similar to Questions 5 and 6, questions 7 and 8 sought to determine which evangelical-associated social issues journalists support and which they do not. Furthermore, question 5, 6, 7, and 8 allowed me to more deeply probe the sentiments the journalists relayed in Question 4 by forcing them to stratify their answers into clearly delineated pro and con opinions.

9. What sources have provided you with most of your information about evangelical Christians?

By asking where journalists get their information about evangelicals, as Question 9 does, I was able to postulate whether journalists are adequately and accurately informed about the evangelical faith and its members. The question also allowed me to explore connections between where journalists get their information about evangelicals and what opinions they hold about evangelicals.

DATA ANALYSIS

The data obtained from the questionnaires were analyzed using the guidelines for categorizing suggested by Yvonna Lincoln and Egon Guba in their text *Naturalistic Inquiry*.[32] Specifically, journalists' responses were scrutinized for commonalities. When common elements were noted, these were reassembled into related categories and subcategories. Smaller groupings, in turn, were combined into overarching categories that best described "what happens" at the level of specific questions' responses and at the aggregate level of the survey responses as a whole. Finally, conclusions were drawn for use in theory building.

Although the answers to the questionnaire were intended to provide qualitative insights into journalists' perceptions, there were elements in the responses given that proved amenable to a degree of reliable, statistical summation. Where appropriate, these quantitative findings are highlighted in Chapter 7 of this book so that the reader might judge more precisely the extent to which certain themes and issues were evident across the survey sample.

MERGING THE DATA FROM THE FRAME ANALYSIS AND THE SURVEY

To address the question whether linkages exist between the stories national television journalists produce about evangelicals and the attitudes they hold about them, the data from the frame analysis and the survey were considered collectively. Specifically, evidence of correlations between frames and attitudes was determined by identifying and then comparing the news reports' most prevalent frames to the journalists' most prevalent attitudes. When a prevalent frame was accompanied by a corresponding prevalent attitude, a relationship between these two variables was deemed to exist.

CHAPTER 6

News Reports about Evangelicals: The Good, the Bad, and the Neutral

Human nature being what it is, it is quite likely that many readers of this book will begin their perusal of the text here at this chapter. It is here that the first findings of my research—the results from the analysis of the news reports—are presented and thus, the question "What did you find out?" begins to be answered. For those who put forth the effort and read Chapters 1 through 5 before arriving here, I appreciate your patience and admire your endurance. Some of the preceding chapters, particularly Chapter 4 with its heavy theoretical focus, are tough sledding. What follows is straightforward. We will now look at the kinds of news stories that evangelicals have been featured in and how they have been portrayed in those stories.

NUMBER OF REPORTS BY YEAR

From January 1994 to January 2005, evangelicals were featured in a total of 119 national television news reports. For the most part, the reports were fairly evenly distributed over the 11-year period; 10 reports per year was the median and 11 was the mean. However, in the year 2000 the number of reports took a sharp rise, increasing to 19. In 2000, evangelical politician Stockwell Day took over the leadership of the Canadian Alliance Party and campaigned to become Prime Minister; 17 of the 19 "evangelical" stories that year focused on Day and his performance in the federal election campaign. At five reports, 2001 saw the fewest number of news stories featuring evangelicals (see Figure 1).

FIGURE 1
NUMBER OF NEWS REPORTS PER YEAR

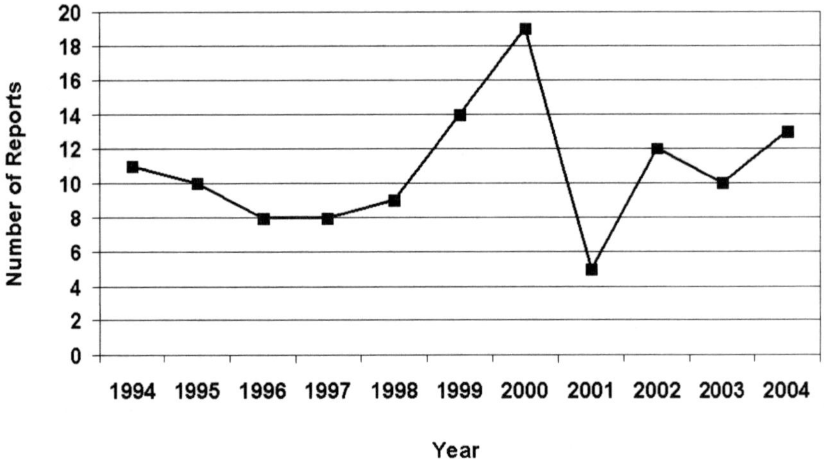

REPORTS BY NETWORK AND NUMBER OF WORDS

Divided according to their respective network, CTV covered evangelicals most often, featuring them in 58 stories; Global had 33 stories in which evangelicals were featured and CBC had 28. However, for CBC, running fewer stories did not equate to less airtime devoted to evangelicals. In fact, because CBC's news stories tended to be longer than those of CTV or Global, the number of words (and therefore the total amount of airtime) that network dedicated to coverage of evangelicals was greatest of all. Combined, CBC's 28 stories contained 38,133 words while CTV's 58 stories had a total word count of 24,741.

At about 12,622 words Global devoted the fewest words to the coverage of evangelicals.

REPORTS BY FORMAT

Most, or 83%, of the reports featuring evangelicals were in the longer format of Reporter's Pre-recorded Package. Broken down by network, about 89% of CBC's news reports about evangelicals were packages, 83% of CTV's, and 79% of Global's reports were in the package format.

Just under 6% of all reports were in the Live Interview or Commentary format. Divided by network, about 11% of CBC's, 9% of Global's, and 2% of CTV's reports were in this format. Similarly, just under 6% of reports were Anchor Reads. Global had 9% in this format, and CTV had about 7%; CBC had no reports in this format. Only 5% of reports were in the Anchor Read to Clip format. By network, just under 9% of CTV's reports were in this form and 3% of Global's; CBC had no reports in this format.

REPORTS BY THEOLOGICAL REFERENCES

About one-third of the reports contained one or more theological reference. Of those, the vast majority contained just one reference. Of the minority, 5 reports contained two references, 1 report contained three, and 1 atypical report contained 17 theological references, of which 16 related to end-times prophecy. By network, about 35% of CTV's, 46% of CBC's and 18% of Global's reports referenced theology one or more times.

Almost half (49%) of the theological references were contained in the interview clips of evangelical sources, while 43% were found in reporters' narration. Non-evangelical sources were responsible for 8% of the theological content in the reports.

Tenets of belief that were at odds with contemporary scientific or cultural perspectives received the most attention, with 54% of reports containing theological content of this nature. For example, six separate reports contained Bible-based arguments against homosexuality, five reports included references to scripture or statements of belief that affirmed creationism and cast dispersion on Darwin's theory of evolution, four highlighted end-times prophecy, and four provided biblical reasons why women should submit to their husbands. The belief that other faiths are inferior to Christianity was also referenced as was biblical support for corporal punishment.

REPORTS BY MAIN FOCUS/TOPIC

As detailed in Table 1, reports featuring evangelicals involved in political actions or issues dominated coverage: about 29% focused on this topic. These stories showed evangelical politicians or evangelical citizens involved in politics mostly at the federal level. A story was not considered eligible for the "evangelicals involved in politics" coding category if the political issue related to education or was connected to a court action; there were more specific categories for stories of that nature.

Table 1
Topic of News Reports

Topic	%	N
Politics	29.4	35
Crime/Immorality	16.8	20
Social Activism	14.2	17
Rel. Observ/Theology	14.2	17
Legal Actions	8.4	10
Education	6.7	8
Proselytizing	4.2	5
Church Business	2.5	3
Charity Work	2.5	3
Celebrity Evangelical	.8	1
Total	100	119

NEWS REPORTS ABOUT EVANGELICALS

After politics, evangelicals were most often featured in stories involving criminal or immoral activity: almost 17% fell into this category. These stories focused primarily on evangelicals perpetrating sexual or physical abuse or engaged in sexual or financial impropriety. However, 4 of the 20 crime-related stories showed evangelicals as victims of crime.

Next, just over 14% of reports showed evangelicals involved in social action or protest. These stories were about demonstrations, marches, petitions, sit-ins or other actions. If the social actions were exercised through the courts, related to education or had an overtly political focus, the report was not placed in this category, but in another more attuned to the specific content.

At slightly over 14%, reports featuring evangelicals involved in religious observance or theological discussion tied those showing social protest. Many of these stories were about special church services, though stories about conferences or seminars by evangelical leaders for an evangelical audience also appeared.

Reports focusing on evangelicals involved in legal actions or issues comprised a little over 8% of the population of scripts. Evangelicals were shown using the courts to stop or challenge decisions made by government, regulatory bodies, businesses or community organizations. If the court action was related to educational matters, the story was placed in the education category. If the court action was related to an evangelical having committed a crime, the story was placed in the crime category.

Evangelicals involved in educational issues made up almost 7% of reports. Stories focused on all levels of education, including university. Most showed evangelicals trying to implement new or change existing school practices and curriculum.

Evangelicals involved in proselytizing comprised about 4% of reports. Reports in this category showed evangelicals actively trying to influence the religious lives/religious beliefs of people locally and abroad. Stories were about missionaries working abroad and large local concerts held with the specific goal of teaching non-Christians/non-evangelicals about Jesus and Christianity.

Evangelicals involved in church business or governance made up 2.5% of reports. The non-theological discussions and decisions of a church or denomination were the focus of coverage. Stories were about new building construction, hiring or firing of a minister, or two churches or denominations amalgamating.

Similarly, just 2.5% of reports focused on evangelicals involved in charity or volunteer work. Stories in this category showed evangelicals helping others locally or abroad to live a better *material life.*

One report (about 1%) focused on a celebrity evangelical. To qualify for this category a report had to highlight biographical information about a famous evangelical over any overt Christian message they were relaying. If an evangelical was famous due to political activity, the report was placed in the political story category.

FRAMES EMPLOYED

In the total population of news reports, evangelicals were negatively framed as being somewhat intolerant (M=2.17, SD=1.19), somewhat politically threatening (M=2.29, SD=1.16), somewhat criminally-minded (M=1.75, SD=1.01), somewhat un-Canadian (M=2.08, SD=1.08), and slightly unintelligent (M=2.44, SD=1.23). They were framed in a balanced or neutral fashion between superstitious and spiritual (M=2.69, SD=1.18), as balanced between vengeful and forgiving (M=2.81, SD=1.25), balanced between pushy and respectful when presenting social views (M=3.09, SD=1.50), balanced between having outdated values and beliefs and contemporary ones (M=3.22, SD=1.71), balanced between insincere and sincere (M=3.24, SD=1.59), and balanced between neglectful and responsible (M=3.37, SD=1.31). The one specifically positive frame depicted evangelicals as being somewhat undeserving of media and societal bias (M=4.21, SD=1.05).

An average of the scores for all frames produced a mean of 2.83 (SD=1.30), or an overall rating of "neutral/balanced." In terms of actual number of frames used in the 119 reports, 241 frames were identified of which 128 were negative (65 somewhat; 63 very), 30 were neutral, and 83 were positive (45 somewhat; 38 very).

On a network by network basis, the news reports that aired on CBC TV employed the most negative frames; collectively, they generated a mean of 2.42 (SD=1.27) or an overall rating of slightly negative. An average of the scores for all frames used in the reports of CTV produced a mean of 2.93 (SD=1.28) or an overall rating of neutral, and the frames used in the reports of Global TV produced a mean of 3.14 (SD=1.25) or an overall rating of neutral.[1] A more detailed examination of the frames used by the individual networks is included at the end of this chapter.

As was explained previously in Chapter 4, when a frame's frequency (that is, how often it is used) and exclusivity (that is, not being opposed by a contradicting or competing frame) are high, it becomes more salient and, therefore, more influential in terms of *how* an audience thinks about an issue. By those criteria, it can be said that the negatively charged "intolerant," "criminally-minded," and "un-Canadian" frames and the positively charged "undeserving of media and societal bias" frame were more likely to influence audience opinion than others that appeared in the news reports about evangelicals (see Figure 2). However, in Chapter 8 it will be discussed why, in terms of influence, the positive "undeserving of media and societal bias" frame would likely have less of an impact on audience opinion than any of the dominant negative frames above.

The "evangelicals as intolerant" frame appeared in about 24% of all reports (10.1% somewhat intolerant; 14.2% very intolerant), while 7.5% of news reports framed evangelicals in a neutral or balanced fashion in relation to tolerance and about 6% framed them as tolerant (4.2% somewhat tolerant; 1.6% very tolerant). An example of a news report that coders determined framed evangelicals as "intolerant" was a profile piece about evangelical politician, Stockwell Day. At the time, Day was leader of Canada's official opposition and the report, which ran during the federal election campaign of 2000, referred to Day as racist, sexist and homophobic. One source in the piece accused Day of having a hidden agenda of intolerance, stating:

> I don't think that the Stockwell Day that Canadians are seeing on the hustings is the true Stockwell Day, as to what his reaction will be, if he is ever Prime Minister of this country and [has] to make decisions about matters relating to women, about matters relating to ethnic groups, particularly religious minority groups, about how he would react in matters clearly related to homosexuality.[2]

Another source attacked Day for opposing a government grant earmarked to fund research into the history of gays and lesbians in Day's home province of Alberta. She said his decision was "inconsistent with an agenda of tolerance."[3] Coders noted that Day was not interviewed for the report and was therefore not given the opportunity to respond to his accusers and give his version of events.

Elsewhere, during the voiceover narration of the report, the reporter pointed out that before entering politics Day had worked at a Christian school that was situated just 30 kilometres down the road from a known holocaust denier.[4] Coders saw the reporter's segue from the holocaust denier to Day as further evidence of negative framing—a type of guilt by association. They noted that the report gave no examples of anti-Semitism on the part of Day; his only connection to the holocaust denier was that they shared the same geographic location.

A final observation was made by the coders regarding news reports employing the intolerant frame. It was found that in reports where evangelicals were featured together with gays and lesbians or gay rights activists, the intolerant frame was far more likely to be employed than in any other type of story. In total, 20 stories were identified as juxtaposing evangelicals against homosexuals or their supporters; in 60% of those stories evangelicals were framed as intolerant to a greater or lesser degree. Four reports featuring evangelicals and homosexuals together were from CBC, 11 were from CTV and five were from Global. In relation to main focus or topic, these reports spanned the categories from politics, to social protest, to court, to education stories. In most of the stories featuring evangelicals and homosexuals, the intolerant frame was also accompanied by one or all of these other frames: the "pushy with social views frame," the "outdated values and beliefs frame," or the "unintelligent frame".

FIGURE 2
FRAMES WITH GREATEST FREQUENCY AND
EXCLUSIVITY, ALL NETWORKS

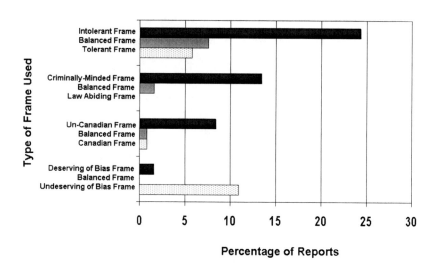

The frame of "criminally-minded" was used in just over 13% of reports (5.8% somewhat criminally-minded; 7.5% very criminally-minded). Regarding neutral and opposing frames, under 2% of reports employed a neutral frame in relation to criminal or ethical situations and under 1% framed evangelicals as somewhat law-abiding. No report framed evangelicals as very law-abiding.

One news report that coders determined employed the frame of "criminally-minded" featured evangelicals visiting the Holy Land at the turn of the millennium. Specifically, the piece focused on members of the faith who wanted to see the Jewish temple rebuilt on Mt. Moriah where a major Muslim mosque stands. The building of this new temple would, they believed, hasten the second coming of Christ.[5] The reporter portrayed the evangelicals in the piece as willing to use illegal means to bring about the destruction of the mosque so as to make way for the temple. For example, in his narration he warned that evangelicals were prepared to do "[s]tupid violent things that will lead to the chaos that will, in turn, [in their minds] lead to paradise."[6] He also noted that the secret plots of evangelicals' were making "Israeli police and intelligence services terribly nervous."[7] However, the reporter did not support any of his claims with a single example of an evangelical found plotting or committing illegal acts against the mosque. The coders also noted that those evangelicals who were quoted in the report gave no indication they endorsed illegal or immoral measures; in fact, it was exactly the opposite. They insisted they were opposed to violence and believed "any human efforts to clear the Mount right now would be futile, destructive and wrong."[8]

Evangelicals were framed positively as undeserving of media and societal bias in about 11% of reports (1.6% somewhat undeserving of media and societal bias; 9.2% very undeserving of media and societal bias). Under 2% of reports framed evangelicals as deserving of media and societal bias (1.6% somewhat deserving; 0 very deserving). No report employed the "neutral" frame in relation to societal and media bias. A report deemed to employ the "undeserving of media and societal bias" aired during the election of 2000, and like the previous example of a story from the federal campaign trail, it too focused on evangelical politician Stockwell Day. However, this second report defended Day's religious beliefs. The reporter in the piece stated:

> Our last five Prime Ministers were all Catholics, Trudeau in particular very devout, trained by Jesuits, Tommy Douglas was a devout minister. No one asked them for a moral accounting. So why are we doing the same in a case of an Evangelical Christian[?] Why are his beliefs so suspect and the beliefs of others not?[9]

Apart from the frames listed above, no other single frame possessed high exclusivity while also appearing in 10% or more of reports. The "sincere" frame and the "politically threatening" frame both appeared in almost 18% of reports. However, these frames did not possess exclusivity. Regarding sincerity, the competing "insincere" frame was used in over 13% of all reports; regarding political activity, almost 7% of reports framed evangelicals in a neutral fashion in relation to their political activity and 5% framed them as politically reassuring. Therefore, despite their significant frequency at about 18%, the influence of the two aforementioned frames was muted—or "cancelled out"—by competition from their respective oppositional frames.

Of those frames appearing in fewer than 10% of reports, only the "un-Canadian" frame stood out for its high exclusivity. Specifically, evangelicals were framed as un-Canadian in over 8% of reports (5.8% somewhat un-Canadian; 2.5% very un-Canadian). While not reaching 10%, this was still a strong showing. On the other hand, the "very Canadian" frame and the neutral frame appeared in under 1% of reports, respectively. No frames appeared for "somewhat Canadian".

By way of example, a CBC report about Canada's first evangelical television station—The Miracle Channel—was coded as employing the "un-Canadian" frame. The piece portrayed the station and its operators as purveyors of American culture, despite the fact that the station's programming schedule was predominantly Canadian. Just before cutting to a clip of American televangelist Jimmy Swaggart (shown begging TV viewers for more financial support), the CBC reporter stated: "The channel joins a host of American stations already beaming up over the border. The station will air many U.S. programs, providing the stars of the right-wing religious world with a Canadian platform."[10] The fact that the bulk of the station's content was home grown was *not* missed by CBC's competitor, CTV news. In that network's coverage of the launch of The Miracle Channel, the reporter noted that "about a third of the programming is American" while all other shows are "produced by Canadians."[11] Furthermore, in contrast to the CBC report which inferred that the station would employ aggressive fundraising techniques like those used by televangelists from the U.S., the CTV report observed that it was The Miracle Channel's expressed policy to "fundraise in a restrained manner."[12] This fact was emphasized by the CTV reporter who commented, "...no one expects the Miracle Channel to imitate the high pressured tactics of some American televangelists."[13]

CHANGES TO FRAMES OVER TIME

As demonstrated in Table 2, most of the frames used in the coverage of evangelicals changed very little over time. It was never the case that a "switch" occurred in which evangelicals were predominantly framed one way for a series of years and then suddenly framed the opposite way for another span of time. Furthermore, it was rarely the case that an inactive frame—that is, one seldom used in coverage—became a highly active frame. Only the "Threatening Politically," "Undeserving of Societal and Media Bias" and the "Un-Canadian" frames experienced uncharacteristic spikes (see Figures 3, 4, and 5). These short-lived spikes occurred in 2000 and directly corresponded with the federal election campaign of evangelical politician Stockwell Day.

TABLE 2
FREQUENCY OF FRAMES BY YEAR

FRAMES	1994	1995	1996	1997	1998	1999	2000	2001	2002	2003	2004
Intolerant	5	2	2	1	2	3	5	1	1	5	1
Balanced					1	1			3	1	3
Tolerant			2		2	2			1		
Insincere	4	1	2	1		2	2		2	2	
Balanced	1	1	1								
Sincere		3		1	4	4	2	1	1	1	4
Unintelligent					1	2	2		1	1	
Balanced											
Intelligent		1								1	
Neglectful						1		1	2		1
Balanced	1				1	1					
Responsible		4			1				1	1	
Pushy w Social Views		1		1		2	1			2	
Balanced			2				1				
Respectful w Social Views	1	1	3	1			1	1	2	1	
Threatening Politically	2		1		2	1	9		2	2	2
Balanced		1					5				2
Reassuring Politically							3				3
Criminally-Minded	2	2		2		3	1	3	1	1	
Balanced		1	1								
Law Abiding						1				1	
Superstitious	1			1	1	1			2	1	
Balanced			1								
Spiritual	1	2			1			1			
Vengeful	1	1				2				3	
Balanced											
Forgiving							2				1
Un-Canadian		2			1	1	4			1	1
Balanced							1				
Canadian											1
Deserving of Bias							1			1	
Balanced											
Undeserving of Bias	2	1	1				5			1	2
Outdated Values & Beliefs				1		1	1				
Balanced											
Contemporary Vs & Bs	2	1							2		1

Please Note: On this table the "very" and "somewhat" manifestations of each frame have been combined into a single positive or negative category. For example, frames coded as "very intolerant" and "somewhat intolerant" have been tabulated together under the frame category "Intolerant".

FIGURE 3
CHANGE IN THE "THREATENING POLITICALLY" FRAME

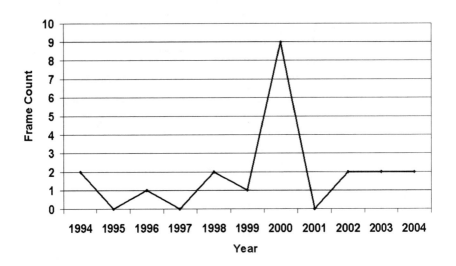

FIGURE 4
CHANGE IN THE "UNDESERVING OF MEDIA AND
AND SOCIETAL BIAS" FRAME

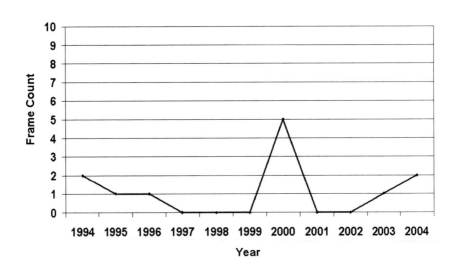

FIGURE 5
CHANGE IN THE "UNCANADIAN" FRAME

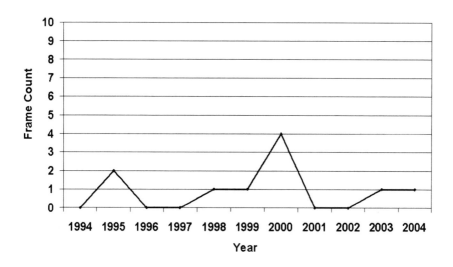

FRAMES BY NETWORK—CBC

As mentioned previously in this chapter, an average of the scores for all frames used in the reports of CBC produced a mean of 2.42 (SD=1.27), or an overall rating of slightly negative. In terms of actual number of frames used in the 28 CBC reports, 77 frames were identified, of which 51 were negative (18 somewhat; 33 very), 5 were neutral, and 21 were positive (10 somewhat; 11 very).

Evangelicals were most frequently and most exclusively framed as intolerant, politically threatening, criminally-minded, insincere and un-Canadian in the reports of CBC news (see Figure 6). However, the positive "undeserving of media and societal bias" frame also appeared with significant frequency and exclusivity. The seeming paradox of this "mixed message" is discussed in Chapter 8 under the section titled "Explaining the Dominant Positive Frame".

Evangelicals were framed as intolerant in almost 36% of CBC's reports (3.5% somewhat intolerant; 32.1% very intolerant); conversely, the use of neutral and oppositional frames was far less frequent. Just 3.5% of reports framed evangelicals in a neutral fashion, or as balanced between intolerant and tolerant and about 7% framed them as somewhat tolerant. No reports employed the "very tolerant" frame.

Evangelicals were framed as politically threatening in 32% of CBC's reports (14.2% somewhat politically threatening; 17.8% very politically threatening), while a "neutral" frame was used in about 7% of reports related to political involvement and the "somewhat politically reassuring" frame in 3.5%. The frame of "very politically reassuring" was not used.

On the CBC, evangelicals were framed positively as undeserving of media and societal bias in 25% of reports (3.5% somewhat undeserving of media and societal bias; 21.4% very undeserving of media and societal bias). Just 3.5% of reports framed evangelicals as somewhat deserving of media and societal bias. No report highlighting media or societal bias employed a "neutral" frame or the "very deserving of media and societal bias" frame.

The "criminally-minded" frame was used in just over 21% of CBC's reports about evangelicals (3.5% somewhat criminally-minded; 17.8% very criminally-minded). No neutral or positive oppositional frames were employed in this category.

Evangelicals were framed as insincere in just over 21% of CBC's reports (3.5% somewhat insincere; 17.8% very insincere). The opposing "sincere" frame was used in 7% of reports (3.5% somewhat sincere; 3.5% very sincere). No "neutral" frames were used in relation to evangelical sincerity.

FIGURE 6
FRAMES WITH GREATEST FREQUENCY AND EXCLUSIVITY, CBC

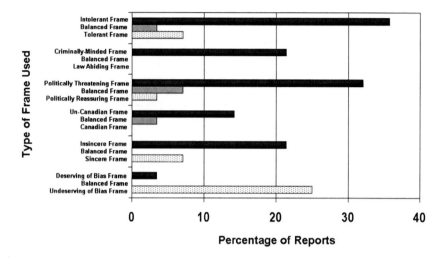

Only two other frames appeared in 10% or more of CBC's reports. Evangelicals were framed as un-Canadian in just over 14% of reports (3.5% somewhat un-Canadian; 10.7% very un-Canadian). A "neutral" frame was used in 3.5% of reports referencing national identity; no positive oppositional frames were used.

Evangelicals were also framed as respectful when presenting their social views in about 14% of reports (7.1% somewhat respectful; 7.1% very respectful). However, unlike the frames above which suffered little enervation from competition, the influence of the "respectful when presenting their social views" frame was muted due to a strong showing by its oppositional frame: almost 11% of CBC reports framed evangelicals as pushy when presenting their social views (3.5% somewhat pushy; 7.1% very pushy). A "neutral" frame was used in 3.5% of reports highlighting social views.

FRAMES BY NETWORK—CTV

An average of the scores for all frames used in the reports of CTV produced a mean of 2.93 (SD=1.28), or an overall rating of balanced. In terms of actual number of frames used in the 58 CTV reports, 113 frames were identified, of which 57 were negative (33 somewhat; 24 very), 15 were neutral, and 41 were positive (25 somewhat; 16 very).

Evangelicals were most frequently and most exclusively framed as intolerant, politically threatening and criminally-minded in the reports of CTV news (see Figure 7).

Evangelicals were framed as intolerant in about 26% of CTV's reports (13.7% somewhat intolerant; 12% very intolerant). Just about 7% of reports framed them neutrally or as balanced between intolerant and tolerant and about 5% framed them as tolerant (3.4% somewhat tolerant; 1.7% very tolerant).

Evangelicals were framed as politically threatening in about 17% of CTV's reports (6.8% somewhat politically threatening; 10.3% very politically threatening). A "neutral" frame was used in just over 3% of reports related to politics and the "somewhat politically reassuring" frame in almost 2%. The frame of "very politically reassuring" was not used.

The "criminally-minded" frame was used in just over 10% of CTV's reports about evangelicals (6.8% somewhat criminally-minded; 3.4% very criminally-minded). A little over 3% of reports in this category employed a neutral frame and none employed positive oppositional frames.

Evangelicals were framed as sincere in about 24% of CTV's reports (10.3% somewhat sincere; 13.7% very sincere) and neutrally or balanced between insincere and sincere in 5%. However, the influence of the sincere frame was muted slightly by the opposing "insincere" frame which was used in just over 15% of reports (8.6% somewhat insincere; 6.8% very insincere).

Apart from those frames listed above, no other single frame was used in 10% or more of CTV's reports.

FIGURE 7
FRAMES WITH GREATEST FREQUENCY AND EXCLUSIVITY, CTV

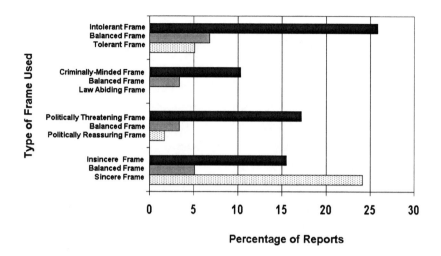

FRAMES BY NETWORK—GLOBAL

An average of the scores for all frames used in the reports of Global produced a mean of 3.14 (SD=1.25), or an overall rating of balanced. In terms of actual number of frames used in the 33 Global reports, 51 frames were identified, of which 20 were negative (14 somewhat; 6 very), 10 were neutral, and 21 were positive (10 somewhat; 11 very).

Unlike the news reports of CBC or CTV in which a single frame, such as that of "intolerance," could appear in a quarter or more of reports in highly exclusive fashion, Global's reports used a more equally distributed, diverse repertoire of frames. As such, even the frames found to appear most frequently were used in just 15% of reports or fewer. Only the "sincere" and the "criminally-minded" frames enjoyed higher levels of exclusivity, all others suffered enervation from competing frames (see Figure 8).

Evangelicals were framed as sincere in 15% of Global's reports (6% somewhat sincere; 9% very sincere). The oppositional frame, "insincere," gave little competition, appearing in just 3% of reports (3% somewhat insincere; 0 very insincere). No "neutral" frames were used in this category.

The frame of "criminally-minded" was used in 12% of Global's reports (6% somewhat criminally-minded; 6% very criminally-minded) and was opposed by the "law-abiding" frame in just 3% of reports (3% somewhat law abiding; 0% very law abiding). Reports that activated this category did not employ any "neutral" frames.

More dominant than others, yet less influential than the two afore-mentioned frames, was the "politically reassuring frame." Evangelicals were framed as politically reassuring in 12% of Global's reports (9% somewhat reassuring; 3% very reassuring) and neutrally or balanced between politically reassuring and politically threatening in 12% of reports. The oppositional frame "politically threatening" was used in 6% of reports (3% somewhat threatening; 3% very threatening)—enough of a showing to mute the "politically reassuring" frame slightly.

Evangelicals were framed neutrally or as balanced between intoler-ant and tolerant in 12% of Global reports. They were framed as intoler-ant in 9% (6% somewhat intolerant; 3% very intolerant) and as tolerant in 6% (3% somewhat tolerant; 3% very tolerant) of reports. The relative equality (or lack of exclusivity) among these competing frames muted the influence of all.

Apart from those frames listed above, no other single frame was used in 10% or more of Global's reports.

NEWS REPORTS ABOUT EVANGELICALS

FIGURE 8
FRAMES WITH GREATEST FREQUENCY AND EXCLUSIVITY, GLOBAL

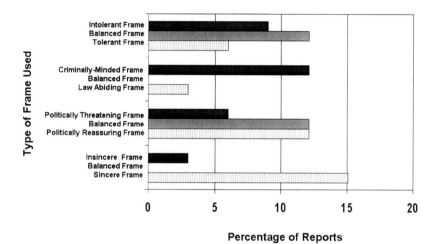

CHAPTER 7

How Journalists Feel about Evangelicals and its Affect on Coverage

Having presented the findings of the frame analysis in the last chapter, we now turn to the results of the survey. After the presentation of the survey outcomes, the findings of the merged data—that is, the conclusions generated from the comparison of the frame analysis results to those of the survey—are tendered. Where applicable, the survey outcomes are expressed in terms of percentage of respondents (%) and numbers of respondents (N=) so that the reader can most clearly visualize the results the data relay.

GENDER, NETWORK, AND JOB TITLE OF RESPONDENTS

As indicated in Chapter 5, 21 national television news personnel completed this study's questionnaire. Eleven of the respondents were men and 10 were women. By network, 10 surveys were completed by CBC personnel, seven by CTV employees, and four by journalists at Global. Question 1 on the survey asked which job the journalists performed for their national news program. A majority of respondents, over 70% (N=15) were reporters, while about 30% (N=6) performed other functions related to the written content of the news reports (for example, news directors, anchors, producers, writers).

RELIGIOUS BELIEFS AND PRACTICES OF JOURNALISTS

Question 2 asked if the journalists considered themselves practicing members of any religion and Question 3 asked if their religious beliefs led them to perform rituals or routines such as prayer or attending religious services. For a strong majority of journalists, religion played little or no role in their lives. Two-thirds (N=14) of respondents stated that they were not practicing members of any religion. Respondents working for the CBC were very uniform in their embrace of secularism; 90% (N=9 of 10) from that news outlet said they were atheist, agnostic or non-practicing, compared to 45% (N=5 of 11) of respondents working for the private stations, CTV (N=4 of 7) and Global (N=1 of 4). As might be expected, in response to Question 3, most of these irreligious respondents also indicated that they performed no religious routines or rituals, though two indicated they had looked at sacred texts for educational purposes and on occasion prayed or meditated. However, the latter activity was not directed toward a god. As one of the two put it, "I sometimes pray to something in the hopes that somebody is listening. I read old texts from various religions to better understand differences . . . realizing that we are not all that different."

The one third (N=7) of respondents who considered themselves practicing members of a religion claimed Christianity as their faith. Two were members of the United Church of Canada (1 from CBC; 1 from CTV), two were Roman Catholic (1 from CTV; 1 from Global), one was Anglican (from CTV), and two were evangelical Christians (both from Global). The first evangelical was a member of the Christian and Missionary Alliance Church; the second did not indicate his/her specific denomination.

Of the 33% (N=7) of journalists who considered themselves practicing members of a religion, just 19% (N=4) gave evidence of that practice. Those demonstrating traditional actions of faith were the two evangelicals from Global, the Anglican from CTV, and the Roman Catholic journalist from CTV. They wrote of weekly or even bi-weekly church attendance; the evangelicals and the Catholic mentioned reading the Bible or religiously-focused material weekly, along with praying daily as part of a set routine. The struggle to keep one's "faith life" vibrant was referenced in this excerpt from the Roman Catholic journalist:

> Prayer and meditation are important facets of my life—and I try to make them part of my daily routine—often without success because of the busyness of the day. I also read newspapers—*The National Catholic Reporter* from the U.S. and try to read books from informed Christians.

The religiously active Anglican journalist stated that prayer outside of church and the study of sacred texts "occur on an ad hoc basis."

Conversely, the United Church members employed at CBC and CTV, respectively, and the Roman Catholic from Global did very little to exercise their faith. All said they did not go to church often, none mentioned reading the Bible, and prayer was described as irregular typically taking place when the journalist or a loved one was in need.

Summarizing the journalists' responses to Questions 2 and 3, one could make the broader assessment that a minority of respondents (19% or N=4) were religious believers who actively practiced their faith, while a strong majority (81% or N=17) had no religious faith at all or did not actively practice the faith they said they held.

EVANGELICALS' DEFINING TRAITS— JOURNALISTS' OPINION

Question 4 asked the journalists to state what they saw as the main beliefs, characteristics and attitudes of evangelical Christians. The hope was to capture what was "top-of-mind" for the journalists in relation to evangelicals. In a sense, the question was asking, "When you picture an evangelical, what are the first things that you think of?" The responses to this question total greater than 21 (the number of partici-

THROUGH A LENS DARKLY

pating journalists) because most journalists listed two or more traits as the main beliefs, characteristics or attitudes of evangelicals. Given the wide diversity of the responses, only those traits that appeared in the answers of five or more journalists are listed.

The two traits the journalists most strongly associated with evangelicals were haughtiness and intolerance toward homosexuals.

Specifically, 38% (N=8) of the respondents saw arrogant self-righteousness as one of the dominant traits of evangelical Christians. This trait was usually mentioned in conjunction with what was perceived to be the evangelicals' desire to impose their values and beliefs on others. Half of the respondents from CBC (4 non-religious; 1 inactive United) cited this trait, as did three respondents from the private stations (2 non-religious from CTV; 1 non-religious from Global). The response from a CBC journalist was typical of others; he/she said evangelicals are people "who believe it is their right and duty to promote their beliefs on others. They feel (or at least give the impression of feeling) superior to others in their faith and practice of faith."

Similarly, evangelicals' opposition to homosexuality was mentioned as a dominant trait by 38% (N=8) of respondents; three were from CBC (all non-religious), five were from the private stations (1 non-religious; 1 inactive United; 1 active Catholic; 1 active Anglican from CTV and 1 evangelical from Global). Unlike the non-religious and religiously inactive respondents who tended to describe evangelicals as being "against homosexuals," the evangelical and religiously active respondents tended to describe the evangelicals' opposition as being directed toward gay-marriage making such remarks as: evangelicals are "against the idea of same-sex marriage," and "evangelicals support the traditional definition of marriage," and they recognize "traditional marriage only."

Evangelicals' high view of scripture was cited as a dominant trait in almost 29% (N=6) of responses. Three CBC respondents (all non-religious) made reference to evangelicals "literal belief in the Bible," as did one respondent from CTV (non-religious). The two evangelical respondents from Global described specific creedal statements they held to be true as defining elements. For example, "the death and resurrection of Christ" was referenced by one and "belief in the Holy Trinity (Father, Son, and Holy Spirit)" was mentioned by both.

Also mentioned as a dominant trait in nearly 29% (N=6) of responses was evangelicals' desire to spread the message of the Gospel. Two CBC respondents (both non-religious), two CTV respondents (1 inactive United; 1 active Anglican) and two Global respondents (both evangelical) referenced this characteristic. The two evangelical respondents from Global and the religiously active Anglican from CTV elevated this trait above others, citing it as the single most important defining feature. One evangelical respondent pointed out that "[a]n evangelical shares God's love and spreads the gospel. Evangelical itself is Greek for messenger." While the active Anglican saw spreading the Gospel as the core trait of an evangelical, he felt the definition of evangelical needed to be expanded:

> I would take issue with your characterization of evangelical Christians as conservative Protestants. The Anglican Church in Canada, you might be interested to know, has been charging its flocks to become more evangelical. There is a feeling among Church leaders we don't do enough proselytizing so the call has gone out to us to "talk up" joining the Anglican Church, a church which . . . would certainly not be characterized as 'conservative'.

Unlike the three religiously active journalists who spoke of evangelicals spreading the Gospel as a positive trait, the three non-religious journalists saw it as a negative. This comment from the religiously inactive CTV respondent was typical: "They are mainly out to convert you. To put a notch in their belt. They'll tell you you're going to hell to get you to make a decision to accept Jesus. It's psychological blackmail."

Evangelicals' stand against abortion was described as one of their main traits by close to 24% (N=5) of respondents; these included two journalists from CBC (both non-religious), two from CTV (1 active Anglican; 1 inactive United) and one from Global (inactive Catholic). Evangelicals' devotion to God/Christ or relationship with God/Christ was also deemed a main trait by about 24% (N=5) of respondents; these included three from CBC (2 non-religious; 1 inactive United), one from CTV (active Catholic) and one from Global (inactive Catholic).

EVANGELICAL RELIGIOUS BELIEFS SUPPORTED BY JOURNALISTS

Question 5 asked the journalists how they were most similar to evangelical Christians in terms of their religious beliefs. The most popular answer to this question echoed by well-over half of respondents (57% or N=12) was: "I am in no way similar." All but one of the journalists from the CBC gave this answer; two journalists for CTV answered in this fashion as did one from Global. Perhaps not surprising, the respondents who could find nothing in common with evangelicals were journalists who had stated previously that they practiced no religion. In the words of one CBC employee, "I am agnostic . . . I cannot imagine God, and therefore cannot believe he has a son."

Close to 29% (N=6) of the respondents suggested trivial or incidental similarities. The religiously inactive United Church members from CTV and CBC, and the inactive Catholic from Global, somewhat tongue-in-cheek remarked that they "use the same Bible" as evangelicals; the United member at CBC also noted that neither he/she nor evangelicals pay homage to the Pope. The religiously active Anglican at CTV noted that he/she and evangelicals "probably" share a belief in the Nicene Creed. In a sincere attempt to find common ground, two of the non-religious respondents from CTV suggested that they were similar to evangelicals in regards to strong "support for family."

On the other hand, slightly over 14% (N=3) of the respondents acknowledged significant affinity with evangelicals. The religiously active Catholic at CTV recognized a bond between him/herself and evangelicals saying that they were similar "[i]n welcoming the grace of God and in following the footsteps of Jesus Christ as best we can." As stands to reason, the two evangelical journalists from Global showed the strongest identification with evangelical religious belief; one summed up the situation saying:

> As an evangelical myself, my beliefs are a reflection of evangelicals at large. The biggies for me, like most evangelicals, are faith in Christ, telling others about God's love, belief in the resurrection, eternal life through Christ, loving my neighbour, believing that the Bible is God's word for my life, I believe all the stuff in the creeds . . . you get the picture.

Summarizing the responses to Question 5, one could say that a strong majority (86% or N=18) of journalists in the sample felt they shared little or no similarity to evangelicals when it came to religious beliefs.

EVANGELICAL RELIGIOUS BELIEFS OPPOSED BY JOURNALISTS

To further probe the journalists' feelings toward evangelicals' religious beliefs, Question 6 negatively inverted Question 5 and asked the journalists how they were most at odds with evangelical Christians in terms of their religious beliefs. One third (N=7) of respondents saw their disbelief in God as the main difference between them and evangelicals; five were from CBC (all non-religious), one from CTV (non-religious) and one from Global (non-religious).

Another third (N=7) suggested that they were most at odds with the evangelicals' belief that theirs was the only "true" faith and that Jesus was the only way to salvation; three journalists from CBC (all non-religious), three from CTV (all non-religious) and one from Global (inactive Catholic) were of that opinion. A respondent from CTV put it this way: "The belief that all other religions . . . billions of people around the world . . . have it wrong. That theirs is the only true path to paradise. I can't even begin to understand how that is possible." Respondents sometimes suggested that the belief they preferred over the evangelical's belief. A journalist from the CBC stated: "I value ideology from

ALL religions . . ." Responses of this nature elucidate why journalists tend to see evangelicals as arrogantly self-righteous.

Just over 14% of respondents (N=3)—the religiously inactive United Church members at CBC and CTV and the religiously active Catholic at CTV—said they were least similar to evangelicals when it came to Biblical literalism. The CBC employee remarked:

> I do not believe in the literal interpretation of the Bible, as I think more conservative churches do. The stories of the Bible are ancient, written and re-written and interpreted many times. The essence of the stories are about faith, kindness, generosity etc . . . The morals are important. The details are not. This is a very liberal interpretation of the bible readings. I am comfortable with this, I don't imagine evangelical Christians would be.

Slightly over 14% (N=3) of journalists stated they were at odds with evangelicals' religious beliefs regarding homosexuality; two were non-religious journalists from CBC (one of whom also saw her disbelief in God, mentioned above, as a dissimilarity), the other, somewhat surprisingly, was one of the evangelical respondents from Global. He/she explained his/her position saying:

> I would not say that I'm at odds with evangelicals because I am one myself. You should know that there is a diversity of beliefs among evangelicals. What I believe, other evangelicals might not. For example, many of my friends and I (all evangelicals) are strong supporters of gay rights and we don't think a loving monogamous life-partnership between gay men or lesbians is a sin.

Considering their responses to Question 4 solidly showed that they saw evangelicals' intolerance toward homosexuals as a major, defining trait—the weakness of the journalists' response here in this subsequent question seems odd. A possible explanation may be that most of the respondents did not see evangelicals' opposition to homosexuality as relating to religious belief. Instead, they may have seen it as a conservative social perspective held by evangelicals—akin to the prohibitions against dancing and playing cards that members of the faith enforced in decades past. This notion appears to be confirmed later in the survey. In Question 8, when respondents were asked to discuss which *social issues* of evangelicals they opposed, the answers that related to homosexual rights outstripped all others.

The religiously active Anglican from CTV felt he/she was most at odds with evangelicals' belief that women should be excluded from church ministry. The second evangelical respondent from Global found no dissimilarities between his/her beliefs and those of evangelicals at large.

EVANGELICAL SOCIAL ISSUES SUPPORTED BY JOURNALISTS

Moving away from the straight religious beliefs of evangelicals to the actions those beliefs inspire, Question 7 asked the journalists, "On which social issues do you find yourself in agreement or mostly in agreement with evangelical Christians?" Reflecting what could be considered the recurring theme of incompatibility, the most popular response to this question was "none," "no comment," or variations on that theme. Thirty-eight percent (N=8) of respondents answered in that fashion; most were non-religious respondents from the CBC, though one respondent was from CTV (active Anglican) and one was from Global (non-religious).

More positively, almost 29% of respondents (N=6) said they shared evangelicals' concern for the vulnerable in society; one was from CBC (non-religious), three were from CTV (1 non-religious; 1 inactive United; 1 active Catholic) and two were from Global (both evangelicals). Most of these respondents mentioned specific initiatives such as "relief programs for the homeless" or "emergency aid" for victims of disaster. The religiously active Catholic, speaking more broadly, said he/she and evangelicals were participating in "[t]he quest for a just society."

Almost 24% of respondents (N=5), including the religiously inactive Catholic from Global, three non-religious respondents from CTV and one from CBC, saw commitment to strong families and healthy communities as the social issue they shared with evangelicals. The inactive Catholic wrote, "Like evangelicals, I put a high priority on spending time with my family and teaching my children what I consider to be good and true." The CBC respondent stated that he/she was "profoundly in agreement" with evangelicals who made their communities better environmentally and with those who "incorporate Christ's teachings to make their community a kinder and more compassionate one."

One non-religious respondent from the CBC said "honesty and truth in thoughts and actions" was the social issue he/she and evangelicals agreed on most. The religiously inactive United Church member from CBC said he/she and evangelicals were aligned in their support for the death penalty "for certain types of crimes" and for religion being taught in schools (though he/she explained that he/she preferred that all religions be part of the curriculum).

EVANGELICALS SOCIAL ISSUES OPPOSED BY JOURNALISTS

In order to dig further into journalists' perceptions of evangelicals' social activism, Question 8 negatively inverted Question 7 and asked, "On which social issues do you find yourself most at odds with evangelical Christians?" The responses to this question total greater than 21 because most respondents expressed two or more social issues for which they were at odds with evangelicals.

In the most unified response for any of the attitudinal questions on the survey, almost three-quarters (71% or N=15) of respondents said that they felt evangelicals were wrong to oppose homosexual rights and gay marriage; six respondents from CBC (all non-religious), six from CTV (4 non-religious; 1 inactive United; 1 active Anglican) and three from Global (1 non-religious; 1 inactive Catholic; 1 evangelical) held this opinion. The evangelical to voice criticism of his fellow believers was the same evangelical from Global who had expressed support for gays in his answer to Question 6. While the other journalists were brief and to the point in their answers to this question, the evangelical respondent gave a detailed explanation of his/her position:

> I know I am at odds with many of my Christian brothers and sisters on this one but I think that people who are gay have no choice in the matter. I wouldn't (and couldn't) ask someone to change their skin colour and likewise, it is unfair to ask a gay man or woman to change their sexual orientation.

Most journalists also felt that evangelicals' were wrong to oppose abortion. With 57% (N=12) of participants voicing this opinion, of the attitudinal questions on the survey it was the second most unified response (tied with Question 5's response, "My beliefs are in no way similar to evangelicals' religious beliefs"). Six journalists from CBC (5 non-religious; 1 inactive United), five from CTV (3 non-religious; 1 inactive United; 1 active Anglican), and one from Global (non-religious) were of this opinion.

Interestingly, in their answers to Question 8, half (N=11) of the journalists surveyed mentioned evangelicals' opposition to homosexual rights and women's access to abortion together. That is, in their minds (and sentences) the two issues were linked—it seems both issues provided evidence of evangelicals' penchant for "quashing the rights of others." This shorter response from a CTV journalist was typical: "I'm at odds with evangelicals' stand against a woman's access to abortion and with their stand against homosexuals' rights, e.g. right to marry."

Three journalists, two from CBC (both non-religious) and one from CTV (active Catholic) gave no response. Two respondents, one from CBC (non-religious) and one from CTV (active Anglican), said they were at odds with evangelicals when it came to rights of women in general. Another two from CBC (both non-religious) viewed the proselytizing that evangelicals engage in as a social ill that needed to be stopped. One CBC respondent (inactive United) said he/she did not agree with evangelicals mixing religion and education, while another CBC journalist (non-religious) said he/she disagreed with the way evangelicals sometimes mix God and politics. Finally, the other evangelical respondent from Global stated that there were no social issues for which he/she was at odds with evangelicals.

WHERE JOURNALISTS GET THEIR INFORMATION ABOUT EVANGELICALS

Having completed the attitudinal probing of journalists, Question 9 asked, "Which sources have provided you with most of your information about evangelical Christians?" Nearly three-quarters (71% or N=15) of respondents cited the mainstream news media as one of their main sources; this was the case for eight respondents from CBC (7 non religious; 1 inactive United), five from CTV (4 non-religious; 1 inactive United) and two from Global (1 non-religious; 1 inactive Catholic). The non-religious journalist from Global remarked, "Like everyone else, I read about evangelicals in the newspaper and see them on the TV news."

Many journalists also said that conservative Christians they had contacted through work—that is, those they had interviewed for news stories—were a main source of information about evangelicals and evangelicalism. Fifty-seven percent of journalists in total (N=12)—six from CBC (5 non-religious; 1 inactive United), four from CTV (3 non-religious; 1 inactive United), two from Global (1 non-religious; 1 inactive Catholic)—made this claim.

Almost 24% (N=5) of journalists had personally explored elements of evangelical faith and culture. A respondent from the CBC (non-religious) and one from CTV (active Anglican) said they had attended evangelical church services. Two other respondents, again from the CBC (non-religious) and CTV (non-religious) said they read evangelical publications or explored evangelical news and current affairs sites on the internet. The religiously active Catholic from CTV said he occasionally watched televangelists on Sundays, but admitted it was "not exactly a bona fide guarantee of accurate impressions."

Interestingly, very few journalists mentioned intimate contact—that is, friendship with an evangelical—as one of their key ways of knowing about this faith and its adherents. The religiously inactive United Church member from CBC said, "I know some evangelicals," but did not go so far as to call them friends. Another journalist from CBC remarked that he/she had a "very close high school friend who was born-again." However, the way the journalist described his/her friend suggested the companion was not highly esteemed, saying: "No books other than the Bible allowed in [her] house. Constant, tedious attempts to convert me." Only three journalists, one respondent from CBC and the two evangelicals from Global stated unequivocally that intimate relationships with evangelicals were a source of information about this faith and its members.

MERGING OF THE SURVEY AND FRAME ANALYSIS FINDINGS

A key goal of this research was to determine if the attitudes journalists hold toward evangelicals affect the way that they frame evangelicals in their news stories. As set out in the methodology of this study, evidence of a correlation between reporters' feelings and reporters' framing was to be attained by comparing the results of the survey and the results of frame analysis. In particular, the journalists' most prevalent attitudes were compared to the news reports' most prevalent frames. A relationship between these two variables was deemed to exist if the prevalent attitudes were accompanied by corresponding prevalent frames.

The survey responses clearly show that the journalists' dominant attitudes toward evangelicals were negative. Summarizing the survey data we can say, without exception, the majority of news personnel characterized the specific religious beliefs and social positions of evangelicals as foreign at best, and offensive at worst.

Did these perceptions of evangelicals as "foreign" and "offensive" infiltrate the frames of the news reports? Indeed. While journalists did use positive and neutral frames in large measure, the frame analysis determined that the journalists used the evangelicals as "intolerant," evangelicals as "criminally-minded," and evangelicals as "un-Canadian" frames most frequently and most exclusively of all.[1]

And while this simple comparison of results of the survey and the frame analysis is enough to suggest that the perceptions journalists have of evangelicals manifest as negative coverage of evangelicals, to prove this assertion more conclusively a corroborative test, or side-analysis, is needed and, accordingly, was conducted.

According to the survey findings, the evangelical position that journalists disagreed with most was their opposition to homosexuality in general, and gay marriage in particular. Several of the survey questions reveal this attitude. For example, 71% of journalists said they felt evangelicals were wrong to hold the social views on homosexuality that they do. Therefore, if attitudes affect coverage, coverage that juxtaposes evangelicals and homosexuals (or their supporters) should feature more negative framing than coverage of evangelicals on the whole.

Earlier, during the analysis of all the news reports, 20 stories featuring evangelicals and homosexuals together had been identified and isolated from the rest of the sample (as was explained in Chapter 6, these 20 reports were examined for the frame of intolerance). For this side-analysis, the scores of all frames appearing in those 20 reports were averaged and that mean was compared to the mean score for the coverage as a whole.

As noted previously, the mean score for all frames in all reports was 2.83 (SD=1.30). That is to say, on a scale of 1 to 5, coverage on the whole had a rating of balanced. However, an average of the scores for the frames found in just those reports featuring evangelicals and homosexuals together produced a mean of 2.20 (SD=1.07), or an overall rating of somewhat negative. Therefore, it is the case that coverage pitting evangelicals against homosexuals (or their supporters) is subjected to more negative framing than coverage of evangelicals on the whole. A two-sample t-test determined the difference between the ratings was statistically significant (t=2.05, d.f.=137, p<0.05).

The outcome of this side-analysis is noteworthy. It shows that the negative perceptions journalists have of evangelicals manifest as negative portrayals of evangelicals. Equally as important, it proves that evangelicals are depicted most negatively in those situations where their beliefs and values are in opposition to the deepest beliefs and values of journalists.

CHAPTER 8

Interpretation and Implications
of the Findings

vangelicals in Canada have claimed that the news media are
biased against them and, as stated at the outset, one of my goals in
analysing 11 years of news reports was to empirically test the validity
of that charge. It would have been more dramatic if the results of the
analysis of CBC's, CTV's and Global's coverage provided unmistakably
clear evidence to support or refute the evangelicals' claim, but they do
not. In fact, the results tell two divergent tales.

Evangelicals were, in terms of overall mean rating for frames,
portrayed in a neutral fashion in nightly, national television news
reports. This finding suggests that Canada's national television journalists, in the main, strive to provide coverage that is balanced. However,
the frequent use of the intolerant, criminally-minded, and un-Canadian frames —usually without significant competition from opposing
frames—and the high number of negative frames used overall, suggests
that there is still room for improvement in their coverage of evangelicals.
Indeed, in certain circumstances where the social values of evangelicals
are in strong opposition to those of the journalists—like in situations
involving gay marriage—media personnel routinely abandon neutral
frames and the pursuit of professional objectivity. In these cases they:
1) do not consistently relay to their audience the ideas that the subjects

of the reports are putting forward as *the subjects intended* those ideas to be understood; 2) do not consistently place events in perspective by providing relevant background; 3) sometimes fail to allow those who are criticized in the body of a report to respond fully to the accusations of their critics and; 4) sometimes fail to indicate when opinion, and not fact, is being relayed.

WHY THE NEGATIVE FRAMES "COUNT" MORE

While it is true that the results of the frame analysis tell two tales, the tales, to my mind, are not of equal significance. Namely, in terms of audience perceptions, the concentrated negative frames (because of their increased saliency) wield more influence over viewers' attitudes than the numerically plentiful, yet thematically disparate, collection of positive and balanced frames. Here is a very simple example that illustrates this point: Imagine a new person, Betty, just moved onto your street, but you are yet to meet her. Your first neighbour tells you she is energetic. Neighbour Two tells you she loves to laugh. Neighbour Three tells you she is obnoxious. Neighbour Four tells you that she is quite pretty. Neighbour Five tells you she is obnoxious. Neighbour Six tells you she is very intelligent. Neighbour Seven tells you she is obnoxious. Neighbour Eight tells you she has short blond hair and round glasses. Five of the comments about Betty were positive or neutral and three were negative. Now, from the list, what do you remember most about Betty? If you are like the majority of the population, the three matching comments penetrate your consciousness more than the numerically superior, yet thematically varied positive and neutral comments.

While the above example is evocative, on a more formal level, research has shown that a correlation exists between the repetitive viewing of specific, similar content on television and the holding of specific perceptions or beliefs about the world. For example, Alan Rubin, Elizabeth Perse and Donald Taylor determined that regular viewers of daytime soap operas (which often feature villains with hidden agendas and ulterior motives) tend to score lower in their per-

166

ceptions of altruism and trust in others.[1] Similarly, other studies have established that regular exposure to crime-saturated local television news promotes the perception that the crime rate is rising even when it is actually going down.[2] By extension, concentrated depictions of evangelicals as intolerant, criminally-minded and un-Canadian likely causes many viewers to accept those messages as valid.

It is true that the effect of these negative frames on viewers' perceptions of evangelicals may be somewhat muted, given that reports featuring this faith group air much less frequently than soap operas or crime stories on daily local TV news. On the other hand, the negativity of the frames themselves causes them to resonate more strongly with audiences. Specifically, negative information has been shown to more greatly affect observers' formation of impressions than positive information. For example, as an experiment, researchers Wayne Wanta, Guy Golan, and Cheolhan Lee had participants view negative, neutral and positive television news stories about specific countries. Their goal was to determine how the reports would affect the participants' opinion of each country.[3] What they found was clear evidence of media influencing perceptions. However, only the negative reports had any impact. On this disconnect, the researchers commented, "Since the more negative news stories a nation received the more negative it was viewed, it is logical to assume that the opposite relationship would be found with positive attributes. The more positive news stories a nation received, the more positively it would be viewed. This was not the case."[4] In a similar experiment, researcher Yuki Fujioka surveyed Caucasian students who had been exposed to negative, neutral and positive portrayals of African-Americans on television. He found that the "perceived negative portrayals affected White students' stereotypes, but perceived positive portrayals did not."[4] He concluded, "This can be explained by the "negativity effect" which refers to the fact that unlikeable or negative information receives more weight in observers' formation of impressions."[5]

THE GREAT DIVIDE—JOURNALISTS AND EVANGELICALS

The goal of this study's survey was to determine the attitudes national television journalists hold toward religion and evangelicals in order to gauge whether those attitudes influence their coverage. Reviewing the major survey findings, it was determined that 81% of journalists who responded to the survey had no religious faith or did not actively practice the faith that they said they held. When asked how they were most similar to evangelical Christians in terms of their religious beliefs well over half of respondents said they were in no way similar. When asked what they saw as the main characteristics, beliefs or attitudes of evangelical Christians, "arrogant self-righteousness" was tied for first as the top response. When journalists were asked "On which social issues do you find yourself in agreement or mostly in agreement with evangelical Christians?" the most popular answer, was "none," "no comment" or variations on that theme. However, when asked how they were at odds with evangelicals when it came to social issues the journalists were not so tongue-tied. A strong majority of respondents, 71%, said they felt evangelicals were wrong to oppose homosexual rights and gay marriage. This was the most unified response to any attitudinal question on the survey. Similarly, over half thought evangelicals' stand against abortion was wrong. These finding suggest that, overall, national television journalists have little personal interest in religion and, for the most part, view those who do—certainly the most devout—negatively.

In terms of secularism, the journalists are not only quite divergent from evangelicals but also from the public-at-large. Just 19% of all Canadians say that they practice no religion (Statistics Canada, 2006), compared to 66% of the respondents to this study's survey. These results corroborate Lydia Miljan and Barry Cooper's and Marsha Barber and Ann Rauhala's findings regarding the religious outlook of Canada's elite journalists.[6]

Now let's take a look at the survey findings more closely. When journalists think of evangelicals, one of the dominant images that comes to their minds is that of a self-righteous person trying to impose his beliefs and values on others. If one considers the worldview of evangelicals versus the worldview of journalists, one can understand how journalists might come to this perception. Evangelicals hold that there is such a thing as "absolute truth"; they take Jesus at his word when he says in the Gospel of John 14:6 that he alone is "the way, the truth, and the life" and not just *a* way or *one of many* truths. Evangelicals reason that if their beliefs are "true," then other faiths and values systems that oppose Christ's teachings cannot be. However, a claim to absolute truth would be considered heresy by journalists who embrace the post-modern notion that truth is relative and situational. To the post-modern journalists there are many "truths" and all are equally valid; one would have to be either stupid, or arrogantly self-righteous, or both, to say that they knew "the truth". As the journalist from CTV put it: "That theirs is the only true path to paradise. I can't even begin to understand how that is possible."

Regarding their impressions of evangelicals, it was interesting to note that the respondents who were actively religious yet not evangelicals themselves—the Catholic and Anglican from CTV—were more temperate in their assessment of evangelicals' main characteristics. These two respondents' more temperate approach to evangelicals is understandable. In his theory of rhetoric, Kenneth Burke outlined the concept of identification which insists that the more overlap there is between a speaker's substance (that is, his/her physical characteristics, background, personality, beliefs, values and method of rhetorical delivery) and an audience's substance, the greater the chance the speaker will be viewed favourably by the audience (as demonstrated by the acceptance of the speaker's message).[7] More recent research in the field of homophily has likewise shown that connection and acceptance between similar people occurs at a higher rate than among dissimilar people.[8]

While a few of the respondents could recognize similarities between themselves and evangelicals, most could not. When asked how they were most similar to evangelicals in terms of religious belief, over half of respondents said "in no way." Similarly, over one- third said they could not think of any social issues that they and evangelicals both supported. When commonalities were cited, it was often the case that the responses were insincere or made in jest. Overall, the lack of effort to find common ground, combined with the tone of the answers suggested that many of the journalists were content to be estranged from evangelicals. This "contented estrangement" is unfortunate: a relationship of respect can never be built when similarities are ignored and only differences are emphasized.

Of course, if many of the television journalists were unable to think of commonalities between themselves and evangelicals it is probably due, in large part, to the fact that they tend not to know many evangelicals personally; those evangelicals they do know are acquaintances that they have interviewed for stories. Only one respondent, apart from the evangelical journalists from Global, indicated close friendships with evangelicals.

That most of the journalists do not know any evangelicals personally becomes increasingly problematic when one considers that a majority of respondents, over 71%, said their key source for information about evangelicals was the mainstream news media. Most mainstream media, as this study and others in the United States have shown, tends to depict evangelicals "coolly" overall (that is, to the negative side of neutral) and in certain instances negatively. That being the case, if Canada's national television journalists are relying on mainstream media to learn about evangelicals, chances are good that the perception they will come away with will not be favourable. In fact, chances are very good journalists will come away with unfavourable impressions of evangelicals. In their survey of Canadian journalists David Pritchard and Florian Sauvageau found, "Canadian journalists overwhelming use CBC and Radio-Canada [the French-language branch of CBC] as their principle source of television news."[9] Elsewhere they note, "It is difficult to overstate CBC/Radio-Canada's influence on Canadian journalists. It is by far the Canadian news organization Canadian journalists admire the most, our survey found."[10] Too bad for evangelicals: the news network that depicts them most negatively also has the greatest role in shaping the perceptions of all journalists in the country.

There is more bad news for evangelicals. Because many Canadian journalists do not know any evangelicals personally, they are even more prone to accept the media messages as valid. Research has found people are more apt to accept the media's portrayal of a group if they have no first-hand knowledge of the group members themselves.[11] For example, a 1999 study showed that Japanese university students who had seen African-Americans on TV but had seldom met them in person were more likely to hold negative stereotypes about them than other students who had regular personal contact.[12] In relation to evangelicals and the news media, it is possible that a vicious circle of negative coverage has developed: journalists accept evangelical stereotypes promoted in past stories; propagate them in current stories; and thereby ensure their presence in future stories.

WHEN AND WHY JOURNALISTS GO ASTRAY

A comparison of the survey responses to the results of the frame analysis showed it is indeed the case that journalists' attitudes toward evangelicals affected their coverage of that faith group. In particular, journalists found it most difficult to report in a dispassionate, neutral manner when evangelicals' beliefs and values directly contradicted their own heart-felt convictions about what constitutes right and wrong within a just society. This finding—the most significant of the study— must be explored in relation to the body of theoretical work that has preceded it, if its implications are to be understood fully.

As mentioned in Chapter 3, up to now, only Miljan and Cooper had empirically examined whether the personal values of Canadian journalists influence the coverage they produce. After surveying the attitudes of Canadian journalists regarding social, political, and economic issues, these researchers content analyzed national news reports related to those issues and concluded that the causes and ideals news personnel support are championed in their stories.[13] Although some of Miljan and Cooper's survey questions touched on religion, they did not gauge journalists' attitudes toward evangelicals, nor did they content analyze any news content related to religious issues. The findings of this study, therefore, build on Miljan and Cooper's work by measuring journalists' attitudes about religion in general, and evangelicals in particular. Furthermore, it extends Miljan and Cooper's work by showing that the attitudes journalists hold about religion and evangelicals affect the stories they produce.

And while the findings of this study tell us a great deal about individual journalists in Canada, they also highlight the role Canada's media plays in the preservation of dominant ideologies and distribution of power. It has been argued by others that news coverage is framed so as to circulate and reflect cultural values and ideologies while simultaneously defining and legitimating those values and ideologies.[14] In Canada, the most revered cultural value is tolerance and the dominant ideology is pluralism.[15] With terrific zeal, national journalists embrace this value and ideology—as Miljan and Cooper determined, more so than the population-at-large.[16] The data from this research show journalists sought to reinforce tolerance and the pluralism (as they understand these concepts) by framing evangelicals negatively in those situations where they were deemed to have compromised those sacred cultural conventions. Most notably, in reports where they were thought to be limiting the rights of others—by opposing homosexuality or abortion, for example—evangelicals were subjected to the most negative framing. By depicting the evangelicals negatively, the validity of their position was undermined and their ability to influence society was mitigated. Conversely, the journalists' definition of what constitutes tolerance and pluralism was reinforced and legitimated.

WHAT JOURNALISTS MEAN BY "TOLERANCE"

When I speak of journalists' "heartfelt convictions regarding pluralism and tolerance" it is important that a point of clarification be made: how most Canadian journalists define tolerance and pluralism differs from the way Canadian evangelicals define these concepts. We have established that Canadian journalists resort to framing evangelicals negatively when they *perceive* that evangelicals have contravened these sacrosanct laws of the land. In most cases, evangelicals would perceive a different reality, believing that no breach had occurred. Evangelicals in Canada *do* subscribe to the principals of tolerance and pluralism; as highlighted in Chapter 2, the research of Sam Reimer has shown this to be so.[18] However, in the minds of evangelicals, tolerance and pluralism are equated with respecting the humanity of persons with differing beliefs and values; the concepts are not equated with accepting opposing beliefs and values as valid. Put most simply, for Canadian evangelicals pluralism and tolerance are embodied in the notion that one must be "willing to agree to disagree." This does not seem to be the understanding of Canadian national television journalists (as is evidenced by the situational conditions that result in the use of their greatest number of negative frames, and also by their responses to the attitudinal survey). It would appear the journalists feel to be truly tolerant and truly accepting of pluralism one needs to view the beliefs and values of others as equally valid to one's own. To claim another's beliefs and values are wrong is a serious transgression in their eyes. Put most simply, for Canadian journalists, pluralism and tolerance are embodied in the notion "we all have a different understanding of what truth is, and while my idea of truth is different from yours, both our ideas of truth are equally valid." Despite its arbitrary, socially constructed nature, when one crosses the definitional boundary line journalists have established, real world consequences follow. This clash of worldviews that Canadian evangelicals and journalists experience is explored more fully later in this chapter.

TWO CRITERIA FOR NEGATIVE FRAMING

This research found that when a story possessed two distinct criteria, there was a far greater likelihood that journalists would subject the featured evangelical(s) to negative framing. First, the featured evangelical had to espouse a belief, or demonstrate an action, that ran contrary to the journalist's worldview. Second, the evangelical's belief or action had to somehow, according to the journalist's perception, threaten the public good. If the second criterion was not present, it was far less likely (though not out of the question) that the evangelical would be framed negatively. For example, evangelicals engaged in ecstatic behaviours, like speaking in tongues or being "slain in the spirit," were framed neutrally, for the most part, despite the fact that Canadian national journalists (as suggested by the findings of this study's survey) would have found that kind of activity unusual at best and disturbing at worst. The idea that evangelicals must be deemed a threat to society (in the journalists' eyes) and not just simply "odd" before the media will subject them to negative coverage is reminiscent of Kevin Carragee's observation about coverage of national issues in the U.S. As discussed in Chapter 4, Carragee states that the media is more easy-going with "outsider" groups when their actions are not likely to affect the social and political foundations of the country.

GOVERNMENT INFLUENCE?

As I stated in Chapter 4, I personally do not subscribe to the media hegemonic perspective. However, to a limited extent those working from that perspective might believe that their position is reinforced by the results of this study. They could argue that certain parallels exist between the established policies of the Canadian government and the dominant frames used in the coverage of evangelicals. Pluralism (most often in the form of multiculturalism) has been federally promoted and financed since the 1960s, and tolerance (including tolerance toward sexual orientation) has been enshrined in Canada's Charter of Rights and Freedoms since the 1980s—though tolerance itself has been a major component of the Canadian identity since the country's inception. Therefore, insofar as they promote tolerance and pluralism, the Canadian media are advancing the government's agenda. Expressed in relation to this study's findings, it could be argued that by subjecting evangelicals to highly negative framing, when they are thought to have contravened accepted standards of tolerance and pluralism, the Canadian news media are exercising the government's will. However, despite this evidence, it is more probable that media professionals frame evangelicals as they do, not to advance government policy, but to promote their own heartfelt convictions regarding pluralism and tolerance. While it is likely that the convictions journalists hold toward tolerance and pluralism have been elevated in importance because of the influence and pervasiveness of related government policies, this is hardly the same thing as being the government's toadies.

If more proof is required that Canada's elite journalists are loath to fall in line with government policy when it contradicts their own social and political views, one need only review news coverage of the same-sex marriage debate. Stephen Harper's Conservatives took power from Paul Martin's Liberals in 2006. Unlike the Liberals, the Conservatives did not support redefining marriage to include same-sex couples. Official conservative policy was more akin to a middle-path: it proposed that the term "marriage" be applied to unions of heterosexuals, and the term "civil unions" be applied to homosexuals who formally united. The rights, privileges and benefits from either of these unions would be identical.

When the Conservatives moved from Opposition to form the Government of Canada, their policy on civil unions became *the government's* policy. Despite its new status as the official policy of the governing party, the media did not suddenly embrace civil unions over full-scale marriage for homosexuals. Indeed, the Conservative's policy received little support from media prior to their elevation to government and it received even less after the fact.

Incidentally, I owe my knowledge of news coverage of the same-sex marriage date to a study I conducted that examined evangelical involvement in the issue. In the final chapter of this book, the Afterword, that study is discussed at length.

MUTING METHODS OF THE MEDIA

Heretofore, we have established that in news reports where evangelicals attempted to limit the rights of others, journalists subjected them to the most negative framing so as to minimize their influence on society. In Chapter 4, I highlighted some of the specific framing strategies the news media employ to mute dissonant voices; let us now turn our attention to those strategies as they apply to the findings of this study.

Other researchers have shown that journalists can devalue the message of a particular speaker by presenting the speaker's statements as paraphrases. Paraphrased statements are seen by an audience as less authoritative and less factual because they lack the instant legitimacy afforded quotes that have come unadulterated "right from the horse's mouth."[19] Given that paraphrases have been judged to contribute to the muting of an oppositional group's message, one might expect that Canadian television journalists would have used few direct quotes from evangelicals when covering issues related to them. (In those instances where evangelicals were seen to be threatening the dominant ideologies of pluralism and tolerance, one would assume the fewest direct quotes would be used). Certainly, this phenomenon has been witnessed in the U.S. Content analyses of American TV news reports have found conservative Christians are quoted directly less frequently than liberal Christian and secular sources.[20] However, in the Canadian television news reports examined for this study there was no scarcity of quotes from evangelical sources. In fact, a simple count of the interview clips showed that evangelicals were quoted directly more often than non-evangelical sources. Even in those reports where evangelical ideology clashed most with dominant ideologies, evangelicals were quoted directly (that is, featured in interview clips) more often than other sources.

While this finding, at first glance, seems to weaken the position that Canadian journalists marginalize evangelicals in those situations where they are deemed to be threatening, a more detailed examination of the principals behind quote selection shows otherwise. In his analysis of news report quote selection, Steven Clayman determined quotes or sound bites are chosen for inclusion in a news piece based on their narrative relevance, conspicuousness and extractability.[21] In the reports examined for this study, the direct quotes from evangelicals most often met the second criterion; that is, the interview clips from evangelicals inserted into the news reports tended to be of a conspicuous or sensationalistic nature, positing ideas foreign to, or at odds with, popular convention. Here is the crucial point. A direct quote or interview clip, when of a culturally dissonant nature, is more likely to frame a speaker negatively then to grant him greater esteem and authority in the public's eyes. (In my discussion of the theological content of the news reports, found later in this chapter, I provide some specific examples of the culturally dissonant ideas contained in the quotes of evangelicals).

We must remember that the reporter is able to choose which evangelical source will provide the voice for her entire religious community. Knowing journalistic convention holds that negative, extreme, and unusual (weird) views are more newsworthy it would go against a reporter's training and inclination to choose a source who presented a moderate, well-reasoned evangelical view when a more extreme source, willing to spout outrageous quotes on camera, was available. As anyone with experience in the news industry, like myself, will confirm, certain rules apply when constructing a story. If a group has a duly appointed spokesperson, then that person's view gets priority. However, in a situation where no clear group leader exists, radical and dramatic individuals become the prime choice for an interview.

In his book examining the news practices of CBS national television news, Bernard Goldberg concluded that journalists will promote one side of an issue over another, not through blatantly stating their opinion in their news report, but by choosing sources who agree with their personal opinion or somehow exemplify their take on a situation.[22] We see a similar process taking place in the coverage of evangelicals. To promote the idea that evangelicals are deviant, reporters can choose to interview only those believers who corroborate their personal thesis. Because every community has its share of "blacksheep," the reporter looking for a deviant source will seldom be disappointed.

Like the sources chosen for a news report, language too can shape a story's frame. As mentioned previously, many scholars contend that special attention must be paid to word usage because some terms are ideologically "loaded" and their usage influences audience perceptions.[23] In my examination of the coverage of evangelicals, one turn-of-phrase in particular stood out for its potential marginalizing effect. In 20% of the reports (N=25) the conservative Protestants featured were referred to as "fundamentalists"—a term that calls forth images of militancy and backwardness. The fundamentalist moniker was seldom used in conjunction with other monikers. Only 4 of the 25 reports referred to their featured conservative Protestants as fundamentalist Christians and then by another descriptor. Specifically, three used the term fundamentalist and evangelical interchangeably to describe their featured Christians; one used fundamentalist and Pentecostal Christian interchangeably.

As we shall see, it is highly unlikely that Canadian journalists reporting during the 1990s and beyond would not know "fundamentalist Christian" was a term of derision; there is reason to believe the term was knowingly used to stigmatize and marginalize those to whom it was applied.

During the fall of 1993, Brian Stiller, at the time head of the Evangelical Fellowship of Canada, launched a public relations campaign directed specifically at the media; he requested that they stop using the term fundamentalist Christian as a synonym for evangelical. Stiller's open letter, sent to all major news organizations, was blunt and to the point:

> For you to label an evangelical a 'fundamentalist' is like calling
> an Afro-Canadian a 'nigger' or a Canadian aboriginal with mixed
> ancestry a 'half-breed.' 'Fundamentalism' is a code word, signifying
> [to] people that the media elite have judged you to be less than legit-

imate, and view you as having no place in the public mainstream of our culture.[24]

Fundamentalist, he conceded, was once used as a religious term to denote conservative Protestants but it now stood for "bigoted, narrow, dogmatic and war-like people and is used to convey contempt and ridicule."[25] Stiller concluded his letter by insisting that the media place a moratorium on the offending term and he requested that journalists "call us 'evangelicals' and not resort to unfair names and innuendoes which the term 'fundamentalist' triggers."[26]

Stiller's letter got media attention and also generated discussion within Canada's newsrooms. As a direct response to the letter, two major news outlets, CBC Radio (the radio division of Canada's public broadcaster) and Canadian Press (Canada's largest news wire service) instituted policies whereby their journalists were not to use the word "fundamentalist" to describe Christians unless the Christians themselves used that term self-referentially.[27]

Given the amount of publicity Stiller's campaign for correct nomenclature was afforded and given the results that it achieved nationally, it seems unlikely that journalists working in Canada after the fall of 1993—including those that created the reports analyzed for this study—could apply the term fundamentalist to an evangelical Christian without knowing the marginalizing effect of that word.[28]

EXPLAINING THE PREDOMINANT POSITIVE FRAME

In light of the evidence showing journalists' penchant for marginalizing evangelicals and their message, how does one account for the fact that 10.9% of their reports framed evangelicals positively as undeserving of media and societal bias? Of the different possible explanations, I believe two are more probable than others.

Scholars Thomas Nelson, Rosalee Clawson, and Zoe Oxley's made the observation that:

Frames may originate within or outside the news organization. Journalists' common reliance on sources for quotes, insight, analysis,
and information means that the media often serve as conduits for
individuals eager to promote a certain perspective to a broader
public audience.[29]

That is to say, there are times when a source's interpretation of an
event or issue is adopted by the reporter as the "right" interpretation.[30]
It may be that in 10.9% of reports, evangelicals stayed on message and
argued vociferously that the treatment they were receiving in the media
and from others in society was prejudicial. In the end they were so
convincing that their "version of reality" was adopted, or favoured, in
the news reports.

It could also be that journalists employed this positive frame in a
concentrated fashion as a means of placating evangelicals and others
disgruntled by previously negative coverage. Interestingly, over half of
the reports in which the "undeserving of societal and media bias" frame
aired near the end, or shortly after, the Canadian federal election of
2000—an election that many defined in terms of its hostility toward
evangelicals. After his party's defeat, Stockwell Day himself publicly
accused the media of an anti-evangelical bias. Regarding journalists'
occasional "change of heart," media critics Edward Herman and Noam
Chomsky argue it is not uncommon for media personnel to sporadically
criticize the very ideas and ideals that they themselves have propagated.
Doing so creates the illusion of diversity and debate and enables the
media to discount claims of imbalance and bias while allowing them
to proceed unencumbered in their promotion of values and ideologies
they esteem. [31]

DO SOME NETWORKS LIKE EVANGELICALS MORE THAN OTHERS?

Variations among the networks, with regard to how each framed
evangelicals, deserves some attention. Of the three networks, the CBC
was the only one to register an overall frame rating below balanced in

the "slightly negative" range. Furthermore, in terms of CBC's dominant frames (that is, evangelicals as intolerant, criminally-minded, politically threatening, un-Canadian, and insincere), the network's negative depictions of evangelicals were seldom (in some cases never) challenged by opposing neutral or positive frames. Put another way, CBC's reports employed the "purist" negative frames of the three networks. It is true that CBC reports, more so than the others, employed the "undeserving of media and societal bias" frame. However, this frame primarily appeared in reports airing just after the 2000 election and thus the motivation for its presence is suspect. In keeping with Herman and Chomski's theory, it may have been the case that after airing particularly slanted reports—for which they were publicly criticized—journalists at the CBC wanted to take the heat off themselves and so decided to incorporate some pro-evangelical frames into their post-election stories.

Given the concentration of negative frames in their reports (relative to the other networks) it is perhaps not surprising to see that CBC journalists held the most uniformly negative attitudes toward evangelicals of all survey respondents. It was confirmed that respondents working for the CBC were more secular than respondents from the two other networks; 90% of CBC respondents said they were atheist, agnostic or non-practicing, compared to just under half of the respondents from the private networks. The one reporter of ten from CBC who did espouse a religious faith said he/she did not partake of regular religious activities like praying, reading the Bible or attending church. When asked how they were most similar to evangelical Christians in terms of their religious beliefs, 90% percent of CBC journalists said they were in no way similar compared to about 30% of the private network journalists. When journalists from CBC were asked "On which social issues do you find yourself in agreement or mostly in agreement with evangelical Christians?" 60% said "none" or gave no comment compared to about 20% of private network respondents.

Viewed by network affiliation, the seven journalists from CTV and even the four journalists from Global possessed a greater diversity of opinion regarding evangelicals (some pro and some con) than all ten journalists from the CBC who were, for the most part, unsympathetic to evangelicals and their beliefs. Such high uniformity of random respondents from CBC suggests that there may not be many journalists at that network who *are* sympathetic to evangelicals. This suggestion finds support in the studies by Miljan and Cooper and Barber and Rauhala which found CBC journalists to be the most secular in all Canada.[32] Miljan and Cooper suggest that the attitudinal uniformity among CBC employees arises from owners and managers with strong ideologies hiring and promoting front-line journalists who demonstrate similar ideologies.[33] Anecdotal evidence, as well, suggests this is so. Long-time CBC employee, turned newspaper columnist, Robert Fulford had this to say about his colleagues at the nation's public broadcaster:

> For generations, they have been constructing a body of impregnable, self-regenerating opinion. As employees they are pre-selected and their views are pre-recorded, like most of their programs. A single rule governs all personnel selection: Like hires like. That principal, followed for seven decades, produces seamless intellectual agreement in all corners of the staff.[34]

Trying to determine why journalists at Global News were the most likely to frame evangelicals positively or in a balanced fashion involves more conjecture. However, it too might have a great deal to do with the hiring and firing practices of owners and managers. It may not be sheer coincidence that two of Global's survey respondents were evangelicals themselves; perhaps management at Global are inclined to hire news staff with evangelical traits. This idea becomes more credible in light of two important facts: one, evangelicals tend to be strong supporters of the state of Israel, and two, the owners of the Global Network expect their employees to support the state of Israel in their coverage.

Evangelicals' support for Israel stems from their belief that the establishment and continuation of the state of Israel is a necessary prerequisite for the second coming of Christ. It is estimated that evangelicals from the United States and Canada contribute more than $20 million a year in aid to Israel. About 400,000 evangelicals travel to the Holy Land each year, contributing millions of dollars to Israel's economy. In fact, Israeli Tourism Minister Benny Elon credited evangelicals with saving his country's tourist industry from bankruptcy.[35] American evangelicals also use their considerable political influence to lobby the U.S. government to adopt pro-Israel policies.[36] Similarly, evangelicals in Canada were given some of the credit when this country's newly elected Conservative government came out strongly in favour of Israel during the 2006 conflict in Lebanon.

Regarding Global's stand on Israel, it is well documented that the Asper family, the owners of CanWest Global, Global Television's parent company, are strong supporters of the state of Israel, both politically and financially.[37] It is equally well-known that journalists working for the Aspers, especially those employed at their newspapers (CanWest owns 14 major dailies and 136 smaller papers), are expected to privilege their owner's position on Israel in their editorial and opinion content.[38] *Montreal Gazette* reporter Bill Marsden summarized the Asper's editorial policy saying, "[t]hey do not want any criticism of Israel. We do not run in our newspaper op-ed pieces that express criticism of Israel and what it is doing."[39] Upper managers at CanWest newspapers who have not toed the Asper's party line editorially, and reporters who have written pieces criticizing the policies of the state of Israel have been punished. For example, the publisher of the *Montreal Gazette*, Michael Goldbloom, was fired "after deviating from CanWest Global's pro-Israel stance."[40] Doug Cuthand, a columnist for the *Regina Leader Post* was not fired, but he had an essay "sympathetic to the plight of Palestinians in Israel" pulled from the paper.[41] It was the first time in 10 years of freelancing for the paper that Cuthand had had his column terminated. While management gave him no explanation, he said he believed it was because "what [he] wrote went against the corporate policy of CanWest."[42]

Again, the proposition that Global news executives are more amenable to hiring evangelicals because of their ideological leanings is highly conjectural and would require further research to be proven conclusively. Less fanciful (though still in need of empirical verification) is the notion that journalists at Global TV and other CanWest news outlets are more favourable in their depictions of evangelicals because they know their top bosses value them as comrades in the defence of Israel. It seems credible that someone hoping to get ahead in their career would be wise to adopt the motto, "The enemy of my boss is my enemy and the friend of my boss is my friend."

ARE BAD NEWS STORIES LONGER?

Regarding the format of the reports, studies of national television news coverage of religion in the U.S. found reports that showed religious individuals in situations of conflict or controversy tended to be longer running, reporter-based stories while those that showed them in positive situations tended to be brief anchor-reads.[43] Similarly, the Fraser Institute's study of religion stories on Canadian national television news determined that reports featuring Christian faith groups tended to be shorter than those reports featuring non-Christian religious groups—except when the Christian groups were involved in conflict.[44] In contrast to the aforementioned studies, my research found that news reports featuring evangelicals in a positive light were not given short shrift. That is, positive stories were not primarily relegated to the shorter-running formats. As was noted in the results, just 13 of the 119 reports about evangelicals were anchor reads or anchor reads to clips. When I examined these shorter pieces more closely, 10 of the 13 were negative in their portrayal of evangelicals (as evidenced by a preponderance of negative frames). If the shortest stories in this study were primarily negative it is a given that the more positive reports about evangelicals are found among the 103 stories that were broadcast as the longer running reporter packages and live interviews.

THUS SAITH THE LORD—PREDICTING THEOLOGICAL CONTENT

The format of the reports for this study defied conventional wisdom—so did the theological content of the stories. With a presence in almost one third of reports, the amount of theological content contained in the television news about evangelicals was higher than one might expect. Studies of religion coverage in the U.S. have found theology to be nearly absent from reports; only about 7% of faith-related news stories reference religious beliefs or doctrines.[45] However, there are some possible explanations as to why theology was included as often as it was in Canadian TV news reports.

In their study of American religion coverage, Lichter and colleagues observed that stories about non-mainstream religious groups like Buddhists, Moonies, or Wiccans, were the exception when it came to the inclusion of theological references.[46] The reason doctrinal information is included in stories about such groups is obvious: the average person watching or reading the news report is not familiar with the tenets of the featured "fringe" faith, so journalists feel obligated to pad their stories with theological background. In Canada, evangelicals and evangelical culture are far less prevalent than in the U.S.; thus, to the majority of Canadians, evangelicalism is as foreign as any Eastern religion. Having been raised in "culturally" Christian homes, where vestiges of religious practice and belief are still present (for instance, Christmas and Easter celebrations might include a foray to a church service), most Canadians would be familiar with such basic theological principles as: God watches over his followers, heaven awaits the faithful, love your neighbour as yourself and forgive others as you have been forgiven. However, only the highly devout, the theologically trained, or regular attendees of conservative Protestant churches would have a grasp of the biblical foundation upon which the more obscure, and sometimes "culturally divisive" beliefs of Christianity rest. That is, what the Bible says (and what many evangelicals believe) about homosexuality, creationism, end-times prophecy, and the submission of wives to husbands would need to be explained to the "average Canadian." Of course, the "oddness" of these beliefs alone might be the reason they receive so much attention. As has been discussed already, the more unusual an idea, the more newsworthy it becomes. Being "culturally dissonant" (that is, at odds with majority sensibilities), as these beliefs are, increases the likelihood that they will get mentioned in a story.

Interestingly, in his study of religion coverage in Ontario newspapers, Larry Cornies also found that almost one-quarter of Canadian faith-related news stories contained theological content.[47] While he did not indicate which faith group was featured in these theologically-rich stories, he did note that theology often related to contentious issues such as the contest between evolution and creationism. Considering the character of the references, it is likely that many of the theologically-rich stories Cornies identified were about the exploits and beliefs of evangelicals. Again, it may have been the case that the journalists saw certain evangelical beliefs as "foreign" and thus in need of explanation.

It might also be the case that Canadian news reports contain more theological content than American news reports because Canadian reporters do journalism differently than their American counterparts. As part a larger research project, Gertrude Robinson and Armande Saint-Jean measured what Canadian journalists saw as their most important role and then compared the Canadian responses to those of American journalists.[48] More than any other answer, Canadian journalists chose providing analysis of complex issues as a very important role; 63% were of this opinion. Conversely, just 49% of American journalists saw providing analysis of complex issues as very important; a higher percentage saw "investigating government claims" (66%) and "getting information to the public quickly" (60%) as very important (1996).[49] It could be that Canadian journalists' desire to explain the "why" behind the "what" of a news event leads them to include more background information in all their reports. For stories about evangelicals (or religion in general) this overriding tendency may be evidenced in the greater inclusion of scriptural and doctrinal content.

MOVING THE MOUNTAIN—FRAMES' PERSISTENT NATURE

Regarding the consistency of the frames, the results showed that apart from the uncharacteristic spikes in frequency that the "Threatening Politically," "Undeserving of Societal and Media Bias" and the "Un-Canadian" frames experienced in 2000 (on account of strife over the federal election), the frames identified in this study did not change dramatically over time. This finding lends support to the idea that once a frame becomes set, or engrained on society, it is unlikely to be replaced by an opposing version of reality.[50] This may be disheartening for evangelicals. It suggests that in those situations where they are persistently and consistently negatively framed there is little hope for a change in perspective.

Let's briefly turn our attention to the spikes that were recorded. They suggest something very interesting was going on in the fall of 2000. As discussed previously in this chapter, this research found that when a story featured an evangelical espousing a belief that ran contrary to the journalist's worldview *and* when the evangelical's belief was deemed to threaten the public good (in the eyes of the journalists), then the evangelical was far more likely to be framed negatively. In the spikes to the "Threatening Politically" and "Un-Canadian" frames we see further support for this study's claim of predictive criteria for negative framing. In 2000, national television journalists deemed evangelical politician Stockwell Day a serious threat to the public good. If he was successful in his bid to become Prime Minister, his strong opposition to abortion, same-sex marriage and other such religiously-informed positions might gain exposure and increased credibility nationally. Seeing his views as antithetical to their own and realizing the influence he would wield if he won, the media appeared to do everything in their power to ensure that he did not. The evidence of their concerted effort is visibly perceptible in the sudden and prolific use of the "Politically Threatening" and "Un-Canadian" frames in the lead-up to the election.

In so far as the media's course of action greatly contributed to the governing Liberal's campaign agenda (that is, to paint Stockwell Day and his Canadian Alliance party as "scary" and thus, illegitimate political players), an argument for the governmental hegemonic thesis could be made. However, as the evidence below indicates, the intense coverage on Day's beliefs was not due to governmental influence but due to the influence of a single network.

CBC made Stockwell Day's evangelical faith an election issue for Canadians who watch TV news. While the print media in Canada had made Day's faith one of their major agenda items as early as March 2000 it was not until mid-November when CBC's *The National* aired its documentary "The Fundamental Day" that the politician's evangelical beliefs became a hot issue for TV news. Up to that time, only short, innocuous references to Day being a Pentecostal and a former lay preacher had been included in national TV reports. However, after the CBC aired its documentary, Day's religious beliefs—particularly his belief in creationism—became the focus of coverage on both CTV national news and Global national news. All three networks kept Day's faith high on their agendas for several days. Subsequent stories tended to be reaction pieces featuring politicians, sociologists, theologians commenting on and discussing—not Day's faith per se—but what CBC's documentary *had said* about Day's faith. In this case, CBC national news not only set the agenda, it became part of the story.

HAVEN'T I SEEN THIS STORY BEFORE?

The TV coverage of Day during the 2000 election is emblematic of the types of evangelical-related issues and events that made the national media's agenda over the longer period of 1994 to 2005. My continuing analysis of the evangelicals in the news suggests the detected trends are still prevalent today. So, in which situations are evangelicals most likely to receive coverage? Past and present trends suggest evangelicals are more apt to be included in a news report when involved in non-religious situations rife with conflict (for example, politics, crime, and social protests). Conversely, they are less likely to receive coverage when involved in distinctly "positive" situations where harmony is exemplified (for example, charity and volunteer work). Distinct from how they are framed in these situations, the situations themselves are primarily negative. In terms of topic or subject matter, it could be that the media's preference for covering evangelicals in non-religious, controversial situations is linked to biased attitudes toward this faith group. However, the media's preference for covering stories of this nature is probably more a case of established precedent than overt prejudice. As discussed, journalistic convention holds that certain types of events and issues possess a greater range of "news values" and, therefore, are more worthy of coverage than others.[51]

We should not be surprised, then, that most of the television news stories about evangelicals focus on negative situations and lack complexity given that most news stories, regardless of the subject, are like that as well. However, we must consider whether the media's defence that "this is just the way we *always* do our job" is sufficient justification for the choices they have made in relation to coverage of evangelicals. On closer inspection, the media's argument comes up wanting.

While the media cannot be faulted for placing stories that contain "tried-and-true" news criteria (for example, negativity or conflict) on their agenda, in the case of evangelicals they can be faulted for focusing on certain conventional criteria to the exclusion of others. It would appear that the media believe that "negativity" is the only (or at least most important) news criterion by which an evangelical-related event or issue should be deemed worthy of coverage. Indeed, they tend to overlook those evangelical stories in which the news criteria of "uniqueness" and "significance" are present. In Canada, evangelicals devote more time to volunteer organizations and more money to charities than other any other single community of citizens, and this measure of volunteer work and charity giving does not include the time and money they contribute to programs within their own churches.[52] These two activities of evangelicals are both "unique" and "significant" in the Canadian context. However, news stories related to their volunteer and charity work comprised just 2.5% of all coverage in the last decade, the lowest amount of coverage for any single topic category. Many Canadians may be surprised to learn that, after their government, evangelical aid agencies are the greatest contributors to their country's social welfare system.

In relation to their agenda-setting function, the media, for the most part, are highly successful in making us think about evangelicals in terms of conflict and controversy and, whether intentional or not, this adds to the impression that they evangelicals are deviant. Even when the reporting is fair and balanced, the content of most of the news stories with its "us-versus-them structure" necessarily leaves news consumers with a feeling of negativity. It cannot be helped that the negativity surrounding an issue is transferred onto the antagonists of the story through the process of "guilt by association." In short, evangelicals are seen as contentious because of the issues with which they are associated.

Whatever the reasons for their aversion to substantively covering evangelicals involved in unique and significant positive acts, it seems incumbent upon Canada's journalists to work towards rectifying this imbalance. If non-evangelical Canadians are to ever truly understand who Canadian evangelical Christians *really are*—that is, if they are ever to see them in terms of more than one of two incidental traits—the news media must begin to define them in a manner more reflective of how they define themselves.

Recently, there have been some signs that Canada's news media are willing to make a concerted effort to provide a broader picture of who evangelicals are. For example, in December of 2006, CBC's *The National* ran an extensive, documentary featuring reporter Mark Kelley living among American evangelicals for seven days.[53] Similarly, in March 2005 the *Globe and Mail* ran a series of lengthy feature articles by writer and CBC radio host Ian Brown cataloguing his experiences travelling throughout America's Bible-belt.[54] Unfortunately, Canadian evangelicals are not American evangelicals and thus, while a step in the right direction, neither of these journalistic efforts did anything to illuminate evangelicalism in its northern context. Worse, both of these pieces focused primarily on the novelty-side of American evangelical culture. For example, both Kelley and Brown gave extensive coverage to a Bible-based amusement park, but devoted no airtime or ink to the thousands of evangelical charity and relief organizations in the U.S. that contribute thousands of workers and billions of dollars in aid around the world.

One thing that this current study's findings about story topics makes clear is that evangelicals have very little power over the media's agenda. In terms of controlling which events and issues the media will cover, this faith group appears to wield almost no influence. While research has determined that some special interest and advocacy groups are able to influence the media's agenda through the sending of media releases, evangelicals—at least from what the data suggest—are not among "the chosen few." To be sure, certain anecdotal evidence provides further proof that Canadian news outlets pay little heed to information subsidies originating with evangelicals. In August of 2005, popular U.S. televangelist Pat Robertson made headlines for suggesting on national television that Venezuelan President Hugo Chavez should be assassinated. Following the incident, the Evangelical Fellowship of Canada (EFC), on behalf of the more than 140 evangelical organizations and denominations it represents, sent out a media release to all major news outlets in Canada condemning Robertson's comments. The intent of the EFC was to relay to non-evangelicals in Canada that Canadian evangelicals were not "cut from the same cloth" as their more radical American cousins. However, the statement was not picked up by radio, TV, or the papers, nor did the EFC receive any calls from reporters seeking to clarify where Canadian evangelicals stood on the issue. According to EFC executives, the media's behaviour in this case was reflective of other instances.[55]

CHAPTER 9

Affixing Evangelicals'
Negative Image

B ack when I was a reporter, I would sometimes finish a story and
hand it to my News Director who, after giving it a quick read,
would declare, "So what?!" Those two words were loaded with meaning.
It was her way of telling me I had not yet drawn a connection between
the facts of my story and the concerns of my audience. I had yet to
make it clear why the average person should care about what I had just
written. I think of this as the "So what?" portion of the book. It is here
that I make the transition from "this is what we know" to "this is why
we should care."

Let's quickly tally what we know. We can say that Canadian national
journalists tend to be irreligious but, when it comes to liberal Western
ideologies and values, especially the ideology of pluralism and the
cultural value of tolerance, they resemble fundamentalists (for example,
they seem to insist that their interpretation of sacred doctrine—the
doctrine of pluralism and tolerance—is the only correct one). We can
also state that the firmly held beliefs of journalists are promoted in
the news coverage that they produce. Specifically, in order to ensure
their own ideological system prevails in society, they tend to negatively
frame those groups that challenge their beliefs and values. By depicting
those groups that they find personally offensive as deviant and undesir-

able, they are able to coax the population-at-large into rejecting their message.

However, holding beliefs and values at odds with those held by the media does not guarantee a group will become a target for negative framing. It is when a group's beliefs or values imperil or threaten to compromise what journalists see as the public good or as a "just society," that an onslaught of negative frames is most likely to be launched.

As well, it is very likely that the way media personnel define tolerance and pluralism brings them into conflict with groups holding more conservative values than themselves. Journalists seem to take a broader, more encompassing view of what these concepts entail. Conversely, groups like Canadian evangelicals tend to define tolerance and pluralism more narrowly. Of course, there is a certain irony in the media's negative framing of groups that they deem to have broached the boundaries of pluralism and tolerance. That is, they seem to be contravening their own rule that "one must accept all views as equally valid." One would guess that they are able to rationalize their behaviour using the logic that it is alright to be intolerant to the "intolerant."

Let's now move to why we should care. It has been more than three hundred years since Scottish politician Andrew Fletcher made his famous quip, "If a man were permitted to make all the ballads, he need not care who should make the laws of a nation." Fletcher recognized that stories have as much power to shape the culture and ideology of a society as political policies. Indeed, when someone or some group has the power to transmit their stories into the living rooms of almost every Canadian, the effects are far very reaching indeed. Given the extent and intimacy of their reach, the news media play a truly crucial role in deciding which groups in society will be valued and which will be devalued. By deciding whether to cover an issue or event, in choosing sources and then portions from their interviews, through word use, and through inclusion and exclusion of information, the media shape a group's message and even their identity for an audience. With that in mind, we recall the statistic from Chapter 1 which noted that 31% of Canadians surveyed said they would be uneasy meeting an evangelical.

In that chapter, it was also suggested that the unflattering stereotypes of evangelicals promoted by the media may be contributing to the negative perception non-evangelical Canadians have towards that faith group. While we cannot claim causation based on the findings of this study, the results fuel the fires of speculation. Should we be surprised that nearly one-third of Canadians feel uncomfortable with evangelicals, when for more than a decade the news media's most memorable (or most resonant) messages about this faith group have stressed that they are intolerant, criminally-mined, politically-threatening and un-Canadian? At the very least, we must admit, in light of this study's findings, a statement like "I don't know an evangelical personally but I've seen them on the news" now takes on ominous overtones.

HOW NEWS REPORTS ABOUT EVANGELICALS AFFECT NON-EVANGELICALS

To tell the truth, when it comes to the affect Canadian news reports about evangelicals have on non-evangelicals, we are able to do more than just speculate. While the original research that comprises the bulk of this book does not empirically show that the media's portrayal of evangelicals lead non-evangelical Canadians to view them negatively, other experimental work I have conducted does establish just such a connection.

Shortly after concluding the major research for this book, I decided to test the affect that exposure to television news reports about evangelicals would have on an audience of non-evangelicals Canadians. The full results of that later study were published in the fall 2007 volume of the *Journal of Media and Religion.*[2] I will provide a précised version of the study's methods and results here.

To explore the influence that media coverage of evangelicals has on non-evangelicals' perceptions, I recruited a small pool of undergraduate student coders to examine national television news reports featuring evangelicals. (As described previously, a "coder" is a study participant asked to examine textual material and identify, or code, the presence of specified phenomenon.) The reports analyzed by the undergraduate coders were those that had been collected and examined for the frame analysis that has been detailed extensively in this book. After reading each report, the coders were asked to rate (code) their impression (positive or negative) of the evangelicals presented in it.

Because this new study was concerned with the affect news reports have on a person's perceptions regarding evangelicals, the attempt was made to enlist participants who had no formed opinion of evangelicals. After an initial interview process with over 100 potential candidates, only four were deemed eligible. A more formal attitudinal survey completed by the eligible participants revealed that none were evangelicals Christians themselves. All stated that religion was "unimportant in their lives." A formal, face-to-face interview with each coder revealed that none had personal experience with evangelicals or evangelicalism and, as such, all reported having "no opinion" on evangelicals prior to the study. The interview also revealed that the personal values of the coders were in keeping with the liberal-pluralistic values to which demographers and sociologists say the majority of Canadians ascribe. Namely, the coders were found to be in favor of multiculturalism, tolerance and ecumenism, homosexual rights, equality for women, and a woman's right to an abortion.

Before they began their examination of the reports, the participants were given a brief lesson about evangelicals. Using value-neutral language, evangelicals' core religious beliefs were explained and their identifying characteristics were highlighted. When performing the actual analysis, the participants worked independently without consultation or guidance. They read each transcript in full and then gauged their impression of the evangelicals using a five-point rating scale. Specifically, they were asked to indicate whether a report made them feel very positively (rated 5), somewhat positively (rated 4), neutrally (rated 3), somewhat negatively (rated 2), or very negatively (rated 1) toward the evangelicals. Each of the five rating categories was explained in detail in a guidebook that was provided.

And how *did* the coders feel about evangelicals who appeared in the news? The combined scores for all reports garnered a mean rating of 2.75 (SD=1.30) on a scale of 1 to 5. Inching toward the territory of slightly negative as this rating does, suggests that, overall, coders felt "cool" or "guarded" toward the evangelicals featured in the reports though not necessarily antagonistic toward them. This is good news for evangelicals. An impression that is anchored far into negative territory (or positive territory for that matter) is one that is hard to change.[3] The relative weakness of the coders' opinion suggests that it would be open to revision. Incidentally, a discussion of the means by which the public's perception of evangelicals might be pulled into more positive territory is found in the next chapter of this book.

In addition to empirically gauging the affect national television news reports had on non-evangelicals' perceptions of evangelicals, my secondary research also produced four other very interesting findings.

First, I determined that one-third of news reports about evangelicals that had aired on Canadian national television news featured American, and not Canadian, evangelicals. In concrete numbers, 64.7% (N=77) featured evangelicals from Canada, 32.7% (N=39) featured evangelicals from the United States. Just 2.5% (N=3) featured evangelicals whose country of origin was outside North America; specifically, evangelicals from Russia, Britain and Brazil were each the focus of one report.

Second, by analyzing each of the reports for the specific situation in which the evangelicals found themselves, and by coding what the evangelicals said and the actions they were described as performing, I was able to determine that the more tolerant nature of Canadian evangelicals and the less tolerant nature of American evangelicals manifests itself tangibly in the coverage. In short, the more irenic nature of Canadian evangelicals that sociologist Sam Reimer discovered in his research (see Chapter 2 for details) was visibly present in television news reports. For example, Canadian and American evangelicals alike received a significant amount of coverage for their demonstrations against homosexual rights or same-sex marriage. However, in the reports featuring American evangelicals the rhetoric used by demonstrators was significantly more pejorative. Slurs such as "faggott" and references to "filthy lifestyle" and "burn[ing] in hell" were present in their quotes.[4] No such slurs or references were present in the reports featuring Canadian evangelicals. Instead, their statements tended to be more defensive than offensive. For example, regarding her stand on homosexuality an evangelical woman explained, "It sort of goes against our own values," to which her husband added, "We love a lot of folks but, you know, why is it we have to be forced down a certain road?"[5]

Third, I determined that an audience (specifically, the non-evangelical coders of my study) exposed to national television news coverage of evangelicals actually perceives Canadian evangelicals more favourably than American, due to the observable expressions of the Canadians' tolerant nature. To make this determination, I divided the coders' news report rating sheets into two groups and performed separate calculations. In the first group, I placed the ratings for those news reports that featured Canadian evangelicals; in the second group were the ratings for those that featured American evangelicals. The news reports featuring Canadian evangelicals alone yielded a mean rating of 2.92 (SD=1.20) on a scale of 1 to 5. In other words, reports featuring just Canadian evangelicals left coders feeling neutral toward this faith group. Conversely, reports featuring American evangelicals alone produced a mean rating of 2.41 (SD=1.43), indicating that coders felt slightly negatively toward this faith group. A two-sample t-test determined that the difference between the ratings of Canadian and American evangelicals' stories was significant (t=1.91, d.f.=114, p<0.05).

My fourth finding is the one that Canadian evangelicals are likely to find the most depressing. A week following their analysis of the news report, I had the coders complete a questionnaire consisting of a single open-ended question. It asked:

> Having completed your coding of the TV scripts about evangelicals, are you left with the impression that evangelicals everywhere share common attitudes and characteristics (if yes, what are the commonalities) or, are you left with the impression that distinct communities of evangelicals differ in their attitudes and characteristics

(if yes, what were the communities and what are the differences).
Or, are you left with an impression that was a mix of option one and
option two above? (Explain).

The completed questionnaire showed that the coders did not notice
any difference in attitudes or characteristics between various evangelical populations. As these excerpts from their responses prove, when the
coders rated Canadian evangelicals more favourably than American,
their preference for the Canadians did not register consciously.

Excerpt from Coder 1's response:

> I was mainly left with the impression that all evangelicals shared
> the same beliefs, and most shared a common attitude toward the
> beliefs of others when [those beliefs] did not conform with evan-
> gelical faith. They all had strong views on religion, gay marriage,
> abortion, and other topics, and they did not appear to be willing to
> adapt their views.

Excerpt from Coder 2's response:

> While participating in this study, I noticed that I began to expect
> certain responses from evangelical groups regarding the issues
> that the news stories were about. I would begin to read the script
> and understand the story, and sometimes even before the evangeli-
> cal voice was introduced, I'd have a good idea of what stance he
> or she would take on the topic. I found in my personal experience
> that evangelicals do generally share common attitudes. Evangel-
> icals--as I read of them--are not an open-minded people. They
> feel very strongly that their opinion is the right one and that they
> are carrying out God's will in choosing to stand up against such
> modern institutions as abortion, gay marriage, etc.

Excerpt from Coder 3's response:

> From the readings, I found that most of the evangelicals shared
> the same beliefs. I thought that many had very traditional values
> (non-acceptance of gays etc.) and were not willing to budge on their

beliefs. It seemed that they were unwilling to even consider pro-
gressing towards accepting gays, etc. I did find that most were the
same.

Excerpt from Coder 4's response:

I think my biggest impression from these news stories was that
evangelicals share a very strong belief, and are willing to go to great
lengths to get their views across to other people. I didn't really
notice any differences between different communities of evangelicals.

As the excerpts above show, in the minds of the coders Canadian
evangelicals are indistinguishable from their American counterparts.
It appears that Canadian evangelicals are forced to share the collective reputation of their extended faith group. If news coverage shows
American evangelicals behaving badly, Canadian evangelicals will
be tarred with the same negative brush despite their more tolerant
nature.

Finally, it should be noted that the coders' questionnaire responses,
like their overall rating for the news reports, show that their attitude
toward evangelicals was "cool" or "guarded." As we can see from
their own words, the dominant impression coders were left with after
exposure to the TV reports was that evangelicals are intolerant of those
who disagree with them. Equally interesting is what the coders did not
say. None of their responses contained an overtly positive statement
about evangelicals. The acts of volunteerism and charity that were
featured in 2.5% of the television news reports, if they were remembered at all, were certainly not top-of-mind for the coders.

CHAPTER 10

Fixing Evangelicals' Negative Image

This research should be viewed as a first step in a long progression to illuminate the relationship between evangelicals and the media in Canada. To convincingly determine if this faith group's concerns over media bias are justified, further research is warranted. For example, the depiction of evangelicals in Canadian newspapers, magazines and even entertainment media should be subjected to analysis

Furthermore, it would be beneficial if future studies were to examine the relationship between the Canadian media and other faith groups using a methodology comparable to that used in this research. Similarly focused studies on "stand-alone" faith communities would allow for comparison of data between religious groups, and in the end, provide a clearer and more complete understanding of the news media's overall treatment of religion. In particular, similar research examining the media's treatment of conservative Catholics and conservative Muslims would be very useful for evaluative purposes. An examination of media coverage of conservative Catholics—who, over the last few decades, have become increasingly similar doctrinally and ideologically to evangelicals—would allow researchers to determine whether conservative Christian faith groups, in general, share a common media profile. Conversely, a similarly conducted study of coverage of orthodox Muslims would allow researchers to determine if journalists—known for their support of the underdog—are more sympathetic in their treatment of non-dominant (that is, non-Christian) conservative faith communities.

It must be said, the results of this study would be put to poor use if they served only to heighten the tension that already exists between evangelicals and the news media. I think that the findings would be better employed as a catalyst to positive action.

WHY OBJECTIVITY IS GOOD FOR JOURNALISTS

The results of my research show that Canadian television journalists, in certain cases, fail to cover evangelical Christians in a balanced and objective fashion. Media personnel would be wise to rectify this situation. Allowing their journalistic objectivity to erode could eventually lead to an erosion of their most prized privilege: freedom of the press. The reason that media outlets in most democratic countries are allowed to produce and disseminate their messages with little government involvement is that it is assumed that they will police themselves when it comes to balance and fairness. When they forgo neutrality in favour of advocating a specific cause or ideology, they risk losing their privileged status. Furthermore, news media organizations that become known for abandoning their objectivity, risk alienating sources and their audiences. Sources might cease to make themselves available to "biased" outlets for fear that their comments would not be accurately or fairly relayed to the public. (As discussed previously, to a certain extent this practice is already being employed by members of the federal Conservative Party.) Likewise, audiences might cease to view, read or listen to the news from those outlets that they perceive are trying to influence their opinion. Anecdotally, I know many evangelicals who have stopped watching CBC television news because they feel it "is anti-Christian and promotes a left-wing agenda." Similarly, many of my colleagues at the university where I teach refuse to read the *National Post* newspaper because they feel it is "a propaganda tool for the far-right."

Lydia Miljan and Barry Cooper note that abandoning attempts at objectivity in order to advocate a particular agenda is dangerous for one other reason. They explain that when journalists write "[t]o promote social change, which means always to promote specific social change . . . [they] justify their advocacy on the grounds that they believe they are right, and that what they advocate will improve society."[1] However, Miljan and Cooper argue, unless journalists possess psychic abilities that allow them to see into the future, they cannot know for certain when they are right. In fact, history suggests that many of the causes and ideals promoted by journalists in the past turned out to be detrimental to society in the future. The glowing—and deeply flawed—coverage the Soviet Union that Walter Duranty produced in the early 1930s comes to mind. As the Moscow correspondent for the *New York Times*, Duranty reported on Josef Stalin's Five-Year Plan to industrialize the Soviet Union. He idealized Stalin—thinking a strong man was just what the Soviet people needed to turn their country around—and his infatuation affected his reporting. When Stalin's regime purposely caused a famine in 1932 to force Ukrainian peasants into surrendering their land, Duranty underreported the resulting devastation and death. Believing that the communist government would know what was best for the country he was able to rationalize his slanted coverage. One sees parallels between Duranty's obsequious treatment of Stalin and many contemporary American journalists' treatment of George W. Bush and his administration in the early days of the Iraq war. Even some of the most trusted, and well-known names in American news became cheerleaders for their government which, unbeknownst to them, was feeding them false information about the dangers posed by Iraq.

STRATEGIES TO HELP JOURNALISTS IMPROVE THEIR COVERAGE

While past and present events show that there are no foolproof means of guaranteeing journalistic objectivity, three simple strategies could help television networks in Canada be more balanced and fair in their coverage of evangelical Christians. First, they could hire a faith specialist—an individual with extensive knowledge in the field of religion. In stories involving evangelicals, such a person would be more able to explain the theological motivation behind their beliefs and actions moving beyond the "what" of a story to the "why".

From June 2001 to July 2002, CTV national television news did have a faith specialist on staff. Mark Schneider was the first; he was later replaced by Anne-Marie Mediwake. Schneider and Mediwake were required to produce a weekly news feature called the "Horizon Report" (I am not sure if the title was meant to invoke the mental image of the sun coming up which arguably has some religious connotations). The report was billed as CTV's "weekly look at issues of ethics and spirituality."[2] While some of the pieces had a superficial and manu-factured feel (one gets the sense that the reporter was under pressure to find some "wacky" religious trend or event that would tickle the audience's fancy), the majority dealt with topical religious issues in a thorough and sensitive manner. Unfortunately, for whatever reason, the Horizon Report's plug was pulled just after a year. It does, however, provide a model that could be followed.

Second, the networks could begin hiring reporters who are evan-gelicals, or at least religious. The results of this study's survey suggest that religious individuals from all faiths are significantly underrepre-sented in Canada's national television newsrooms. The survey findings also showed that reporters who are religious, though not necessarily evangelicals themselves, tend to be more open-minded toward those believers who are evangelicals. Having more people of devout faith on staff would bring greater knowledge and balance to stories about evangelicals and religion in general. If there is any question of the efficacy of such a measure, one need only look at the benefits that affirmative action strategies have already brought to newsrooms across the country. At one time, the voices of women and non-whites were excluded from the popular discourse—now those perspectives have been integrated and our popular discourse is much richer. I am a strong proponent of Hegel's notion that the best ideas come to the fore in an environment that allows and promotes thesis, antithesis, and synthesis. News organizations are greenhouses for ideas—unfortunately, in terms of religious belief, our greenhouses continue to sow a monoculture. Should news media employers be taking proactive measures to ensure that their employees represent a diverse mix of religious orientations as well? I think yes. Those who would disagree must answer this question: Why is encouraging racial diversity in the newsroom good (and it is) but not religious diversity?

Third, when secular news personnel cover evangelicals, they should try to explore the religious angle of the story—that is, its theological foundation—by asking questions and *reporting answers* related to beliefs and faith. It is true that journalists are already inclined to include in their reports references to religious beliefs when those beliefs are tied to controversial practices. However, this interrogatory approach is seldom used when covering "good news" stories about evangelicals. For example, when evangelicals receive coverage for volunteer or charity work they are rarely asked what motivates their actions. During my days as a TV reporter I became aware of such behaviour. When evangelicals (or other people of devout faith) voluntarily offered one of my colleagues their religious reasons for doing some good deed or another, their comment was ignored. My fellow reporter might smile and nod at the time of the interview, but when it was time to write the story, the comments that related to religious motivations were left out. I can recall a time when I was sitting in an editing booth with a co-worker. He was working on a story about a farmer in Ontario who was donating hay to other draught-stricken farmers in Alberta. I watched the TV monitor as my associate reviewed the interview he had just done with the farmer. Several times, without prompting, the farmer said with great conviction, "Jesus tells his followers to do unto others as you would have other do unto you. We've got to reach out to our neighbours like Jesus says in the story of the good Samaritan. That's why I'm doing this. I'm following Christ." Later, I was surprised by the finished report my colleague produced. It explained, down to the kilogram, how much hay the Ontario farmer was sending and it said exactly where it was going. It even talked about the plants that comprise hay (clover, alfalfa and some rye grass, if I remember correctly). However, as to the farmer's motivation for giving the hay away, that comment was boiled down to a sterile paraphrase: he felt moved to help others because of his "religious beliefs."

I am not alone in noticing that reporters downplay "faith" as a legitimate reason for someone's positive behaviour. At an Ottawa conference on Faith and the Media held in the late 1990s, former CBC radio host and reporter Leslie Hughes commented on the news coverage Joyce Milgaard received while fighting her protracted legal battle to have her son, David, exonerated for a murder that he did not commit. Hughes remarked:

> Here was a woman with absolutely no legal training whatever, who managed to move mountains. She managed to do this and with almost no resources except her Christian Science faith. She explained how it energized her, how again and again and again it gave her the courage and the strength and the good cheer to go back and forgive everybody who was resisting what she was trying to do, everybody, including herself and her own errors, and how she was able to persist until she got the changes that she wanted in the case against her son. It was interesting to see that in the stories about her, though, in radio and television, newspaper, that Christian Science didn't appear, probably because it wasn't accepted as an authentic answer.[3]

Interestingly, the media's aversion to citing faith as a motivator for positive behaviour was noticed as early as the 1960's by none other than civil rights leader and Baptist minister Martin Luther King Jr. Professor of American Religious History, Patrick Allitt, says this about King and the news media:

> Throughout the late 1950s and early 1960s the civil rights movement was clearly both a political and religious movement but the American media, because they didn't want to get into the religious aspect of it too much, systematically downplayed the degree to which it was accomplished through evangelical excitement. King and the others would talk about the way in which the TV cameras would come and often they would remain turned off

while a sermon an hour long would be preached. Then at the end, when there was a 10 minute passage about actual political objectives, the big flood lights would go on and the cameras would roll and that would be the passage that appeared on the TV news. It gave the appearance to outside observers that it was relatively less of a religious movement than was experienced by people who had been physically present at the time.[4]

Of course, there are other measures that could be implemented to ensure evangelicals and other people of devout faith receive fairer news coverage but, taking a cue from my friends who are priests and pastors, here I will limit myself to a "three-point sermon." After three points, my collared friends tell me, people start to doze off.

BIBLICAL-OBJECTIVITY VERSUS DISCLOSURE JOURNALISM

However, I must admit, I am skeptical that any of the above recommendations will gain traction. I find it hard to believe that news professionals will change the way that they cover evangelicals simply because I have asked them nicely. And there are other reasons to be pessimistic. Frame theory itself, and its ideological cousin, the social constructionist position, insist that journalists—indeed, all of us—must necessarily interpret (or filter) events and issues through the lens of our own values, beliefs and opinions. (Though, as has been discussed, "good" journalism, as it is understood today, requires that a reporter try to keep her personal biases in check). It is only if our values, beliefs and opinions change that our interpretations of reality can or will change. By that logic, it is fair to say that unless the majority of Canadian news professionals experience personal conversions to evangelical Christianity, it is highly unlikely that their values, beliefs, and opinions toward members of that faith group will significantly change. I can suggest ways for journalists to change the way that they write about evangelicals, but getting them to change the way that they think about evangelicals is quite another matter. Knowing that the perceptions of journalists become the reality of their audience, it is only the latter action that will lead to conclusive and lasting results in terms of coverage of evangelicals. That is to say, if journalists' worldviews do not change, then their coverage—at its deepest level, the level of the frame—cannot. It is this conundrum that causes me to consider, at least briefly, what might be described as more radical strategies. I begin with an approach advocated by Dr. Marvin Olasky, professor of journalism at the University of Texas at Austin.

Olasky, an evangelical himself, does not believe that a devout Christian is able to get "accurate" or "objective" information from a secular news source. His solution, therefore, is for Christians to get their news from Christian news outlets that specifically subscribe to the principal of "Biblical-objectivity."[5] Olasky defines the principal of Biblical-objectivity as:

> faithful reflection of the biblical view, as best we can discern it
> through God's Word . . . Biblical-objectivity does not fall into rela-
> tivism or situational ethics, however, because its sole ethic is to
> reflect biblical positions. In that way its philosophical base is dia-
> metrically opposed to the prevailing liberal theory of objectivity,
> which assumes that there is no true truth on any issue.[6]

Olasky states that to non-evangelicals and secularists his principle may appear biased and subjective because it categorically promotes the Biblical position. However, his feeling is that the Bible is True (in that it contains the thoughts of *all-knowing* God), and therefore, the rules, values and actions it promotes qualify as an objective gauge by which events and issues in this world can be measured. Furthermore, he states that secular journalists who criticize *his* model of objectivity should be aware of their own hypocrisy when it comes to fairness and balance. He remarks, "Many reporters privately acknowledge that they put their hands on the scales, but try to do so in subtle ways unnoticed by readers."[7] For Olasky the choice is unequivocal:

> Christian journalists, in situations where the Bible shows us the
> right path (and it does so most of the time), should reject both the
> theory and the farce [of objectivity as mainstream media see it].

Biblically, there is no neutrality: We are either God centered or man centered.

Olasky's assertion that Christians should get their news from Christian news sources that are dedicated to, and informed by, an evangelical worldview seems to find support in the social constructionist position. In a manner reflective of my own argument above (in which I question whether the hope for improved coverage of evangelicals might be naïve), Olasky, through his Biblical-objectivity principle, takes the social constructionist position to its logical conclusion. While he does not expound the theoretical foundation for his position explicitly, he appears to posit the following: Because reality is a social construction influenced by one's beliefs, values, and culture, what is reality for people within one community cannot be the same reality for those in another who possess different beliefs, values and culture. That being the case, the best a journalist can ever hope for when she creates a news report is to reflect the reality of her community back upon itself. To be exact, it is only when the journalist creates news for those who share the same beliefs, values and culture as herself that it will be taken as fair, accurate, and balanced: in other words, True. It is inevitable that those who are outside the journalist's "worldview community" will see her coverage as misrepresenting most events or issues (especially those that pertain to them personally) because their criteria for truth (what is real) has been set by their own worldview. In short, for news coverage to ever be taken as an objective account of reality, both the journalist and the audience must be willing participants of the dialectic: the reporter must speak the truth, but, more importantly, the audience must hear the truth. Only those who share the journalist's worldview—or perception of reality—are predisposed to hearing the truth of the news report.

However, the solution Olasky proposes—that evangelicals only get their news from evangelical newspapers, radio programs and TV shows—is problematic for a number of reasons, not the least of which is that, if put into practice, it would contribute to the cultural retardation and isolation of evangelicals in North America. Another obvious concern has to do with how evangelicals interpret the Bible. Olasky assumes that there is a unified evangelical worldview and that is simply not the case. For example, many conservative Mennonite denominations in Canada include evangelicals who are pacifists and abhor war; conversely, many Baptist denominations in Canada include evangelicals who feel war, under certain circumstances, can be just—both groups base their beliefs on a literal interpretation of scripture (these are no "liberal" Christians). How does one cover a war in a Biblically-objective fashion—that is, from God's perspective—when evangelicals themselves are diametrically opposed over what God's perspective truly is on that issue? Despite Olasky's claim that Biblical-objectivity transcends the capriciousness of "secular" journalistic objectivity, it is obvious that it too is influenced by the subjective opinions of individual journalists.

The last flaw I will focus on is of a more practical nature. At present, there are just not that many evangelical news outlets in existence. If one wanted to rely on evangelical news agencies for the bulk of one's news, one would be terribly under-informed. Even in the U.S., where the evangelical community possesses the greatest financial and human resources, there is not, at this time, a daily national evangelical newspaper, or an all-news evangelical radio network. The evangelical TV networks that exist, like CBN and Trinity, devote relatively little time in their schedule to the reporting of news. Evangelical publications and broadcast programs operating in local markets tend to be more focused on commentary and analysis than on coverage of day-to-day issues and events. In Canada, daily news from an evangelical perspective is virtually non-existent.

For the reasons stated above, I believe Olasky's solution is not viable. However, I would like to offer another option that is not so radical as Olasky's plan but, admittedly, unconventional in its own right. Increasingly, it is becoming common practice for journalists working at newspapers, radio and television news outlets to publish a blog on their company's Web site; this, in addition to creating standard news pieces. These blogs—a type of informal journal or diary—for the most part, provide behind-the-scenes insights into how particular stories were researched and ultimately published or broadcast. Blogs on a news outlet's Web site are the equivalent of the movie director's commentary on a DVD movie—they provide the story behind the story.

My suggestion is this: journalists should begin using their blogs for another purpose. They should use them to disclose where they personally stand on the issues that they are covering. *Disclosure journalism*, as I call it, recognizes that news professionals are influenced by the values and beliefs that they hold and it further recognizes that it is impossible for them to separate themselves from that influence. Therefore, rather than force journalists to sublimate their worldview, it asks them simply to reveal it. By doing so, the audience is able to weigh a journalist's personal perceptions against his account of an issue and then can judge for themselves how "true" that retelling of events might be. *The greatest problem with news is not that journalists are influenced by their perceptions; the greatest problem is that news audiences do not realize journalists are influenced by their perceptions.* Disclosure journalism awakens news audiences to this phenomenon and thus inoculates them, at least somewhat, to its effects.

In addition to reminding news audiences of the subjective nature of the news, disclosure journalism would combat news bias at its source. That is, it would decrease bias in the creation of news because it would make journalists more self-reflective. A journalist who knew that she would have to disclose where she stood on a particular issue after her coverage of that issue was filed, would be more likely to exercise caution when framing her original news report. As I envision it, disclosure journalism would not reject the journalistic principles of fairness, accuracy and balance. Under this new model, those principles would still be applied to the best of the ability of each reporter. However, while it reveres fairness, accuracy and balance, disclosure journalism realistically accounts for the fact that some reporters are less able (or willing) to apply those principles than others.

Because the profitability of a newspaper or news broadcast is linked to its reputation as an honest purveyor of information, news providers might view disclosure journalism with a modicum of interest. At a time when the public is becoming increasingly cynical toward the media and slanted coverage, it is not unreasonable to think that a news outlet that claimed "our reporters have no *hidden* agenda and we can prove it to you" might prove highly successful.

CLEANING THE LENS—ADVICE FOR EVANGELICALS

To this point, I have suggested how the media might go about conducting "their business" in some new ways; I now will turn my attention to evangelicals, offering them some advice regarding their engagement in the public sphere, especially as that engagement relates to interaction with the media.

If evangelicals hope to get their ideas featured in news reports with a minimum amount of "adjustment" by journalists, then they must approach the task of communicating with reporters more strategically and purposefully. Previously, in Chapter 4, I highlighted the elements a message should possess if it is to be successful. They included: generalizability, an appearance of common sense, and the application of concrete facts coupled with emotional rhetoric or endorsement by official sources.[9] I want to elaborate on those elements now but in a very practical way. My objective is to outline a number of techniques that religious organizations and individuals can use to craft more effective messages.

But from the outset, let me be clear: no technique in the world can render a truly weak argument credible or a bigoted position tolerant in the eyes of the public. While I am the first to defend evangelicals against biased news coverage, I am also clear-headed enough to admit that there are cases where they are the authors of their own trouble. Sometimes, it is a few bad apples tainting the rest; other times the affliction is endemic. Be that as it may, the fact remains that evangelicals have been party to their share of weak arguments and bigoted positions. Let us remember, not every news piece featuring evangelicals behaving badly is slanted reporting! Therefore, I offer this word of advice: before going in front of the media to make a public statement, evangelicals would be wise to critique their intended message using stringent measures. For example, before lobbying for this or that public policy, evangelicals should impartially determine if the measures they are suggesting benefit society as a whole or just those of their religious ilk. If the suggested policy privileges those in their faith community but tramples on the religious freedoms of those in other groups, it should be applied to the evangelical community alone. The crux of the matter is this: unless evangelicals are willing to "do unto others" and support non-evangelicals—Muslims, Buddhists, Hindus and the like—who are seeking to implement laws or public policy based on their particular religious beliefs, they must refrain from insisting it is legitimate for themselves to do so. While I strongly support the notion that believers of all stripes must be able to freely practice the tenets of their faith within their religious community (so long as harm is not done to others), I feel just as strongly that in a plural society, policies and laws that affect everyone must be equitable to everyone and thus must not favour one religious group over another. On this matter, my opinion echoes that of the Supreme Court of Canada, as demonstrated by its rejection of the Lord's Day Act. In its 1985 Queen v. Big M Drug Mart case, the Court struck down the Lord's Day Act (the law that made it a crime for stores to be open for business on Sundays) after finding the law's only justification came from religious belief. On the matter, the Supreme Court Justices ruled that a law based on religious codes or practices was illegal under Canada's Charter of Rights and Freedoms. The Justices' logic was this: under the Charter, Canadians have freedom of religion. Thus, if a law is based on one religion—say Christianity—and someone of another faith is forced to follow it, that law violates the non-Christian's Charter rights.[10]

To be sure, I think evangelicals should give serious consideration to which method of societal transformation they will dedicate themselves to in the future. Will they put their faith in the transformative power of legislation or in the transformative power of personal example? It has been my impression that the official institutional bodies representing Canadian evangelicals have in the recent past devoted the greatest resources to the former method, while the latter method has received little attention. Given that the worth of Christianity lies in its ability to change lives, not change legislation, I feel that there has been an error in emphasis.

In addition to weighing the impartiality of their public pronouncements, evangelicals would be wise to imbue their messages, regardless of content, with a spirit of deep humility, compassion, and love for others. I would say that if a message cannot be crafted in such a way as to resonate with humility, compassion and love for others, it should be scrapped altogether. Evangelicals today must realize that the public's perception of them is severely tainted—thanks to the media but also because of the excesses of certain of their own. Only a radical and concerted effort to distance themselves from their present—mostly negative—persona will enable evangelicals to slowly regain their positive image as light in a dark world.

And one more word about evangelical vigilance when it comes to the "the excesses of certain of their own." In terms of calling ministries to account (especially the ministries of televangelists), rank and file evangelicals in Canada are incredibly negligent. Average evangelicals need to be unified in their insistence that their leaders live lives above reproach (that is, that they live according to the standards the Apostle Paul set out for pastors in 1 Timothy 4: 1-7). In particular, regarding accountability with money, Canadian evangelicals must demand far more from the ministers and ministries they support. There exists a Christian standards organization—the Canadian Council of Christian Charities (CCCC). Similar to the International Standardization Organization, the CCCC requires that its members meet the highest ethical and operational standards. I would suggest that ordinary evangelicals seriously consider supporting *only those ministries* that are members of the CCCC and have been given its official seal of approval. If evangelical leaders with questionable accounting procedures—or any other dubious practices—are denied support, news stories of con-men preachers betraying the trust of their devotees will also decline.

I would also raise a challenge to those not-so-ordinary evangelicals who are in a position to provide a mass broadcast platform for high-profile ministers. I am talking about those individuals who own and operate Canada's Christian television and radio stations. Before you allow ministers to air on your station, ensure that their financial records have been independently scrutinized and found ethical and, where applicable, ensure that their claims to supernatural occurrences (like healings) are impartially verified. Of course, this kind of diligence may result in loss of funds for Canada's Christian television and radio stations—they get paid by clergy to air their programs not cancel them. However, on this matter, Christian media owners and operators must decide if they are more interested in the integrity of the gospel or the integrity of their bank accounts.

With those caveats in mind, let us now turn to the nuts and bolts of message making. Nuts and bolts, by the way, is a fairly accurate description of what follows. The information contained on the next few pages is akin to a "How-To-Guide" for evangelicals (or other persons of faith) who must interact with the news media. So, if interacting with the media is not part of your daily activities, you may want to rush ahead to No Lights Under Baskets, the last section of this chapter.

Communication scholars have divided the methods one can use to enhance a message's acceptability into two types: arguments and cues. Arguments are incorporated into a message to make it more persuasive and include such things as facts, evidence, and examples. Cues, on the other hand, tend to involve the person delivering the message, more than the content of the message itself. Cues include things like the attractiveness, friendliness, and expertise of the spokesperson. These attributes in the source contribute to a receivers' acceptance of the message.[11]

Some receivers (those individuals at whom the communication is directed) find that messages that include arguments are more persuasive, while others are swayed by cues. It is therefore important for the person crafting a message to include both arguments and cues into the discourse they intend to transmit. This mix is especially important when the characteristics of the audience members are unknown. However, if the crafter of the message has reason to believe that their intended audience is more amenable to arguments than cues, or vice versa, they should tailor the discourse accordingly.[12] But some limits apply. In terms of long-term effectiveness, arguments work better than cues. The research suggests that when the receiver of message experiences a change of mind or moves closer toward a certain viewpoint because of an argument, that newly embraced perspective is more persistent over time and is also more resistant to change than when it is caused by cues.[13] This fact is not lost on advertisers. For instance, the producers of beer commercials know that cues such as visuals of girls in bikinis and buff, outdoorsy-types playing extreme sports cause young men to "relate positively" toward their product. But, they also realize that in order to make their pitch stick, their ad must mention the "long tradition of craftsmanship" that has led to "a quality brew" or some other such argument.

The chances are slim that a pro-evangelical message would ever incorporate girls in bikinis (mind you, I never thought I would see Christianity linked with the attainment of worldly riches but evangelicals in the Prosperity Preaching movement have done just that). However, other strategies involving cues of a tamer nature could be used to make average Canadians more willing to listen to what evangelicals have to say. I will be frank. Cues are shallow. They stress appearance over content: style over substance. They also work. Think of them as the foot-in-the-door that lets the rest of your message get through. There are many cues but two stand out for their simplicity and effectiveness. The spokesperson delivering the message should be attractive and possess tangible signs of authority.

The New Testament book of James 2:1–4 makes it clear that Christians are not to judge others by outward appearances. Although, it seems everybody else does. The research shows unequivocally that the messages of physically attractive people are more readily accepted than the messages of less attractive people. For example, studies have shown that juries find arguments more persuasive if they are made by attractive lawyers.[14] Similarly, jurors are more likely to believe the testimonies of attractive defendants than those of unattractive defendants, resulting in more acquittals for the former and more convictions for the latter.[15] The science suggests that we listen and believe the messages of attractive people because we are biologically hardwired to think that they are more intelligent and competent in general. In terms of specific tasks or professions, we view attractive people as having superior abilities to others.[16] Some very influential evangelical Christians have understood the importance of "putting their best face forward" when communicating a message to the un-churched public. Bill Bright, founder of Campus Crusade for Christ, used to caution his frontline staff members about letting their appearance slide. He knew that college students would, on first meeting, respond more positively to outwardly "beautiful people."

Your spokesperson does not have to be fit for the pages of a fashion magazine but all things being equal, if they were, it could only help. However, in those cases where genetics did not deliver the full package, make-up, hairstyle, and clothing can increase a spokesperson's attractiveness quotient.

While most of us have a solid grasp of what attractiveness is (though personal preference might cause us to disagree on some miniscule points in our definition), the idea of a spokesperson having tangible signs of authority is probably much less clear.

A few things qualify as tangible signs of authority. One's speaking style can be a tangible sign of authority. Speech that is delivered in a lower pitch, at a slower pace, in a serious but relaxed tone is far more authoritative than that which is high pitched, fast and harried. One's posture and facial expressions are important too. Slouching, fidgeting and lack of eye contact all diminish one's aura of authority. While research into persuasion verifies these claims, I am basing these comments on my own experiences as a TV reporter. For that matter, anyone who has ever paid close attention to the delivery style of national news anchors Lloyd Robertson, Peter Mansbridge, or Kevin Newman will be able to appreciate the truth of my statements.

One's academic or professional credentials can also be an important outward sign of authority.[17] James Dobson, founder and chairman of the evangelical advocacy group Focus on the Family, has long insisted that he be referred to as Dr. Dobson (he holds a Ph.D. in psychology) in all the communiqués issued from his own organization and also when being interviewed by secular news organizations. He knows the legitimacy such a title confers upon his opinions and he uses it to its full effect.

Arguments are not as cut-and-dry as cues. Because they illicit lasting change, arguments are obviously the technique of choice when constructing a message. However, it is far harder to get an audience to pay attention to an argument. Unlike cues which operate on a very superficial level mentally and thus penetrate a receiver's consciousness quickly, arguments require deep thought and contemplation. Many people do not want to do the work of grappling with a message's argument—when it is introduced, they tune-out.[18] Fortunately, certain measures can be employed to make an audience pay more attention to the arguments in a message.

First and foremost, your audience must be shown how the argument you are making is relevant to them. When people believe a situation or issue will affect them personally, they are much more likely to listen and think carefully about it.[19] Before you begin crafting your argument, ask the question "what is important to my audience?" When that has been determined, demonstrate how the position you are advocating also addresses the needs or wants of your listeners.

As well, express your arguments in terms and concepts that your audience will find simple and familiar.[20] If the information you are presenting is complex or chocked full of "foreign" expressions it will be ignored (non-evangelicals scratch their heads when they hear people use words like "saved," "sin," "witness," "testimony," or "backslider").

Furthermore, your arguments should focus on examples and avoid, for the most part, lists of numbers and statistics. Lists of numbers and statistics are easily forgotten or confused. Conversely, examples are easy to comprehend and, because they make people think more deeply about an issue, they tend to be remembered. Of course, a key number or a single startling statistic can have impact but to ensure it "sticks" it should be paired with a metaphorical description (for example, the average Canadian drinks 40 litres of beer a year, enough to fill a bathtub).

Having explained how the arguments you want to use can be made more "user-friendly" for an audience, let's turn to some specific argument structures and strategies that are particularly effective.

An argument that defends one position but also considers competing views, tends to be more influential than one that advocates a single position. Because arguments of this nature appear to be more fair and balanced, the speaker attains greater credibility in the eyes of the audience. However, it is not enough that competing perspectives are mentioned, they must be shown to be faulty if this method is to be effective. By highlighting the strengths of the favoured position and exposing the weakness of the competing view, the audience is forced to question the validity of the "other" side.[21] When building a two-sided argument like the one discussed above, to bolster the favoured position it is often a good idea to include evidence. However, even on its own, evidence can be strongly persuasive. Unlike the previously mentioned "examples" which can originate with the source of the message, I define evidence as factual statements—often of a scientific or empirical nature—that have been created by an objective, disinterested party. The objective nature of evidence makes audiences more likely to accept it at face value. Ironically, even when members of the audience are not paying close attention to the content of the evidence, it is still influential. They superficially understand that "objective facts" are being presented and they somewhat lazily assume that whatever is being said must be valid.[22]

An argument can also be structured in such a way that it uses people's desire for consistency to its advantage. Simply, the speaker begins by reiterating several positions that he is confident the members of his audience already support. Then, he introduces a final, new position being careful to show how, in many ways, it is similar to those the audience has already endorsed. The audience members, if they are convinced of the similarity, will accept the new position as valid for consistency's sake. People long to be consistent—or perhaps it is more a case of not wanting to seem hypocritical.[23]

Of course, when crafting a message there are some pitfalls to be avoided. For example, it is generally not a good idea to spell out for your audience that your goal is to influence their opinion.[24] People immediately dig in their heels when they get the sense that someone is trying to change the way they think. However, there is an exception to this rule. In those cases where it is clearly the speaker's intent to influence an audience—and the audience knows it—it is counterproductive for the speaker to deny it. In fact, by acknowledging the "elephant in the room," (that is, admitting his true intentions) the speaker gains credibility.

Again, related to what should and should not be said, if it is ever the case that you have to craft a rebuttal because something untrue was said about you or your group, under no circumstances should you include the offending party's slander in your refuting message. You would simply be giving the slander greater exposure. Ironically, those who did not hear the original slur get a second chance, only this time on your dime. Instead, in very general terms acknowledge the offence and then provide your defence, *being sure* to describe yourself or your organization in positive terms. When President Nixon said "I'm not a crook" it was the "crook" that stayed in people's minds. Only say the positive things that you are; not the negative things you are not. Of course if a negative claim is made against you or your organization and it is true, a different strategy applies. You should admit your mistake fully and honestly and do everything necessary to right the situation.

Finally, those crafting a message should keep in mind that it is far easier to bring about small changes in attitude than big changes. That being the case, a message that proposes a radical shift to receivers' values or ideology is far more likely to fail than one that gently nudges their views slightly to the left or right.[25] The old story goes: if you put a frog into a pot of boiling water, it will jump out but if you put it in water at room temperature and turn up the heat gradually, it will stay put. The same principal is at work here (minus the frog soup conclusion).

I have often thought that the slow progress Canada's right-to-life movement has experienced is directly related to its leaders' refusal to craft "watered-down" messages (and policy) that advocate small changes instead of large. Polling data show that a majority of Canadians (between 60 and 70%) already agree that if a baby is old enough to survive on its own outside the womb it is wrong to abort it.[26] Because the majority of the population are already psychologically predisposed to accept a ban on late-term abortions, this particular battle is one that the pro-life lobby could win. Put another way, pro-lifers need to sow their seeds where they are suited to grow. The effects of such a win should not be underestimated. A new status quo would be established: the new moderate, mainstream position would be one that accepted limits to abortion.

Combined, these techniques, strategies and sundry bits of advice will help evangelicals get their message heard. I look forward to the day when I turn on the TV news and see a report featuring an appealing, authoritative evangelical speaker using simple, faith-neutral words to outline compelling arguments, replete with examples and objective evidence.[27] In my mind's eye, I see the reporter nodding in agreement as the speaker describes the evangelical "take on the situation" in terms he, the secular reporter, understands and respects. He "gets it" when the speaker frames evangelicals as a religious and cultural minority who, like other minorities in Canada, simply want to exercise their Charter given rights and protect and promote their particular lifestyle choices. The irony is not lost on me that evangelicals' future approach to public communication should model, in many respects, the approach used by Canada's gay and lesbian lobby over the last two decades.

NO LIGHTS UNDER BASKETS

All this is not to say that evangelicals should deny the source from which their ideas and actions spring. While I think it is best if evangelicals keep doctrine out of the public policies they promote, I also believe that in many other situations, their devotion to Christ and his teachings can be proclaimed boldly. For example, when evangelicals receive media coverage for their volunteer or charity work (admittedly, these are rare occasions) they can be unequivocal as to why they are motivated to do what they do. However, they must be guided by the knowledge that 30 seconds in a television news piece, or a paragraph or two in a newspaper, is not long enough to convince someone of the truth of Christianity. The reality is that non-believers will only become convinced of Christianity's truth when the Christians they know personally reflect Christ in their lives. Knowing that, we come to the most profound observation in this book: if those who believe in the risen Christ, en masse, began practicing the active compassion, deep humility, unconditional forgiveness, and anti-materialism that Jesus calls them to, it would prove so powerful and compelling to today's world that how the media chose to depict them would no longer matter.

Important Findings About Newspapers

While preparing this book for publication, I have had opportunity to explore the relationship between evangelicals and the news media even further. As a result, I now find myself with bit of extra information to impart.

The original research conducted for this book focused on national television news and national television journalists. However, it is my contention that the book's conclusions have applicability to all media personnel working at the national (elite) level. My opinion is supported by the work of researchers like Lydia Miljan and Barry Cooper, who have shown that Canada's elite journalists—be they in print, radio, or television—tend to share a similar attitudinal profile and similar journalistic habits.[1] That said, when drawing conclusions, additional corroborating research is always welcome.

In the spring of 2008, I set out to determine if Canada's national print journalists, were similar to, or different from, their broadcasting colleagues when it came to coverage of evangelicals. Briefly, I will recount the study I conducted and the results that materialized. Incidentally, these findings were originally presented at the "Sacred and Secular in a Global Canada" Conference held from May 9 to 12, 2008 at the University of Western Ontario's Huron College.[2] The full paper is to appear as a chapter in a forthcoming book titled *Religion Unbound,* edited by Dr. William Acres of Huron College.

Whilst planning this new research, I was keen to find a recent event or issue involving evangelicals that had garnered extensive newspaper coverage. In the end, I chose the same-sex marriage debate that raged in Canada between 2004 and 2006.

BACKGROUND

In the summer of 2003, Liberal Prime Minister Jean Chretien announced that his government would be drafting legislation that would change the definition of marriage from the "union of one man and one woman" to the "union of two people." However, the legislation legalizing same-sex marriage—dubbed bill C-38 or the *Civil Marriage Act*—did not move forward until 2004 when Paul Martin, former Liberal Finance Minister, took the reigns of power from retiring Chretien. Interestingly, the bill's first official appearance was not before the House of Commons but the Supreme Court of Canada. Martin, in his new role as Prime Minister, asked the Court to review the bill and determine if it was constitutionally valid. In particular, his government wished to know: if Parliament had the exclusive legal authority to define marriage; if the proposed act was compatible with Canada's *Charter of Rights and Freedoms*; and whether or not the Constitution would protect religious leaders who refuse to sanctify same-sex marriages.

In December 2004, the Court answered in the affirmative to the above three questions. By February 2005, the *Civil Marriage Act* was before Parliament and in July it passed into law. With that, Canada became the fourth country in the world to legalize same-sex marriage.

However, in early 2006, the new legislation came under fire when the Conservative Party, led by Stephen Harper, replaced Martin's Liberals as the government of the day. The Conservatives had campaigned on a promise to re-open the marriage debate. True to their word, a free-vote on the issue was held in December that year. However, Members of Parliament supporting the traditional definition of marriage were again in the minority. In the eyes of the politicians, the issue was put to rest for good.

THE EVANGELICAL LOBBY AGAINST SAME-SEX MARRIAGE

From the outset, evangelicals were strongly opposed to the government changing the legal definition of marriage. In particular, in the year leading up to the initial 2005 vote on the Civil Marriage Act, and again in the lead-up to 2006 vote to reopen and reconsider the Act, three key evangelical organizations—the Evangelical Fellowship of Canada (EFC), Focus on the Family Canada (FOTF), and the Canada Family Action Coalition (CFAC)[3]—waged an extensive campaign of pressure. Specifically, to persuade the public and federal politicians to support their position, these organizations employed a multi-pronged lobbying strategy. For example, in the run-up to the first vote on bill C-38, Defend Marriage Canada, an ancillary body of the CFAC, "hosted 320 rallies (including one of more than 15,000 people on Parliament Hill), made a million protest phone calls to MPs, distributed 1.4 million brochures in five different languages, posted 50 billboards, 11 full-page ads, and united over 200 multifaith organizations."[4] The same intensity of activism was seen throughout 2006 as evangelicals, rejuvenated by the Conservative's electoral win, lobbied MPs to vote in favour of Harper's motion to re-open debate on the definition of marriage.

And while their lobbying techniques were varied and numerous, the arguments that the EFC, FOTF, and the CFAC used to support their stand against redefining marriage were not.

SINGING FROM THE SAME SECULAR HYMN BOOK

In total, just three core arguments were used time and again by these leading evangelical organizations to promote their pro-traditional marriage position. These arguments were worked into information on their respective Web sites, brochures, information sheets, petition letters, manuals, ads, submissions to the Supreme Court and submissions and speeches to committees of parliament. I was able to identify this argumentative triumvirate by analyzing all available public documents these organizations had created in relation to the same-sex marriage debate between the summer of 2003 and the end of 2006. Some of the documents were still available online from the Web sites of the respective organizations, others were found using the internet archive retrieval system.[5] In other cases, texts had to be procured from the organizations' executive staff. In the end, just over 60 documents were collected.[6]

Analysis involved reading and coding each text for arguments for the traditional definition of marriage/arguments against same-sex marriage. Each document was scrutinized to determine if its content correlated with other texts—when common elements were noted these were placed in a common group. Content that was interrelated led to the development of a specific category.

Interestingly, the three arguments which appear in the persuasive discourses of the EFC, FOTF, and the CFAC were specifically designed to appeal to a secular audience and thus did not reference religious belief or doctrine. Instead, they were philosophically or empirically derived and supported. The "religion-free" content of these core arguments reveals that the leaders of the EFC, FOTF, and the CFAC realized statements such as "same-sex marriage is wrong because it goes against the Bible" and other "arguments from faith" would gain little traction in Canada's secular public square.[7]

The three core arguments were not only to be used by the leaders and staff of the three organizations, evangelical pastors and laypeople were encouraged to use them as well. In fact, to facilitate ease of use among the rank and file faithful, the EFC, FOTF, and the CFAC all crafted short "talking points" documents that presented the arguments in concise form (these were downloadable from their respective Web sites). The EFC's document, *Marriage Talking Points* advised readers, "Here are some possible topics to raise with politicians or the media."[8] Similarly, one of the tracts put out by FOTF titled *Defending Marriage: Debate-Tested Sound Bites* announced:

Here is a collection of lines and arguments that Focus on the Family has learned work best in the many public debates we have done on the issue of the same-sex family. These sound bites have also been tested by focus groups and rated very strongly.[9]

EVANGELICALS THREE CORE ARGUMENTS FOR TRADITIONAL MARRIAGE

In my study, I categorized the three core arguments that these evangelical groups used to support traditional marriage as follows:

1. abandoning the traditional definition of marriage will lead to a breakdown of the family and harm children (hereafter the "harms families and children argument");
2. abandoning the traditional definition of marriage will lead to polygamy and other harmful types of unions (hereafter the "polygamy argument");
3. legalizing same-sex marriage will lead to discrimination and lawsuits against traditional Christians, clergy and churches (hereafter the "discrimination argument").

The "harms families and children argument" maintained that heterosexual unions are the most stable, healthy family units. As families are the chief social building block of civilization, it held that society is wise to encourage the healthiest types of families possible. The talking points for the CFAC expressed this argument in these terms: "Research shows that children raised under the influence and parenting of a mother and father do far better in every area of life than children raised under the influence of other forms of relationships."[10]

The "polygamy argument" was more straightforward. It posited that legalizing same-sex marriage set a dangerous precedent because it establishes consenting adults' attraction and affection for each other as the key criteria for marriage. In doing so, it opens the door for other types of relationships between consenting adults—such as polygamy, polyamory (group marriage) or incest—where attraction and affection is felt. On this matter, the EFC's *Talking Points* tract began: "Once marriage has been de-linked from procreation there is nothing to prevent other forms of marriage, such as polygamy."[11]

The "discrimination argument" made the case that as acceptance of homosexuality becomes the norm, those who are opposed to homosexual practice (like evangelicals) will face greater prejudice from society and greater adversity from the courts. Intricate to this argument was the suggestion that clergy would be compelled to perform same-sex weddings against their will. Extant court cases in which Christians were charged or sued for opposing homosexual practices were often cited to reinforce this argument.[12]

SEEK AND YE SHALL FIND (OR MAYBE NOT)

Having determined through analysis that the texts produced by the EFC, FOTF, and the CFAC consistently included the core arguments found above, the function of my study was straightforward. I simply set out to determine if those three "religion-free" arguments—which were so prevalent in all of the evangelical lobbying discourse—got picked up by national newspaper reporters. To that end, I content analyzed all reports about evangelicals and same-sex marriage, published between 2004 and 2006 in Canada's two national newspapers, the *National Post* and the *Globe and Mail*. Letters to the editor were excluded from the sample.

The official hypothesis for my study—that is, what I felt I would find—was this:

> Of those news stories highlighting evangelical involvement in Canada's same-sex marriage debate, a majority will not mention the three core arguments that members of this faith community used to bolster their position in favour of the traditional definition of marriage.

I justified my theoretical hunch that the arguments would, for the most part, be absent from the coverage by citing both my own and others studies (all found in the preceding chapters of this book). To summarize that research, I explained that many studies have shown that the media will manipulate or even omit information to mitigate the messages of groups—including evangelicals—when they perceive them to be outside the mainstream. More pointedly, I highlighted my own research findings, as well as those of Miljan and Cooper, which determined that Canadian national journalists are strident supporters of homosexual rights and gay marriage and, by design, their reports tend to diminish the position of homosexuals' opponents.[13]

My hunch turned out to be right. Between 1 January 2004 to 31 December 2006 a total of 76 news reports, 40 from the *National Post* and 36 from the *Globe and Mail* featured evangelicals in connection with the same-sex marriage issue. In the total population of news reports, 74% (N=56) made no mention of the evangelicals' "religion-free" arguments against same-sex marriage. The majority of the news reports that included the prescribed arguments—20% of the 26%—were published in the *National Post*. Only 6% of were *Globe and Mail* about evangelicals and same-sex marriage referenced the arguments.[14]

On its own or in combination with other arguments, the "discrimination argument" was present most often. An excerpt from a report from the *Globe and Mail* shows how the argument was included in a story. The report itself appeared in the *Globe and Mail* prior to the passage of the *Civil Marriage Act*—the Supreme Court of Canada was still reviewing the legislation to determine if it was constitutionally viable. After mentioning the legal briefs which evangelical and other conservative religious organizations were submitting to sway the Court toward their position, the report commented on the arguments contained in the briefs stating: "[religious conservatives contend] that they may be stripped of their charitable status and other state benefits, penalized by public institutions, branded as hate-mongers and forced into accepting the legitimacy of same-sex unions."[15]

The "harms family and children argument" appeared just slightly less often than the "discrimination argument." A report in the *National Post*, written a few weeks before the Conservative-initiated vote to re-open the marriage debate, illustrates how this argument could be incorporated into a news piece. The story focused on a pro-traditional marriage declaration crafted and supported by over 40 leaders from several conservative faith communities. The expressed goal of the declaration was to convince MPs to reinstate the traditional definition. While the detailed arguments for traditional marriage outlined in the declaration were not quoted in the article, one of the signatories, an evangelical pastor, was. He stated, "Marriage has been recognized in law because it serves society. It [traditional marriage] is the preferred society context for having and raising children."[16]

The "polygamy argument" seldom appeared; in fact, it was found in just two news reports. In one of the reports—a piece from the *National Post* about a speech delivered by an American evangelical leader to an audience in Canada—the reporter noted that evangelicals were wary of same-sex marriage because they felt it "leads to polygamy and consensual incest."[17] It also quoted the evangelical leader himself who said, "If the compelling reason for same-sex marriage is you have a caring loving relationship, how are you going to stop consensual incest, between adults, brothers and sisters, if it is a consensual relationship?"[18]

While three-quarters of the news reports didn't mention the evangelicals' "religion-free" arguments for opposing same-sex marriage, many articles did offer faith-based reasons for the evangelicals' opposition. That is, somewhere in the article it was suggested that evangelicals opposed same-sex marriage because of their religious beliefs. This finding is somewhat ironic given the evangelicals' concerted effort to steer away from "arguments from faith" when conducting their public lobbying. Perhaps not surprisingly, it was most often in reporter paraphrases or columnist commentary, and seldom quotes from the evangelicals themselves, where this suggestion was made. For instance, one columnist explained evangelical opposition to same-sex marriage saying:

> An evangelical church is one that preaches its gospel, like for
> instance the inerrancy of Scripture. And Scripture comes down
> quite hard on the union of man and woman being pretty much the

only sexual union that God allows. Old and New Testament, rather strict. Mean, really.[19]

DÉJÀ VU: NEWSPAPERS TOO

The results of the study revealed a disconnect. Evangelical leaders spent tremendous time and energy crafting a media-savvy and decidedly secular communications strategy composed of three (non-religious) arguments for traditional marriage. Analyzing the documents that were not subjected to news media "filtering"—that is, those documents produced by the evangelical organizations themselves—one finds that they are replete with these three core arguments. Furthermore, evangelical leader's themselves confirm that at every opportunity they relayed to media personnel and politicians their organizations' faith-free public policy arguments for traditional marriage.[20] However, in news coverage the faith-free arguments were virtually absent.

If the prescribed arguments were being relayed faithfully and frequently, one has no other option but to consider that the journalists were the weak link in the communication chain.

Yes, there could be several reasons this particular "blind spot" developed. In some instances, systemic barriers such as turn-around time or column space may have been to blame. And, of course, outright sloppy reporting cannot be overlooked. However, the frequency with which the key arguments were "missed" significantly reduces the credibility of the above explanations. Every working journalist knows and almost all journalism text books insist, for a news report to be considered complete it must, at minimum, answer a checklist of five questions: who, what, when, where, and why. The Five Ws, as this five-word maxim has come to be known, is by strict convention the basic formula for crafting a news report. It is surprising that in almost three-quarters of their stories the most elite, established, reporters in Canada forgot to include the "fifth W." That is, time-and-again they "forgot" to provide the reason why evangelicals said they were opposed to same-sex marriage.

As discussed at length previously, a fair or neutral news report (commonly called "objective") relays to the audience the ideas that the subjects (that is, the people the story is about) are putting forward, as *they intend* those ideas to be understood. The ideas of the subjects are not interpreted or filtered by the reporter according to his personal worldview. By that definition, Canadian national newspaper journalists, for the most part, did not provide fair or objective coverage of evangelicals' involvement in the same-sex marriage debate. Rather than relaying the religiously neutral, pro-traditional marriage messages of evangelicals (as the evangelicals intended), reporters virtually omitted those messages.

Of course, there are occasions when a reporter might feel morally and professionally obliged *not to* relay the ideas her interview subjects are presenting as *they intend* them to be understood. As mentioned in the discussion of "The Neutral Frame" in Chapter 4, when a subject's information is wrong or misleading a reporter is not obligated to present it as true. Showing that an interview subject is incorrect or purposely twisting the truth is not negative framing, it is simply thorough reporting. Perhaps Canada's national print journalists saw evangelicals as dishonest when they provided non-religious arguments to support their opposition to same-sex marriage (in their eyes the true reason for evangelicals' opposition was religious and religious only). As such, rather than give a platform to what they perceived to be lies, they choose to leave out the evangelicals' faith-free arguments altogether. However, if this is what transpired then the print journalists are still guilty of allowing their personal worldview to shape their coverage; they have still strayed from the tenets of objective reporting.

While a reporter is obligated to expose a source who is misrepresenting information, she is also obligated to provide clear, empirical evidence to prove that the source's information is wrong. Not in a single report was evidence given to suggest that evangelicals were being disingenuous when proffering their non-religious arguments against same-sex marriage. In the absence of proof to the contrary, the reporter is left to report the source's perspective as it is given. At the very least, if the journalists covering the same-sex marriage debate suspected that evangelicals were using their non-religious arguments as a socially acceptable means to a religiously motivated end they should have incorporated both perspectives (theirs and the evangelicals) into their coverage. That is, the arguments the evangelicals put forward should have been included the coverage but could have been contrasted with the reporters' assertion that, in addition to their other reasons for opposing same-sex marriage, evangelicals' resistance was also tied to their religious beliefs. Seldom was such a balanced report published.

Having discounted other explanations, one must consider a less innocuous reason for this persistent journalistic oversight. It seems that national newspaper reporters are just as likely as their national broadcasting colleagues to abandon the ideal of objectivity when faced with a group or individual promoting values that run counter to their own values and beliefs. (Again, thanks to the survey work of Miljan and Cooper we know Canada's elite newspaper reporters—like national TV reporters—are strong supporters of same-sex marriage and homosexual rights in general.[21]) By excluding the secular reasons that evangelicals gave for opposing same-sex marriage from coverage, newspaper personnel were able to undermine the evangelicals' ability to influence the public and government and thus bolstered their own preferred policy position (that is, legalization of same-sex marriage). The casual newspaper reader would have been left with the impression that evangelical opposition to same-sex marriage was baseless, or based primarily on religious belief fuelled by interpretation of scripture.

Because my study was not designed to gauge the degree to which the arguments that evangelicals fashioned were logically compelling or emotionally persuasive, I am hesitant to indulge in too much specula-tion about "what might have been." However, one could reasonably make the case that the exclusion of the evangelicals' core ideological arguments from the discourse surrounding same-sex marriage in all probability lessened the "attractiveness" of the pro-traditional marriage position in the eyes of average Canadians. Similarly, it is interesting to note that between 2004 and 2006 polls showed that the population-at-large was in closer alignment with the evangelicals' position on marriage than with the position proposed by the Liberal government. In fact, at the time, between 58% and 65% of Canadians did not agree with the Liberals' plan to legalize same-sex marriage and most would have preferred some other option.[22] Thus, it is possible, had they received more amenable coverage from the media, evangelicals could have leveraged popular discontent over the Liberals' plan into increased support for traditional marriage. However, with the "horse out of the barn," or, perhaps more appropriately, with "the grooms out of the wedding chapel," speculation of this type serves no useful purpose. In fact, on the issue of same-sex marriage I am of the opinion that evangelicals would be wise to "forever hold their peace" and simply move on.

NOTES

INTRODUCTION

1. John G. Stackhouse, "Three Myths about Evangelicals," *Faith Today*, May/June, 1995, p. 28.

2. John G. Stackhouse, "Who's Afraid of Evangelicals?" *Faith Today*, January/February, 2005, p. 29.

3. While the survey used the term "born-again" the results reflect the opinion of the general populace toward evangelicals. As professor George Rawlyk asserts, the term born-again should be "regarded as a litmus test for determining who is, or who is not, an evangelical" for only evangelicals are truly comfortable with the born-again label. George A. Rawlyk, *Is Jesus Your Personal Saviour? In Search of Canadian Evangelicalism in the 1990s* (Montreal, PQ: McGill-Queens University Press, 1996), p. 84.

4. Reginald W. Bibby, *The Boomer Factor* (Toronto, ON: Bastian, 2006), p. 24.

5. For Canadian evangelicals stand on specific social issues, see Sam Reimer, *Evangelicals and the Continental Divide: The Conservative Protestant Subculture in Canada and the United States* (Montreal, PQ: McGill-Queens University Press, 2003), pp. 34, 74-75, 89, 94, 101, 121. For the majority of Canadians stand on social issues, see Michael Adams, *Fire and Ice: The United States, Canada and the Myth of Converging Values* (Toronto, ON: Penguin, 2003), pp. 52, 125; Michael Adams, *Sex in the Snow—Canadian Social Values at the End of the Millennium* (Toronto, ON: Penguin, 1997), pp. 171-173; Bibby, *Boomer Factor*, pp. 19-23; Lianne George, "What We Believe," *Maclean's*, July 1, 2006, pp. 35-38; PMG Consulting, *National Gaming Monitor: Summary of Findings* (Toronto, ON: Canadian Gaming Association, 2006, p. 1).

6. Randy Boswell, "Canadians Object Least to Muslim Neighbour," *National Post*, February 8, 2007, p. A1.

7. Exodus 20:5

8. Aileen VanGinkel, *Evangelical Beliefs and Practices: A Summary of*

the 2003 Ipsos Reid Survey Results (Markham, ON: Evangelical Fellowship of Canada, 2003), p. 7.

9. Evangelical Fellowship of Canada, *Oral Submission to the House of Commons Standing Committee on Canadian Heritage.* (Markham, ON: Evangelical Fellowship of Canada, 2002), p. 2; Ipsos Reid, *Data tables: Survey of Evangelical Beliefs and Practices* (Toronto, ON: Ipsos Reid, 2003). These data tables were obtained by the author from Evangelical Fellowship of Canada staff, March 13, 2004.

10. Neil Macdonald, "Report on Vice-Presidential Candidate Sarah Palin," *CBC's The National,* September 3, 2008.

11. John Fritze, "Palin Did Not Ban Books in Wasilla: City Denies Any Removals as False List Spreads on Net," September 10, 2008, *USA Today,* p. A7.

12. Ibid.

13. Sarah Baxter, "Sarah Palin: Conservatives Find the Girl of Their Dreams," *Sunday Times,* August 31, 2008, p. 23.

14. For example, this comment was posted to the Proud to be Canadian Web site:

> I find it interesting that the CBC is trying to paint Palin as a
> "glassy-eyed fundamentalist bible-thumper" (when interviewed on
> NBC News this is one of the ways CBC reporter Neil McDonald
> suggested she could be portrayed). If they would do any research
> into Palin's background they would note she does not let her faith
> override her duties to the public... The CBC will never make that
> part of their reports on Palin: it doesn't fit the negative image they
> want to create.

Allan MacLeod, "CBC's 'reporter' Neil Macdonald on Sarah Palin: Best at 'talking about hunting moose'," Proud to be Canadian Web site (September 19, 2008), http://www.proudtobecanadian.ca/index/weblog/comments/cbcs_reporter_neil_macdonald_on_sarah_palin_best_at_talking_about_hunting_m/#comments

15. Macdonald, "Report on Palin."

16. FredrickofAmerica, "The Sarah Palin Church Video Part One," YouTube, September 2, 2008, http://www.youtube.com/watch?v=QG1vPYbRB7k&feature=related

17. For example, while governor, Palin applied pressure to subordinates to get her former brother-in-law, a state trooper, fired. In her defence, the

trooper appears not to have been a model of virtue. In addition to mistreating his wife—Palin's younger sister—and his step-children, *The Washington Post* reported he had been reprimanded and suspended by his superiors for incidents involving shooting a cow moose without a permit, Tasering his stepson and drinking while driving a trooper vehicle. See James V. Grimaldi, "Palin's Ex-Brother-in-Law Says He Regrets Bad Blood," *Washington Post*, September 6, 2008, p. A7.

Nonetheless, Palin's involvement in the dismissal was a violation of her state's Ethics Act. See Serge.F. Kovaleski, "Alaska Inquiry Concludes Palin Abused Powers," *New York Times*, October 11, 2008, p. A1.

18. On his blog, Kay went on to highlight that Macdonald had also falsely reported that Palin used to be a member of the Alaska Independence Party, a fringe political group with designs to breakaway from the rest of the United States. It was Kay's conclusion that Macdonald was orchestrating "a bogus smear on Sarah Palin." Jonathan Kay, "Let the CBC know how you feel about Neil Macdonald's appalling smear on Sarah Palin," *National Post* Web site, September 4, 2008, http://network.nationalpost.com/np/blogs/fullcomment/ archive/2008/09/04/jonathan-kay-let-the-cbc-know-how-you-feel-about-neil-mcdonald-s-appalling-smear-on-sarah-palin.aspx

19. Dianne Haskett, "A Message to Londoners," *London Free Press*, October 22, 2007, p. A10

20. Rachel Giese, "Private Views Should Not Rule Public Office," *Toronto Star*, November 10, 1997, p. A1.

21. Morris Della Costa, "Is Haskett's Obligation to Self or City?" *London Free Press*, October 23, 1997, p.A3.

22. Ibid.

23. Morris Della Costa, "Gay Bashers Find Bravery in Anonymity," *London Free Press*, October 25, 1997, p. A3.

24. Chip Martin, "Mayor Acted Oddly Before Last Election," *London Free Press*, October 24, 1997, p. A3.

25. Ibid. While she does not deny that her religious convictions influenced her decision to enter politics, Haskett does deny that she ever talked with her former business partner about "receiving a calling from God." In his October 24, 1997 article, Chip Martin makes note of this fact.

26. Sandra Dimitrakopoulos and Sara Marett, "Haskett Comes Out for Victory Party," *University of Western Ontario Gazette*, November 11, 1997, p. 1.

27. Gloria Galloway,. "Christian Activists Capturing Tory Races: Some

in Party Worry New Riding Nominees Will Reinforce Notion of "Hidden Agenda," *Globe and Mail*, May 27, 2005, p. A1.

28. Charles Adler, "A Front Page Smear on Christians," *National Post*, May 30, 2005, p. A19.

29. Galloway, "Christian Activists," p. A1.

30. See David Haskell, "Media vs. Evangelicals," *Toronto Star*, June 25, 2005, M07.

31. Tony Gosgnach and Alphonse de Valk, "The *Globe* Panics! Wants Christians Out of Politics!" *Catholic Insight*, July 1, 2005, http://www.highbeam.com/Catholic+Insight/publications.aspx?date=200607

32. Adler, "Front Page Smear," p. A19; Also see Gosgnach and de Valk, "The *Globe* Panics."

33. For example, Sehdev Kumar, "On the Seventh Day, Stockwell Rested," *Globe and Mail*, November 13, 2000, p. R9; Jason Moscovitz, "Report on Stockwell Day," *CBC's The National*, November 17, 2000; Margaret Wente, "Day, Darwin, Darkness," *Globe and Mail*, November 2, 2000, p. A21.

34. John Geddes, "The Scare Factor," *Maclean's*, July 10, 2000, p. 16-19.

35. For example, Gordon Laird, "Can Stockwell Day Separate Church from State?" *Globe and Mail*, July 17, 2000, p. A19; Shawn McCarthy, "Religious Beliefs are Fair Game: Stockwell Day should not be silent when Canadians ask how his faith will influence his political agenda," *Globe and Mail*, November 17, 2000, p. A6.

36. Arthur Sheps, "God has No Place on the Ballot: Canada lacks the U.S. taste for—and protections from—the influence of religion in politics," *Globe and Mail*: October 27, 2000, p. A21.

37. Paul Hunter, "The Fundamental Day," *CBC's The National Magazine*, November 14, 2000.

38. Joe Woodard, "God in Exile, Part 2: The Role of the Media," *Calgary Herald*, January 6, 2001, p. A17.

39. Ibid.

40. Ibid.

41. Dennis R. Hoover, "A Religious Right Arrives in Canada." *Religion in the News* 3, no. 2 (2000), paragraph 15, http://www.trincoll.edu/depts/csrpl/RINVol3No2/canada_religious_right.htm

42. Augie Fleras, *Mass Media Communication in Canada* (Scarborough, ON: Nelson 2003), p. 279; Mark Silk, *Unsecular Media: Making News of Religion in America* (Chicago, IL: University of Illinois Press, 1995), pp. 5-7.

43. Robert P. Vallone, Lee Ross and Mark R. Lepper, "The Hostile Media Phenomenon: Biased Perception and Perception of Media Bias in Coverage of the Beirut Massacre," *Journal of Personality and Social Psychology* 49 (1985), p. 577.

44. Silk, *Unsecular Media*, p. xi.

45. Ipsos Reid, *Data Tables*.

46. Jack Jedweb, *Canadian Media: Trust, Bias and Control*, (Montreal, PQ: Association for Canadian Studies, 2003), pp. 9, 11.

47. For example, Larry Cornies, "Religion Content in Ontario Daily Newspapers, 1986" in *Essays in Journalism,*ed. Heather Hiscox (London, ON: Graduate School of Journalism, University of Western Ontario, 1988). For my research, I accessed the online version at the Centre for Faith and Media Document Archive Web site, http://www.geocities.com/faithmedia/readings/weblarry.html; Fraser Institute, "Religious Character of Canada Not Represented in TV reports," *On Balance* 9, no. 1 (1999), http://oldfraser.lexi.net/publications/onbalance/1996/9-1/; Susan Wilson Murray, *Do Journalists Pay Insufficient Attention to the Role of Spirituality and Organized Religion in Canadian Society and Culture?* (Vancouver, BC: Project Censored Canada, Simon Fraser University, 1996); Joyce Smith, "Faith and Media: 1999 Newspaper Scan," Centre for Faith and Media Document Archive Web site, December 1999, http://www.geocities.com/faithmedia/1999/1999.html

Chapter 2

EVANGELICALS IN CANADA

1. Aileen VanGinkel, *Evangelical Beliefs and Practices: A Summary of the 2003 Ipsos Reid Survey Results* (Markham, ON: Evangelical Fellowship of Canada, 2003), p. 2.

2. Statistics Canada, *2001 Census Analysis Series: Religions in Canada* (Ottawa, ON: Government of Canada, 2003) p. 12; Sam Reimer, *Evangelicals and the Continental Divide: The Conservative Protestant Subculture in Canada and the United States* (Montreal, PQ: McGill-Queens University Press, 2003), p. 192.

3. VanGinkel, *Evangelical Beliefs*, p. 3.

4. Reginald W. Bibby, *The Boomer Factor* (Toronto, ON: Bastian, 2006), pp.199–200.

5. Reginald W. Bibby, *Fragmented Gods: The Poverty and Potential of Religion in Canada* (Toronto, ON: Irwin, 1987), p. 26.; Reimer, *Evangelicals*, p.187. Also see, John H. Redekop, J.H. "Canadian Religious Beliefs and Practices—Part 1," *B.C. Christian News*, December 2003, p. 1.

6. Bibby, *Frangmented Gods*, p. 26; VanGinkel, *Evangelical Beliefs*, p. 5.

7. Quentin J. Schultze, "Evangelical's Uneasy Alliance with the Media," in *Religion and Mass Media: Audiences and Adaptations*, ed. Judith M. Buddenbaum and Daniel Stout (Thousand Oaks, CA: Sage, 1996), pp. 62.

8. For example, Judith M. Buddenbaum, "Mainline Protestants and the Media," in *Religion and Mass Media: Audiences and Adaptations*, ed. Judith M. Buddenbaum and Daniel Stout (Thousand Oaks, CA: Sage, 1996), pp.51–57; Stewart M. Hoover, *Religion in the News—Faith and Journalism in American Public Discourse* (Thousand Oaks, CA: Sage, 1998); Schultze, "Evangelicals Uneasy Alliance."

9. George A. Rawlyk, *Is Jesus Your Personal Saviour? In Search of Canadian Evangelicalism in the 1990s* (Montreal, PQ: McGill-Queens University Press, 1996), p. 80; Reimer, *Evangelicals*, pp.77–78.

10. Rawlyk, *Is Jesus*, p. 95.

11. Ipsos Reid, *Data tables: Survey of Evangelical Beliefs and Practices* (Toronto, ON: Ipsos Reid, 2003).

12. All percentage comparisons in this chapter are between Canadian evangelicals and Canadian non-evangelicals unless otherwise stated; for clarity, responses from Canadian Catholics who held evangelical tenets of faith have been excluded from the 2003 Ipsos Reid figures.

13. Rawlyk, *Is Jesus*, p. 80; Reimer, *Evangelicals*, pp. 59–60.

14. Reimer, *Evangelicals*, p. 61.

15. Ibid.

16. Ipsos Reid, *Data Tables*.

17. Reimer, *Evangelicals*, p.104.

18. Rawlyk, *Is Jesus*, p. 80; Reimer, *Evangelicals*, pp. 60–61.

19. Rawlyk, *Is Jesus*, p. 84.

20. John Blanchard, *Ultimate Questions* (Darlington, UK: Evangelical Press, 1999), pp. 24–27; Rawlyk, *Is Jesus*, pp. 125–126; Reimer, *Evangelicals*, p. 44.

21. Ipsos Reid, *Data Tables*.

22. Rawlyk, *Is Jesus*, p. 104; Reimer, *Evangelicals*, p.78.

23. VanGinkel, *Evangelical Beliefs*, p. 7.

24. Ipsos Reid, *Data Tables*.

25. Rawlyk, *Is Jesus*, pp. 80, 113; Reimer, *Evangelicals*, pp. 43, 78.

26. Tim F. LaHaye and Jerry B. Jenkins, *The Rapture: In the Twinkling of an Eye, Countdown to the Earth's Last Days* (Carol Stream, IL: Tyndale House, 2006); Hal Lindsay, *The Late Great Planet Earth* (Grand Rapids, MI: Zondervan, 1970).

27. Reimer, *Evangelicals*, p.78.

28. Bibby, *Frangmented Gods*, pp.103-104; Reimer, *Evangelicals*, pp. 77–80.

29. Reimer, *Evangelicals*, p.81.

30. Bibby, *Frangmented Gods*, p. 104; Reimer, *Evangelicals*, p.113.

31. Ipsos Reid, *Data Tables*.

32. Reimer, *Evangelicals*, pp.104–106.

33. Ibid., p.113.

34. Ron Rhodes, *The Complete Guide to Christian Denominations: Understanding the History, Beliefs, and Differences* (Wheaton, IL: Harvest House, 2005), pp. 171–193, 311–340.

35. Michael Adams, *Fire and Ice: The United States, Canada and the Myth of Converging Values* (Toronto, ON: Penguin, 2003), pp. 52, 125; Michael Adams, *Sex in the Snow—Canadian Social Values at the End of the Millennium* (Toronto, ON: Penguin, 1997), pp. 171-173; Bibby, *Boomer Factor*, pp. 19–23; Lianne George, "What We Believe," *Maclean's*, July 1, 2006, pp. 35-38; PMG Consulting, *National Gaming Monitor: Summary of Findings* (Toronto, ON: Canadian Gaming Association, 2006), p.1.

36. Reimer, *Evangelicals*, pp.34, 74–75, 89, 94, 101, 121. Also see, Evangelical Fellowship of Canada, "Social issues," Evangelical Fellowship of Canada Web site, http://www.evangelicalfellowship.ca/NetCommunity/Page.aspx?pid=187

37. Ted Byfield, "Paul Didn't Really Mean It: Four Bible-based Denominations Debate Female Ordination," *Western Report*, October 30, 1995, p. 36; Reimer, *Evangelicals*, pp. 13, 78.

38. Adams, *Fire and Ice*, p.51.

39. Janet Epp-Buckingham, "Canadian Charter of Rights and Freedoms,"

Faith Today, March/April, 2001, p. 28.

40. Ibid., p.29.

41. Ibid.

42. Ibid., p. 28.

43. Joe Woodard, "God in Exile, Part 2: The Role of the Media," *Calgary Herald*, January 6, 2001, p. A17.

44. Epp-Buckingham, "Canadian Charter," p. 28.

45. Shawn McCarthy, "Believe It: Faith's a Factor," *Globe and Mail*, May 3, 2003, p. F3.

46. Andrea Wicken, "Airwaves: Playboy Yes, Christians No," *Sunday Magazine* 21, no.2 (2004), pp. 1, 3.

47. Margaret H. Ogilvie, *Discussion Paper #2: Overcoming "The Culture of Disbelief"* (Ottawa: ON. The Centre for Cultural Renewal, 2006), p. 5.

48. Ibid.

49. Kevin M. Grace, "Sunset on Religious Freedom: The Courts Now Claim the Right to Decide the Limits of Christian Conscience," *Report Newsmagazine*, July 22, 2002, p. 22.

50. Ibid.

51. Ian Hunter, "Free Speech Falls Prey to "Human Rights," *National Post*, August 18, 2003, p. A13.

52. Lorne Gunter, "Gay? Cool. Christian? Not So Much," *National Post*, April 11, 2005, p. A16.

53. Lorne Gunter, "Fighting Canada's secularist tide," *National Post*, September 26, 2005, p. A16; Hunter, "Free Speech Falls," p. A13.

54. Robert White, "Christmas Gets the 'Politically Correct' Treatment," *Guelph Mercury*, December 14, 2002, p. C7.

55. Statistics Canada, *Religions in Canada*, p. 6.

56. Ibid., pp. 6-7.

57. Buddenbaum, "Mainline Protestants," p. 52.

58. Ibid.

59. Bob Harvey, "A Church Leader's View of Jesus' Life," *Hamilton Spectator*, November 27, 1997, p. A15.

60. Statistics Canada, *Religions in Canada*, p. 6. However, it should be noted that in Canada, there are two major Lutheran denominations. The Lutheran Church—Canada is conservative in doctrine and the smaller of

the two with about 325 churches under its banner. The Evangelical Lutheran Church, despite the Evangelical in its title, is more liberal in doctrine and has about 624 churches under its banner. Statistics Canada combines the figures for both these denominations. As such, it is impossible to know for sure if the mainline Lutheran denomination, the Evangelical Lutheran Church, has declined more or less than 5%. Given that conservative Protestant churches in general have better membership retention than mainline churches, it is likely the case that if the Lutheran Church—Canada numbers were separated from the Evangelical Lutheran Church numbers, the latter denomination would be shown to have declined more than 5%.

61. Ibid.

62. Stuart Macdonald, "Death of Christian Canada? Do Canadian church statistics support Callum Brown's timing of church decline?" (paper presented at the Congress of the Humanities and Social Sciences, York University, Toronto, Ontario, May 28-30, 2006).

63. Reginald W. Bibby, *Restless Churches: How Canada's churches can contribute to the emerging religious renaissance* (Kelowna, BC: Novalis, 2004), pp.39-40.

64. Bibby, *Boomer Factor*, p.200.

65. Rodney Stark, *The Rise of Christianity* (Princeton, NJ: Princeton University Press, 1996), pp.13-21.

66. Ibid.

67. Ibid.

68. Statistics Canada, *Religions in Canada*, p.1. However, it has been observed that these "religious nones" (as they are often called by sociologists) are proportionately young and as they get older 1 in 3 will come to identify with the religion of their parents. See Bibby, *Boomer Factor*, p.201.

69. Adams, *Fire and Ice*, p.50.

70. Reginald W. Bibby, "Who says God is Dead? Canadians are Going Back to Church in Significant Numbers," *Globe and Mail*, April 17, 2006, p.A15.

71. Ibid.

72. Ibid.

73. Adams, *Fire and Ice*, p.50; Adams, *Sex in the Snow*, pp.30–31, 162–163, 169; Bibby, *Boomer Factor*, p. 205.

74. Lewis A. Coser, *Functions of Social Conflict* (New York, NY: Free Press, 1964), pp. 39–40.

75. Reimer, *Evangelicals*, pp. 100-101.

76. Ibid., p. 232.

77. Ibid., pp. 115; 118–151.

78. Ibid. p. 82.

79. Terrence Murphy, "The English Speaking Colonies to 1854," in *A Concise History of Christianity in Canada*, ed. Terrence Murphy and Roberto Perin (Toronto, ON: Oxford University Press, 1996), p. 342.

80. Ibid.

81. John G. Stackhouse, *Canadian Evangelicalism in the Twentieth Century: An Introduction to Its Character* (Toronto, ON: University of Toronto Press, 1993), p. 196.

82. Reimer, *Evangelicals*, p. 27.

83. Ipsos Reid, *Data Tables*.

84. Reimer, *Evangelicals*, p. 83.

85. Reimer, *Evangelicals*, p. 85. Also see, Reginald W. Bibby, *Restless Gods: The Renaissance of Religion in Canada* (Kelowna, BC: Novalis, 2002), p.67.

86. Adams, *Fire and Ice*, pp. 40, 50; Adams, *Sex in the Snow*, p. 165; Jeffrey K. Hadden, "Paradigms in Conflict: Secularization and the Theory of Religious Economy," University of Virginia, Religious Movements Homepage Project Web site, 2001, http://religiousmovements.lib.virginia.edu/lectures/secular.html. Also see, Murphy, "English Speaking Colonies," pp. 160-164.

87. Hadden, "Paradigms in Conflict."

88. Reimer, *Evangelicals*, pp. 133, 135–6.

89. Adams, *Fire and Ice*, p. 125; Adams, *Sex in the Snow*, p. 183; Reimer, *Evangelicals*, pp. 3, 135.

90. Dennis R. Hoover, "A Religious Right Arrives in Canada." *Religion in the News* 3, no. 2 (2000), paragraph 18, http://www.trincoll.edu/depts/csrpl/RINVol3No2/canada_religious_right.htm

91. Sam Reimer, "A Generic Evangelicalism? Comparing Evangelical Subcultures in Canada and the United States," in *Rethinking church, state, and modernity*, ed. David Lyon and Marguerite Van Die (Toronto, ON: University of Toronto Press, 2000), p. 235. Also see, Reimer, *Evangelicals*, pp. 115, 118–151.

92. Sam Reimer, "A More Irenic Canadian Evangelicalism? Comparing Evangelicals in Canada and the U.S.," in *Revivals, Baptists, and George Rawlyk*, ed. Daniel C. Goodwin (Wolfville, NS: Acadia Divinity College, 2000), p. 159.

93. Reimer, *Evangelicals*, pp. 132–135.

94. Adams, Fire and Ice, p. 125; Adams, Sex in the Snow, p. 171–173.

95. Stackhouse, *Canadian Evangelicalism*, p. 198.

96. Adams, *Fire and Ice,* pp.5, 40; Reimer, *Evangelicals*, p.135.

97. Murphy, "English Speaking Colonies," pp. 137-139; Rawlyk, *Is Jesus,* pp. 10–11.

98. Murphy, "English Speaking Colonies," p. 128; Rawlyk, *Is Jesus,* p. 10.

99. Murphy, "English Speaking Colonies," pp. 137–139; Reimer, *Evangeli-cals,* pp. 25-26.

100. Murphy, "English Speaking Colonies," p. 142.

101. Bruce Clemenger, "How and Why Evangelicals Vote," *Faith Today,* May/June, 2004, p.14; Reimer, *Evangelicals*, pp. 127–128.

102. Adams, *Sex in the Snow,* p.166; McCarthy, "Believe It," p. F3.

103. Maureen Dowd, "Bush is courting the Jesus vote," *Plain Dealer,* December 16, 1999, p. B15.

104. Adams, *Sex in the Snow*, pp. 166–167.

105. McCarthy, "Believe It," p. F3.

106. Ibid.

107. Hoover, "A Religious Right," paragraph 20.

108. Ibid.

109. Jeffrey Simpson, "Leave the Prayer Book at Home, Stockwell," *Globe and Mail*, March 31, 2000, p. A17.

110. Steven Chase, Gloria Galloway, Campbell Clark, "Harper's Lead Takes a Hit; With Tory Leader Straying from Script, Poll Shows Support for his Party Waning," *Globe and Mail*, January 20, 2006, p. A1.

111. Douglas Todd, "A Matter of Faith; Prime Minister Stephen Harper has been Associated with Evangelical Protestantism for Decades, But it is an Aspect of his Political Agenda about which he Seldom Talks Publicly," *Van-couver Sun*, August 18, 2007, p. C1.

112. Mario Canseco, Canadians clearly want religion disconnected from politics, Media Release (Ottawa, ON: Angus Reid Strategies, 2008), p. 1.

113. Reimer, Evangelicals, p. 132.

114. Stackhouse, *Canadian Evangelicalism*, p. 201.

115. Christian Smith, *Christian America? What evangelicals really want* (Berkeley, CA: University of Califoria Press, 2000), pp. 1, 5.

116. Hoover, "A Christian Right," paragraph 5; Reimer, *Evangelicals*, p. 125.

117. Hoover, "A Christian Right," paragraph 5-8. For an in depth look, see David Laycock, *The new right and democracy in Canada: Understanding Reform and the Canadian Alliance* (Toronto, ON: Oxford University Press, 2001).

118. Matthew Coutts, "Study debunks voting myths," *National Post*, September 16, 2008, p. A6.

119. Clemenger, "Evangelicals Vote," p. 14; John G. Stackhouse, "Who's Afraid of Evangelicals?" *Faith Today*, January/February, 2005, p. 29.

120. Dennis R. Hoover, Michael D. Martinez, Sam Reimer, Kenneth D. Wald, "Evangelicalism Meets the Continental Divide: Moral and Economic Conservatism in the United States and Canada," *Political Research Quarterly* 55, no. 2 (2002), p. 355; Reimer, *Evangelicals*, pp. 128, 130.

121. Reimer, *Evangelicals*, p. 96.

122. Ibid., pp. 105, 113.

Chapter 3

EVANGELICALS AND THE NEWS MEDIA: A REVIEW OF PAST RESEARCH

1. Mark Silk, *Unsecular Media: Making News of Religion in America* (Chicago, IL: University of Illinois Press, 1995), pp. 35–36.

2. Silk, *Unsecular Media*, p. 36.

3. S. Robert Lichter, Linda Lichter, and Dan Amundson, *Media Coverage of Religion in America: 1969–1998* (Washington, DC: Center for Media and Public Affairs, 2000), pp. 6–7.

4. Sarah F. Orwig "Substantive and Functional Representations of Religion in Four American Newspapers, 1883–1998" (PhD diss, Boston University, 1999).

5. Orwig, "Representations of Religion," p. 200.

6. Ibid.

7. Ibid.

8. Ibid.

9. Lichter et al, *Coverage of Religion*, p. 1.

10. Ibid., pp. 3–5, 7.

11. Ibid., pp. 9–10.

12. Ibid., pp. 12, 15.

13. Ibid., pp. 11–12.

14. Ibid., pp. 13–15.

15. Ibid., pp. 18–19.

16. Ibid., pp. 28-29.

17. Barry Kosmin, Egon Mayer, and Ariela Keysar, *American Religious Identification Survey* (New York, NY: The Graduate Center of the City University of New York, 2001), pp. 12–13.

18. Lichter et al, *Coverage of Religion*, pp. 28–29.

19. Ibid., p. 27.

20. George A. Rawlyk, *Is Jesus Your Personal Saviour? In Search of Canadian Evangelicalism in the 1990s* (Montreal, PQ: McGill-Queens University Press, 1996), pp. 87–88; Aileen VanGinkel, *Evangelical Beliefs and Practices: A Summary of the 2003 Ipsos Reid Survey Results* (Markham, ON: Evangelical Fellowship of Canada, 2003), pp. 4–6.

21. Tim Graham, *Religion on TV News: More Content, Less context* (Alexandria, VA: Media Research Center, 2004), pp. i, 1.

22. Ibid., pp. 4, 5.

23. Ibid., p. 4.

24. Ibid., p. 7.

25. Ibid., p. 12.

26. Ibid., p. 12.

27. Ibid., p. 7.

28. Tim Graham and Steven Kaminski, *Faith in a Box: The Network News on Religion, 1993* (Alexandria, VA: Media Research Center, 1993), p.16.

29. Ibid., pp. 18-22.

30. Garrett-Medill Center for Religion and the News Media, *Media Coverage of Religion, Spirituality and Values/1999* (Evanston, IL: Garrett Evangelical Theological Seminary, 2000), pp. 3–4, 8.

31. Ibid., pp. 25–26, 27, 28.

32. Ibid., pp. 25–26, 30.

33. Kyle D. Huckins, "Religion, Politics and Journalism: Testing the Theoretical Constructs of Framing," (PhD diss., University of Texas at Austin, 1999); Silk, *Unsecular Media*, p. 135. Also see, Fraser Institute, "Religious Character of Canada Not Represented in TV reports," *On Balance* 9, no. 1 (1999), http://oldfraser.lexi.net/publications/onbalance/1996/9–1/

34. Judith Buddenbaum, "Religious News Coverage in Network News-casts," in *Religious Television: Controversies and Conclusions*, ed. Robert Abelman and Stewart Hoover (Norwood, NJ: Ablex, 1990), p. 255.

35. Ibid., pp. 258–259.

36. Peter A. Kerr and Patrica Moy, "Newspaper Coverage of Fundamentalist Christians, 1980-2000," *Journalism & Mass Media Communication Quarterly* 79, no. 1 (2002), p. 54.

37. Ibid., pp. 58-59, 62.

38. Peter A. Kerr, "The Framing of Fundamentalist Christians: Network Television News, 1980-2000," *Journal of Media & Religion* 2, no. 4 (2003), pp. 228, 230.

39. Ibid., pp. 220–222, 225.

40. Ibid., pp. 220, 231.

41. Huckins, "Religion, Politics, Journlism," pp. 24–32.

42. Ibid., p. 177.

43. Larry Cornies, "Religion Content in Ontario Daily Newspapers, 1986" in *Essays in Journalism*,ed. Heather Hiscox (London, ON: Graduate School of Journalism, University of Western Ontario, 1988). Available online at the Centre for Faith and Media Document Archive Web site, paragraphs 23–26, 28–29, http://www.geocities.com/faithmedia/readings/weblarry.html

44. Cornies, "Religion Content," paragraphs 46, 48, 50.

45. Ibid., paragraph 50.

46. Ibid., paragraph 51–52.

47. Lichter et al, *Coverage of Religion*, pp. 7–8.

48. Cornies, "Religion Content," paragraphs 53, 54.

49. Ian A. G. Barrier, "The Sins of Omission: Reporting Religion," (MJ diss., Carleton University, 1995), pp. 29–30.

50. Ibid., pp. 75–76.

51. Ibid., p. 122.

52. Susan Wilson Murray, *Do Journalists Pay Insufficient Attention to the*

Role of Spirituality and Organized Religion in Canadian Society and Culture? (Vancouver, BC: Project Censored Canada, Simon Fraser University, 1996). Available on the new Centre for Faith and Media Web site, paragraphs 29–32, 49–51, 52 http://faithandmedia.org/articles/show/142

53. Ibid., paragraph 53.

54. Ibid., paragraphs 54–55.

55. Fraser Institute, "Religious Character."

56. Joyce Smith, "Faith and Media: 1999 Newspaper Scan, National Summaries," Centre for Faith and Media Document Archive Web site, December 1999, http://www.geocities.com/jemsmith.geo/99sum4.html

57. Joyce Smith, "Faith and Media: 1999 Newspaper Scan, Religious Summaries," Centre for Faith and Media Document Archive Web site, December 1999, http://www.geocities.com/jemsmith.geo/99rel.html

58. Lichter et al, *Coverage of Religion*, pp. 28–29.

59. Mike Maus, "Believers as Behavers: News Coverage of Evangelicals by the Secular Media," in *American Evangelicals and the Mass Media*, ed. Quentin J. Schulze (Grand Rapids, MI: Zondervan, 1990), p. 225.

60. Stewart M. Hoover, *Religion in the News—Faith and Journalism in American Public Discourse* (Thousand Oaks, CA: Sage, 1998), p. 11.

61. John Dart & Jimmy Allan, *Bridging the Gap: Religion and the News Media* (Nashville, TN: Freedom Forum First Amendment Center, 1993), p. 15.

62. Hoover, *Religion in the News*, pp. 36–37.

63. Johan Galtung and M. Holmboe Ruge, "The Structure of Foreign News. The Presentation of the Congo, Cuba, and Cyprus Crises in Four Norwegian Newspapers," *Journal of Peace Research* 2 (1965), p. 65, 68, 70.

64. Maus, "Believers as Behavers," p. 245.

65. Jacques Bourbeau, "Report on Evangelicals at Parliament Hill," *Global National,* March 27, 2005.

66. Ibid.

67. Michael A. Messner, Margaret C. Duncan & Faye Linda Wachs, "The Gender of Audience Building: Televised Coverage of Women's and Men's NCAA Basketball," *Sociological Inquiry* 66, no. 4 (1996), p. 437.

68. Neil Postman and Steve Powers, *How to Watch TV News* (New York, NY: Penguin, 1992) pp. 23-24, 148, 149.

69. Richard V. Ericson, *Crime and Media* (Aldershot, UK: Brookfield,

1995), p. 20.

70. Barrier, "Sins of Omission," p. 109.

71. Ibid., p. 117.

72. Silk, *Unsecular Media*, p. 141.

73. David H. Weaver, Randal A. Beam, Bonnie, J. Brownlee, Paul S. Voakes, and G. Cleveland Wilhoit, *The American Journalist in the 21st Century: U.S. News People at the Dawn of a New Millenium* (Mahwah, NJ: Lawrence Erlbaum Associates, 2007), p. 17.

74. Ibid., p. 22

75. Ibid., p. 16.

76. Ibid., pp. 14, 15

77. Ibid., p. 15.

78. Annenberg Public Policy Center, *Public and Press Differ on Partisan Bias, Accuracy and Press Freedom* (Philadelphia, PA: University of Pennsylvania, 2005), p. 1.

79. Andrew Kohut, *How Journalists See Journalists: 2004* (Washington, DC: Pew Research Centre for the People and the Press, 2004), pp. 24–27.

80. S. Robert Lichter and Stanley Rothman, "Media and Business Elites." *Public Opinion* 4, October/November (1981), pp. 42–43.

81. S. Robert Lichter, Stanley Rothman and Linda Lichter, *The Media Elite: America's New Powerbrokers* (Bethesda, MD: Adler and Adler, 1986), pp. 29, 31, 32–33.

82. Ibid., p. 22.

83. Ibid.

84. Stanley Rothman and Amy Black, "Media and Business Elites: Still in Conflict?" *Public Interest* 143 (2001), pp. 72–73.

85. Ibid., p. 82.

86. Ibid., p. 83.

87. Ibid., p. 76.

88. Stanley Rothman as cited in Lichter et al, *Coverage of Religion*, p. 26.

89. Kohut, *Journalists See Journalists*, pp. 4, 16, 32. Also see, William Proctor, *The Gospel According to the New York Times: How the World's Most Powerful News Organization Shapes Your Mind and Values* (New York, NY: Broadman & Holman, 2000).

90. Marsha Barber and Ann Rauhala, "The Canadian News Directors

Study: Demographic and Political Leanings of Television Decision-Makers," *Canadian Journal of Communication* 30 (2005), p. 285.

91. Ibid., p. 287.

92. Ibid., p. 289.

93. Ibid., pp. 288–289.

94. Ibid., p. 289.

95. David Pritchard and Florian Sauvageau, "The Journalists and Journalisms of Canada," in *The Global Journalist: News People Around the World*, ed., David. H. Weaver (Cresskill, NJ: Hampton Press, 1996), pp. 383–384.

96. Ibid., p. 383.

97. Lydia Miljan and Barry Cooper, *Hidden Agendas: How Journalists Influence the News* (Vancouver, BC: UBC Press, 2003), pp. 62–63.

98. Ibid., p. 169.

99. See Pritchard and Sauvageau, "Journalists and Journalisms," p. 384.

100. Miljan and Cooper, *Hidden Agendas*, pp. 80, 81, 169.

101. Ibid., pp. 79–80.

102. Ibid., p. 81.

103. Ibid., p. 80.

104. Lydia Miljan, *Survey Data Tables from "Hidden Agendas: How Journalists Influence the News."* This data was obtained by the author from Lydia Miljan at the University of Windsor, May 11, 2004.

105. Miljan, *Survey Data Hidden Agendas*. Also see, Miljan and Cooper, *Hidden Agendas*, pp. 79–80.

106. Miljan and Cooper, *Hidden Agendas*, pp. 69–70.

107. Miljan, *Survey Data Hidden Agendas*.

108. Wesley Pippert, "Worldly Reporters and Born-Again believers: How Each Perceives the Other," in *American Evangelicals and the Mass Media*, ed., Quentin J. Schulze (Grand Rapids, MI: Zondervan, 1990), p. 282.

109. John Schmalzbauer, "Between Professional and Religious Worlds: Catholics and Evangelicals in American Journalism," *Sociology of Religion* 60, no. 4 (1999), p. 367.

110. Ibid.

111. Miljan and Cooper, *Hidden Agendas*, pp. 73, 171.

112. Ibid., p. 74.

113. Ibid., p. 170.

114. Ibid., pp. 74–5, 98–99, 171, 172.

115. Ibid., p. 63.

116. Ibid., pp. 63, 103.

117. Ibid., pp. 155–166.

118. Christoph Clodius, "Does an Institutionalized Left-Liberal Bias in the Culture and Organization of Journalism Generate Imbalance in the News, as Shown by Coverage of the Abortion Issue?" Simon Fraser University's Newswatch Canada Archive Web cite, 1994, http://www.sfu.ca/cmns/research/newswatch/studies/96-leftlibabortion.html

Chapter 4

NEWS AND NEWS FRAMING

1. Jorgen Westerstahl, "Objective News Reporting: General Premises," *Communication Research*, 10, no. 3 (1983), p. 403–405.

2. Michael Schudson, *Discovering the News: A Social History of American Newspapers* (New York, NY: Basic Books, 1978), p. 120, 121–144; Mary Vipond, *The Mass Media in Canada* (Toronto, ON: Lorimer, 1989), p. 14.

3. David T. Mindich, *Just the Facts: How "Objectivity" Came to Define American Journalism* (New York, NY: New York University Press, 1998), p. 115.

4. Ibid., p. 8.

5. David Pritchard and Florian Sauvageau, "The Journalists and Journalisms of Canada," in *The Global Journalist: News People Around the World*, ed., David. H. Weaver (Cresskill, NJ: Hampton Press, 1996), p. 378; Vipond, *Media in Canada*, p.14.

6. Kevin G. Barnhurst & John Nerone, *The Form of News: A History* (New York, NY: Guilford, 2001), pp. 71–72; Mindich, *Just the Facts*, pp. 129–130; Schudson, *Discovering the News*, p. 120.

7. W. Lance Bennett, *News: The Politics of Illusion* (New York, NY: Addison, Wesley, Longman, 2001), pp. 73-74.

8. Peter Berger and Thomas Luckmann, *The Social Construction of Real-*

ity (Garden City, NY: Doubleday, 1966), pp. 1–18, 185–190.

9. Rowland Lorimer and Mike Gasher, *Mass Communication in Canada* (Don Mills, ON: Oxford University Press, 2001), p. 234.

10. Tony Bennett, "Media, 'Reality,' Signification" in *Culture, Society, and the Media*, ed., Tony Bennett, James Curran, Michael Gurevitch, Janet Wollacott (London, UK: Metheun, 1982), p. 303.

11. This idea of objectivity in journalism is revisited in Chapter 10. There, a new model of journalistic practise is discussed.

12 Everett M. Rogers and James W. Dearing, "Agenda-Setting Research: Where has it Been, Where is it Going?" in *Communication Yearbook 11*, ed., J.A. Anderson (Newbury Park, CA: Sage, 1988), p. 556.

13. Bernard C. Cohen, *The Press and Foreign Policy* (Princeton, NJ: Princeton University Press, 1963) p. 13.

14. Maxwell E. McCombs Donald L. Shaw, "The Agenda-setting Function of Mass Media," *Public Opinion Quarterly* 26 (1972), pp. 177–179.

15. Ibid., pp. 179–184.

16. For example, G. Ray Funkhouser, "The Issues of the Sixties: An Exploratory Study in the Dynamics of Public Opinion," *Public Opinion Quarterly* 37 (1973), pp. 62–75; Pamela J. Shoemaker, Wayne Wanta and Dawn Leggett, "Drug Coverage and Public Opinion, 1972-1986." in *Communication Campaigns about Drugs: Government, Media and the Public*, ed., Pamela J. Shoemaker (Hillsdale, N.J.: Lawrence Erlbaum, 1989), pp. 67-80.

17. Shanto Iyengar, Mark Peters, and Donald Kinder, "Experimental Demonstrations of the "Not-So-Minimal" Consequences of Television News Programs," *American Political Science Review* 76 (1982), pp. 848–858.

18. John Bare, "The War on Drugs: A Case Study in Opinion Formation," *The Public Perspective*, November/December (1990), pp. 29–31.

19. For example, Shanto Iyengar and Donald Kinder, *News that Matters: Television and American Opinion* (Chicago, IL: University of Chicago Press, 1987); Wayne Wanta, *The Public and the National Agenda: How People Learn about Important Issues* (Mahwah, NJ: Lawrence Erlbaum, 1997).

20. Julie L. Andsager, "How Interests Groups Attempt to Shape Public Opinion with Competing Frames," *Journalism and Mass Communication Quarterly* 77, no. 3 (2000), pp. 577-592; Julie L. Andsager and Leiott Smiley, "Evaluating the Public Information: Shaping News Coverage of the Silicone Implant Controversy," *Public Relations Review* 24, no. 2 (1998), pp. 183–201.

21. Maxwell McCombs, "News Influence on Our Pictures of the World,"

in *Media Effects: Advances in Theory and Research*, ed. Jennings Bryant & Dolf Zillman (Hillsdale, NJ: Lawrence Erlbaum, 1994), pp. 1-12. Also see, Leon Sigal, *Reporters and Officials* (Lexington, MA: D.C. Health, 1973.)

22. Sigal, *Reporters and Officials*, pp. 120–124.

23. Daniel Berkowitz, "TV News Sources and News Channels: A Study in Agenda-Building," *Journalism Quarterly* 64, no. 3, (1987), pp. 508–513.

24. Stephen Reese and Lucig Danielian, "Intermedia Influence and the Drug Issue: Converging on Cocaine," in *Communication Campaigns about Drugs: Government, Media, and the Public*, ed., Pamela J. Shoemaker (Hillsdale, NJ: Lawrence Erlbaum, 1989) pp. 29–46; Craig. W. Trumbo, "Longitudinal Modeling of Public Issues," *Journalism Monographs* 151 (1995), pp. 1–57.

25. Guido Stempel, "Gatekeeping: The Mix of Topics and the Selection of Stories." *Journalism Quarterly* 62, no. 4 (1985), pp. 791–796.

26. Lydia Miljan and Barry Cooper, *Hidden Agendas: How Journalists Influence the News* (Vancouver, BC: UBC Press, 2003), p. 31; Pritchard and Sauvageau, "Journalists and Journalisms," p. 385.

27. Anne Johnston, "Trends in Political Communication: A Selective Review of Research in the 1980s," in *New Directions in Political Communication: A Resource Book*, ed., David L. Swanson and Dan Nimmo (Newbury Park, CA: Sage, 1990), p. 337.

28. Jim A. Kuypers, *The Art of Rhetorical Criticism* (Boston, MA: Allyn and Bacon, 2005), pp. 189–190.

29. See Walter Lippmann, *Public Opinion* (New York, NY: The Free Press, 1922), pp. 3–4.

30. Erving Goffman, *Frame Analysis* (Boston, MA: Northeastern University Press, 1974), p. 21.

31. Gaye Tuchman, *Making news: A Study in the Construction of Reality* (New York, NY: The Free Press, 1978), p. 1.

32. Todd Gitlin, *The Whole World is Watching: Mass Media in the Making and Unmaking of the New Left* (Berkeley, CA: University of California Press, 1980), p. 7.

33. Maxwell McCombs and George Estrada, "The News Media and the Pictures in Our Head," in *Do the Media Govern? Politicians, Voters, and Reporters in America*, ed., Shanto Iyengar and Richard Reeves (Thousand Oaks, CA: Sage, 1997), p. 239.

34. Robert M. Entman, "Framing: Toward Clarification of a Fractured Paradigm," *Journal of Communication*, 43, no. 4 (1993), p. 52.

35. Kuypers, *Rhetorical Criticism*, p. 189.

36. Gerald Kosicki, "Problems and Opportunities in Agenda-Setting Research: A 20-year Assessment," *Journal of Communication*, 43, no. 2 (1993), p. 113.

37. Nicolaas Van Rijn, "Women Win on Pay Equity: Judge Throws Out Tory Wage Cap on Public Sector Jobs," *Toronto Star*, September 9, 1997, p. A1.

38. James Rusk, "Ontario Loses Pay-Equity Fight: Court Strikes Down Law that Scrapped Hundreds of Millions of Dollars in Raises for Women," *Globe and Mail*, September 9, 1997, p. A1.

39. David Pritchard and Florian Sauvageau acknowledge the ideological orientation of the journalists at these two papers. See Pritchard and Savageau, "Journalists and Journalisms," p. 377.

40. Entman, "Framing: Toward Clarification," p. 52.

41. Ibid., p. 53.

42. John Soloski, "Sources and Channels in Local News," *Journalism Quarterly* 66 (1989), p. 870.

43. Bernard Goldberg, *Bias: A CBS Insider Exposes How the Media Distort the News* (Washington, DC: Regnery, 2001), pp. 70–71.

44. William A. Gamson, *Talking Politics* (New York, NY: Cambridge University Press, 1992), p. 24.

45. Robert M. Entman, *Projections of Power: Framing News, Public Opinion, and U.S. Foreign Policy* (Chicago, IL: University of Chicago Press, 2004), p. 6.

46. I have borrowed this example from Lawrence Wallack, Lori Elizabeth Dorfman, David Jernigan, and Makani Themba. It is found in their book, *Media Advocacy and Public Health: Power for Prevention* (Newbury Park, CA: Sage, 1993), p. 45.

47. Steven Clayman, "Defining Moments: Presidential Debates and the Dynamics of Quotability," *Journal of Communication* 45, no. 3 (1995), p. 124, 126–127.

48. Janet Maybin, "Language, Struggle and Voice: The Bakhtin/Volosinov Writings," in *Discourse Theory and Practice*, ed., Margaret Wetherell, Stephanie Taylor, and Simeon J. Yates (London, UK: Sage, 2001), p. 68–69.

49. Rhonda Gibson and Dolf Zillman, "The Impact of Quotation in News Reports on Issue Perception," *Journalism Quarterly* 70, no. 4 (1993), p. 795.

50. Augie Fleras, *Mass Media Communication in Canada* (Scarborough,

ON: Nelson, 2003), p. 119.

51. Robert M. Entman, "Framing U.S. Coverage of International News: Contrasts in Narratives of the KAL and Iran Air Incidents," *Journal of Communication*, 41, no. 4, (1991), p. 7; Entman, "Framing: Toward Clarification," p. 53.

52. See Iyengar et al, "Experimental Demonstrations."

53. Celeste Condit, *Decoding Abortion rhetoric: Communicating Social Change* (Urbana, IL: University of Illinois Press, 1990), 46–47.

54. Stephen Hiltgarner and Charles L. Bosk, "The Rise and Fall of Social Problems: A Public Arenas Model," *American Journal of Sociology* 94, no. 1 (1988), pp. 65–66.

55. William A. Gamson, David Croteau, William Hoynes, and Theodore Sasson, "Media Images and the Social Construction of Reality," *Annual Review of Sociology* 18 (1992), pp. 381–384.

56. Entman, "Framing: Toward Clarification," p. 54.

57. Dietram Scheufele, 'Framing as a Theory of Media Effects," *Journal of Communication* 49, no. 1 (1999), pp. 114–116.

58. Ibid., pp. 117–118.

59. See Stuart Hall, "Foucault: Power, Knowledge and Discourse," in *Discourse Theory and Practice* ed., Margaret Wetherell, Stephanie Taylor, and Simeon J. Yates (London, UK: Sage, 2001[1997]), esp. pp. 73–74.

60. I am grateful to Jim Kuypers at Dartmouth College for his definition of what constitutes the neutral role of the press. My definition of a neutral frame relies heavily on the ideas he sets out. See Kuypers, *Rhetorical Criticism*, p. 190.

61. Doris A. Graber, *Mass Media and American Politics* (Washington, DC: Congressional Quarterly Press, 1989), p. 288.

62. Tony Burman, "Reporting a Statement Doesn't Prove Bias: Is the Public Broadcaster Anti-American?" *National Post*, June 17, 2005, p. A16.

63. For example, Kevin Carragee, "News and Ideology: An Analysis of Coverage of the West German Green Party by the *New York Times*," *Journalism Monographs*, 1991; Entman, "Framing U.S. Coverage." Also see, Todd Gitlin, *Whole World Watching*; Daniel Hallin, *"The Uncensored War": The Media and Vietnam* (New York, NY: Oxford University Press, 1986).

64. For example, William A. Gamson and Andre Modigliani, Gamson, "The Changing Culture of Affirmative Action," *Research in Political Sociology* 3 (1987), pp. 137–177.

65. Ibid., p. 166.

66. See Lorne Gunter, "Kill Court Challenges Program," *National Post,* September 8, 2006, p. A16; Lorne Gunter, "Fighting Canada's Secularist Tide," *National Post,* September 26, 2005, p. A16.

67. Kevin Carragee, "A Critical Evaluation of Debates Examining the Media Hegemony Thesis," *Western Journal of Communication* 57, no. 3 (1993), p. 333.

68. David Altheide, "Media Hegemony: A Failure of Perspective," *Public Opinion Quarterly* 48 (1984), p. 482-483.

69. Werner J. Severin and James W. Tankard Severin, *Communication Theories: Origins, Methods, and Uses in the Mass Media* (New York: Longman, 2001), p. 282.

70. For example, Amy Binder, "Constructing Racial Rhetoric: Media Depictions of Harm in Heavy Metal Music and Rap Music," *American Sociological Review* 58 (1993), pp. 753-767; Sandra J. Ball-Rokeach and Milton Rokeach, "Contribution to the Future Study of Public Opinion: A Symposium," *Public Opinion Quarterly* 51 (1987), pp. 184–185; Kevin Carragee, "News and Ideology"; William A. Gamson, "Constructing Social Protest," in *Social Movements and Culture: Social Movements, Protest, and Contention, Volume 4,* ed., Hank Johnston and Bert Klandermans (Minneapolis, MN: University of Minnesota Press, 1995), pp. 85–106; Miljan and Cooper, *Hidden Agendas.*

71. Miljan and Cooper, *Hidden Agendas,* pp. 56-58; Silk, *Unsecular Media,* pp. 72, 142–143.

72. Silk, *Unsecular Media,* p. 141.

73. Ibid., p. 142.

74. Gitlin, *Whole World Watching,* p. 792.

75. Gamson, "Constructing Social Protest," p. 102.

76. Hallin, *Uncensored War,* pp. 116–117.

77. Bernadette Barker-Plummer, "News as a Political Resource: Media Strategies and Political Identity in the U.S. Woman's Movement, 1966–1975," *Critical Studies in Mass Communication* 12 (1995), p. 309.

78. Rowland Lorimer and Mike Gasher, *Mass Communication,* p. 236.

79. Daniel Kahneman, Paul Slovic, and Amos Tversky, cited in Oscar H. Gandy, Katharina Kopp, Tanya Hands, Karen Frazer, and David Philips "Race and Risk," *Public Opinion Quarterly* 61, no. 1 (1997), p. 163.

80. Ibid.

81. Barbara McNeil, Steven Parker, Harold Sox, and Amos Tversky, "On

the Elicitation of Preferences for Alternative Therapies," *New England Journal of Medicine*, 301 (1982), pp. 1259–1262.

82. Thomas Nelson, Rosalee Clawson, and Zoe Oxley, "Media Framing of a Civil Liberty Conflict and its Affect on Tolerance," *American Political Science Review* 91, no. 3 (1997), pp. 567–583.

83. Ibid., pp. 570–572.

84. Ibid., p. 567.

85. Ibid., pp. 575–576.

Chapter 5

METHODOLOGY

1. See R. Allan Hedley, "Social Generalizations: Biases and Solutions," *International Journal of Comparative Sociology*, 25, no 3–4 (1984), pp. 159–172.

2. CBC's national news program, *The National*, typically airs at 10pm EST (although, from 1992 to 1995, it had an earlier timeslot and went by the program name *CBC Prime Time News*). CTV's national news program typically airs at 11pm EST. Since 1994, Global's national news program has been assigned airtimes falling between 5:30pm and 6:30pm EST. Although the argument could be made Global's national news program is an evening newscast, for the purposes of this research it was considered "nightly" national news. Also, for clarity, prior to 2001 Global's national newscast was not available in the provinces of Alberta and British Columbia (Carmen Harvey, Global Television News Producer, telephone conversation with author, October 17, 2005).

3. W. Lawrence Neuman, *Social Research Methods* (Toronto, ON: Allyn and Bacon, 2004), pp. 122–125.

4. Etan Viessing, "Canada," *Hollywood Reporter*, March 27, 2001, p. S20. Also see, Statistics Canada, *Television broadcasting, 2004* (Ottawa, ON: Government of Canada, 2005), p. 6.

5. Josephine Mazzuca, "Network and Local TV News Sources Remain Most Popular," *The Gallup Poll* 61, no. 9 (2001).

6. Charlie Gillis, "Pants on Fire: Network News Rathings have CBC and CTV at Each Other's Throats," *Maclean's*, February 13, 2006, p. 38; Bureau of Broadcast Measurement/Nielsen Media Research, *National Program Reports, January 1, 2007–June 17, 2007* (Markham, ON: BBM/Nielsen, 2007).

7. Bureau of Broadcast Measurement, *Programs—Total Canada, September 12, 2005 to May, 26 2006.* (Toronto, ON: Bureau of Broadcast Measurement, 2006).

8. Em Griffin, *A First Look at Communication Theory* (Toronto, ON: McGraw-Hill, 2006), p. 399; Guido Stempel, "Gatekeeping: The Mix of Topics and the Selection of Stories." *Journalism Quarterly* 62, no. 4 (1985), pp. 791–796.

9. Lydia Miljan and Barry Cooper, *Hidden Agendas: How Journalists Influence the News* (Vancouver, BC: UBC Press, 2003), p. 31.

10. For several reasons, a researcher conducting a longitudinal study of Canadian television news stories must use transcripts of the stories and not video dubs. Unlike in the United States, where dubs of news reports are available from the Vanderbilt Video Archive, Canada has no independent body or group that records and stores television newscasts. While the networks themselves archive many of their news reports in video form, some stories— deemed to be of "lesser" interest—are not saved indefinitely on video. Even when a story is saved on video it is difficult to access, as the TV networks do not make their archives open to the public—not even for academic research purposes. Dubs of specific stories can be obtained (if they survive) for a fee of about $50; however, a request for dubs of numerous stories that have aired over an 11-year period would not be approved. Such a request would not be granted because it would prove "too daunting a task for tape library personnel who are already busy with other duties" (Kelly Noseworthy, Global Television Archivist, telephone conversation with the author, April 11, 2005).

11. Statistics Canada, *2001 Census Analysis Series: Religions in Canada* (Ottawa, ON: Government of Canada, 2003) p. 20.

12. Klaus Krippendorff, *Content analysis: An Introduction to its Methodology* (Beverly Hills, CA: Sage, 1980), p. 155.

13. Matthew Lombard, Jennifer Snyder-Duc and Cheryl Bracken, "Content Analysis in Mass Communication: Assessment and Reporting of Intercoder Reliability," *Human Communication Research* 28, no. 4 (2002), pp. 587–604.

14. Abraham Kaplan and Joseph M. Goldsen, *The Conduct of Inquiry* (San Francisco, CA: Chandeler, 1965), p. 83.

15. For example, Garrett-Medill Center for Religion and the News Media,

Media Coverage of Religion, Spirituality and Values/1999 (Evanston, IL: Garrett Evangelical Theological Seminary, 2000); Tim Graham, *Religion on TV News: More Content, Less context* (Alexandria, VA: Media Research Center, 2004); S. Robert Lichter, Linda Lichter, and Dan Amundson, *Media Coverage of Religion in America: 1969–1998* (Washington, DC: Center for Media and Public Affairs, 2000); Sarah F. Orwig "Substantive and Functional Representations of Religion in Four American Newspapers, 1883-1998" (PhD diss, Boston University, 1999).

16. For example, Lichter et al, *Coverage of Religion*. Also see, Larry Cornies, "Religion Content in Ontario Daily Newspapers, 1986" in *Essays in Journalism*, ed. Heather Hiscox (London, ON: Graduate School of Journalism, University of Western Ontario, 1988). Available online at the Centre for Faith and Media Document Archive Web site, http://www.geocities.com/faithmedia/readings/weblarry.html

17. Thomas Koenig, "Frame Analysis: Theoretical Preliminaries," University of Manchester, Cathie Marsh Centre for Census and Survey Research Web site, 2004, paragraph 2, http://www.ccsr.ac.uk/methods/publications/frameanalysis/measurement.html

18. Koenig, "Frame Analysis," paragraph 7. Also see, Claes H. de Vreese, Peter Jochen and Holli A. Semetko, "Framing Politics at the Launch of the Euro: A Cross-National Comparative Study of Frames in the News," *Political Communication* 18, no. 2 (2001), pp. 107–122; Semetko, Holly A. and Peter M. Valkenburg, "Framing European Politics: A Content Analysis of Press and Television News," *Journal of Communication* 50, no. 2 (2000), pp. 93–109.

19. Koenig, "Frame Analysis,' paragraph 9.

20. See, Peter A. Kerr and Patrica Moy, "Newspaper Coverage of Fundamentalist Christians, 1980-2000," *Journalism & Mass Media Communication Quarterly* 79, no. 1 (2002), p. 58.; Peter A. Kerr, "The Framing of Fundamentalist Christians: Network Television News, 1980-2000," *Journal of Media and Religion* 2, no. 4 (2003), pp. 215–218.

21. James W. Tankard, "The Empirical Approach to the Study of Media Framing," in *Framing Public Life*, ed., Stephen D. Reese, Oscar H. Gandy and August E. Grant (Mahwah, NJ: Lawrence Erlbaum Associates, 2001), p. 101.

22. In relation to historical analysis, such works as these were consulted:

Brian Clarke, "English Speaking Canada from 1854." in *A Concise History of Christianity in Canada*, ed. Terrence Murphy and Roberto Perin (Toronto, ON: Oxford University Press, 1996), pp. 261–359; Terrence Murphy, "The English Speaking Colonies to 1854," in *A Concise History of Christianity in*

Canada, ed. Terrence Murphy and Roberto Perin (Toronto, ON: Oxford University Press, 1996), pp. 108–189; Mark M. Noll, *A History of Christianity in the United States and Canada* (Grand Rapids, MI: Eerdmans, 1992); John G. Stackhouse, "Bearing Witness: Christian Groups Engage Canadian Politics since the 1960s," in *Rethinking Church, State, and Modernity,* ed., David Lyon and Marguerite Van Die (Toronto, ON: University of Toronto Press, 2000), pp. 113–130; John G. Stackhouse, *Canadian Evangelicalism in the Twentieth Century: An Introduction to Its Character* (Toronto, ON: University of Toronto Press, 1993).

In relation to similar academic exploration done in the U.S., the studies highlighted in Chapter 3 provide a representative sample of the types of documents consulted. In relation to sociological research examined, the studies highlighted in Chapter 2 provide a representative sample of the types of documents consulted. In relation to interviews with prominent Canadian evangelicals, the following persons were consulted early-on via telephone, email, or in person: Tristan Emmanuel (telephone conversation with author, May 12, 2004); Janet Epp-Buckingham (e-mail to author, March 13, 2003); Ron Mainse (e-mail to author, October 12, 2004); Aileen VanGinkel, (personal interview with author, March 12, 2004).

23. For example, Murphy, "Canada to 1854," pp. 125, 132; Dennis R. Hoover, "A Religious Right Arrives in Canada." *Religion in the News* 3, no. 2 (2000), paragraph 18, http://www.trincoll.edu/depts/csrpl/RINVol3No2/canada_religious_right.htm.

24. George Gray and Neil Guppy, *Successful Surveys: Research Methods and Practice* (Scarborough, ON: Nelson, 2003), pp. 91–92.

25. See Sara Kiesler and Lee Sproull, "Response Effects in the Electronic Survey," *Public Opinion Quarterly* 50 (1986), pp. 402–413; S.D. Loke and B.O. Gilbert, "Method of Psychological Assessment, Self Disclosure, and Experiential Differences: A Study of Computer, Questionnaire and Interview Assessment Formats." *Journal of Social Behavior and Personality* 10 (1995), pp. 255–263.

26. Andrew C. Montgomery and Kathleen S. Crittenden, "Improving Coding Reliability for Open-Ended Questions," *Public Opinion Quarterly* 41, no. 2 (1977), pp. 238–239.

27. Gray and Guppy, *Successful Surveys,* p. 151.

28. Kim Sheehan, "E-mail Survey Response Rates: A Review," *Journal of Computer-Mediated Communication,* 6, no. 2 (2001), http://jcmc.indiana.edu/vol6/issue2/sheehan.html

29. Thomas J. Johnson, "Have New Media Editors Abandoned the Old Media Ideals? The Journalistic Values of Online Newspaper Editors," *New Jersey Journal of Communication*, 11, no. 2 (2003), p. 118.

30. Gray & Guppy, *Successful Surveys*, p. 168.

31. Anne Marie Gringras and Jean-Pierre Carrier, "Public Opinion: Construction and Persuasion," *Canadian Journal of Communication,* 21, no. 4 (1996), http://www.cjc-online.ca/viewarticle.php?id=382&layout=html

32. Yvonna S. Lincoln and Egon G. Guba, *Naturalistic Inquiry* (Newbury Park, CA: Sage, 1985), pp. 347–351.

Chapter 6

NEWS REPORTS ABOUT EVANGELICALS: THE GOOD, THE BAD, AND THE NEUTRAL

1. A t-test determined that by conventional criteria the difference between the means of the CBC and Global was extremely statistically significant (t = 3.94, d.f.=126, p=0.0001). A second t-test determined the difference between the means of CBC and CTV was also statistically significance (t=2.70, d.f.=188, p=0.0075). A third t-test determined the difference between the means for CTV and Global was not statistically significant (t=0.97, d.f.=162, p=0.214)—this stands to reason as both the CTV and Global ratings were in balanced or neutral territory.

2. Paul Hunter, "The Fundamental Day," *CBC's The National Magazine,* November 14, 2000.

3. Ibid.

4. Ibid.

5. Neil Macdonald, "Report on Evangelical Christians in the Holy Land," *CBC's The National*, December 23, 1999.

6. Ibid.

7. Ibid.

8. Ibid.

9. Craig Oliver, "Report on Election Campaign 2000," *CTV National*

News, November 15, 2000.

10. David Gray, "Report on the Upcoming Launch of the Miracle Channel," *CBC Prime Time News,* April 4, 1995. In this citation *CBC's The National* has been replaced by *CBC Prime Time News.* From 1992 until 1995, CBC experimented with an earlier timeslot, different format and different title for its nightly national news program.

11. Mark Sikstrom, "Report on the Launch of the Miracle Channel," *CTV National News,* January 14, 1996.

12. Ibid.

13. Ibid.

Chapter 7

HOW JOURNALISTS FEEL ABOUT EVANGELICALS AND ITS AFFECT ON COVERAGE

1. In addition to the prevalence of the intolerant, criminally-minded, and un-Canadian frames, it should not be overlooked that in terms of overall totals, Canadian national television journalists more often framed evangelicals negatively than positively or neutrally. In very general terms, this phenomenon gives support to the "feelings shape framing" thesis. It is true that the difference between the number of negative frames and the combined neutral or positive frames was small enough (that is, 128 negative frames versus 113 neutral or positive) to not skew the overall rating of coverage from balanced to negative. However, it remains that in raw numbers alone, negative frames were more often employed by journalists.

CHAPTER 8

INTERPRETATION AND IMPLICATIONS OF THE FINDINGS

1. Alan Rubin, Elizabeth Perse and Donald Taylor, "A Methodological Examination of Cultivation," *Communication Research* 15, April (1988), p. 119.

2. Maxwell McCombs and Salma Ghanem, "The Convergence of Agenda Setting and Framing," in *Framing Public Life: Perspectives on Media and Our Understanding of the Social World*, ed., Stephen D. Reese, Oscar H. Gandy Jr., August E. Grant Jr. (Mahwah, NJ: Lawrence Erlbaum Associates, 2001), pp. 83-94; Jack M. McLeod, Katie Daily, William P. Eveland, Zhongshi Guo, Katy Culver, David Kurpius, Patricia Moy, Edward Horowitz, and Mengbai Zhong, "The Synthetic Crisis: Media Influences on Perceptions of Crime," (paper presented at the Association for Education in Journalism and Mass Communication convention, Washington, D.C, August 1995).

3. Wayne Wanta, Guy Golan, and Cheolhan Lee, "Agenda Setting and International News: Media Influence on Public Perceptions of Foreign Nations," *Journalism and Mass Communication Quarterly* 87, no. 2, (2004), p. 374.

4. Yuki Fujioka, "Television Portrayals and African-American Stereotypes: Examination of Television Effects when Direct Contact is Lacking," *Journalism & Mass Communication Quarterly* 76, no. 1 (1999), p.68.

5. Ibid.; also see, Glen D. Reeder & Michael D. Coovert, "Revising an Impression of Morality," *Social Cognition* 4 (1986), pp. 1–17.

6. Lydia Miljan and Barry Cooper, *Hidden Agendas: How Journalists Influence the News* (Vancouver, BC: UBC Press, 2003), pp. 69–70); Marsha Barber and Ann Rauhala, "The Canadian News Directors Study: Demographic and Political Leanings of Television Decision-Makers," *Canadian Journal of Communication* 30 (2005), pp. 285, 287.

7. Kenneth Burke, *A Rhetoric of Motives* (Englewood Cliffs, NJ: Prentice-Hall, 1950), pp. 19–27.

8. See Lee Jussim & D. Wayne Osgood, "Influence and Similarity Among Friends: An Integrative Model Applied to Incarcerated Adolescents," *Social Psychology Quarterly* 52 (1989), pp. 98–112; Miller McPherson, Lynn Smith-Lovin and James M. Cook, "Birds of a Feather: Homophily in Social Networks," *Annual Review of Sociology* 27 (2001), pp. 415–430.

9. David Pritchard and Florian Sauvageau, "The Journalists and Journalisms of Canada," in *The Global Journalist: News People Around the World*, ed., David. H. Weaver (Cresskill, NJ: Hampton Press, 1996), p. 385.

10. Ibid., p. 375.

11. Fujioka, "African American Stereotypes," pp. 52-75. Also see, Maxwell McCombs, "New Frontiers in Agenda Setting: Agendas of Attributes and Frames," *Mass Communication Review*, 24 (1997), pp. 4–24.

12. Fujioka, "African American Stereotypes," p. 63.

13. Miljan and Cooper, *Hidden Agendas*, pp. 26, 173.

14. For example, Amy Binder, "Constructing Racial Rhetoric: Media Depictions of Harm in Heavy Metal Music and Rap Music," *American Sociological Review* 58 (1993), pp. 753–767; Robert Hodge and Gunther Kress, *Language as Ideology* (New York, NY: Routledge, 1979).

15. Michael Adams, *Fire and Ice: The United States, Canada and the Myth of Converging Values* (Toronto, ON: Penguin, 2003), pp. 52, 125; Michael Adams, *Sex in the Snow—Canadian Social Values at the End of the Millennium* (Toronto, ON: Penguin, 1997), pp. 171–173, 183. Also see, Seymour M. Lipset, *Continental Divide: The Values and Institutions of the United States and Canada* (New York, NY: Routledge, 1990).

16. Miljan and Cooper, *Hidden Agendas*, pp. 56–58, 169.

17. Kevin Carragee, "A Critical Evaluation of Debates Examining the Media Hegemony Thesis," *Western Journal of Communication* 57, no. 3 (1993), p. 333.

18. Sam Reimer, "A Generic Evangelicalism? Comparing Evangelical Subcultures in Canada and the United States," in *Rethinking Church, State, and Modernity*, ed. David Lyon and Marguerite Van Die (Toronto, ON: University of Toronto Press, 2000), p. 235; Sam Reimer, *Evangelicals and the Continental Divide: The Conservative Protestant Subculture in Canada and the United States* (Montreal, PQ: McGill-Queens University Press, 2003), pp. 115; 118–151.

19. Rhonda Gibson and Dolf Zillman, "The Impact of Quotation in News Reports on Issue Perception," *Journalism Quarterly* 70, no. 4 (1993), p. 795; Janet Maybin, "Language, Struggle and Voice: The Bakhtin/Volosinov Writings," in *Discourse Theory and Practice*, ed., Margaret Wetherell, Stephanie Taylor, and Simeon J. Yates (London, UK: Sage, 2001), p. 68–69.

20. Tim Graham, *Religion on TV News: More Content, Less context* (Alexandria, VA: Media Research Center, 2004), p. 12; Tim Graham and Steven Kaminski, *Faith in a Box: The Network News on Religion, 1993* (Alexandria,

VA: Media Research Center, 1993), pp. 18–22.

21. Steven Clayman, "Defining Moments: Presidential Debates and the Dynamics of Quotability," *Journal of Communication* 45, no. 3 (1995), p. 124–127.

22. Bernard Goldberg, *Bias: A CBS insider exposes how the media distort the news* (Washington, DC: Regnery, 2001), pp. 70–71.

23. For example, William A. Gamson, *Talking Politics* (New York, NY: Cambridge University Press, 1992), p. 24; Lawrence Wallack, Lori Elizabeth Dorfman, David Jernigan, and Makani Themba. *Media Advocacy and Public Health: Power for Prevention* (Newbury Park, CA: Sage, 1993), p. 45.

24. Stiller, as cited in an article by Michael McAteer, "'Fundamentalist' Dirty Word, Evangelical Christians say," November 6, 1993, *Toronto Star*, p. K17.

25. Ibid.

26. Brian Stiller, "I, too, remember Peter," Official Brian Stiller Web site, [publication date unknown], paragraph 10, http://www.brianstiller.com/view-page.php?pid=29

27. Stiller, "I, too, remember," paragraph 12.

28. I must admit I am of two-minds when it comes to the use of the term "fundamentalist Christian" by journalists. In one respect, I agree with Brian Stiller that the term should not be used at all as it has become so imbued with negative connotations. As it stands today, most non-evangelicals would find the idea that someone is both a good person *and* a fundamentalist Christian to be an outrageous impossibility. Thus, if journalists wanted to be the most fair/non-judgemental in their reporting they would follow Stiller's request and refrain from using the term altogether. Let us call this interpretation "the spirit of the law." However, in another respect, it must be conceded that by strict definition such a creature as a fundamentalist Christian exists— this is a person who is an ultra-conservative evangelical who demonstrates militancy, strict biblical literalism, and separatism from the culture and even other Christians. Is it wrong for a reporter to describe someone as a funda-mentalist when all indications—that is, visible, outward signs—show that they are? I would say, no. While they might be behaving insensitively, journal-ists employing this term (in light of evidence) would not be committing the greater journalistic sin of inaccuracy. Let us call this interpretation "the letter of the law."

A study that I conducted applied this second interpretation when ana-lyzing reporters' use of the term fundamentalist Christian. I concluded that, overall, journalists who used the term did so in an empirically justi-fied manner. See David M. Haskell, "What's in a name?: The use of the term fundamentalist Christian in Canadian televison news," in *Fundamentalisms and the Media*, ed., Stewart M. Hoovers and Nadia Keneva (New York, NY: Continuum, 2009).

29. Thomas Nelson, Rosalee Clawson, and Zoe Oxley, "Media Framing of a Civil Liberty Conflict and its Affect on Tolerance," *American Political Science Review* 91, no. 3 (1997), p. 568.

30. Bernadette Barker-Plummer, "News as a Political Resource: Media Strategies and Political Identity in the U.S. Woman's Movement, 1966–1975," *Critical Studies in Mass Communication* 12, no. 3 (1995), pp. 313–315, 218, 319–321.

31. Edward Herman and Noam Chomsky, *Manufacturing Consent: The Political Economy of the Mass Media* (New York: Pantheon, 1988), pp. 1–2, 32-34, 302.

32. Miljan and Cooper, *Hidden Agendas*, pp 69–70; Barber and Rauhala, "Canadian News Directors," pp. 285, 287.

33. Miljan and Cooper, *Hidden Agendas*, p. 97.

34. Robert Fulford, "The Lessons I Learned at CBC," *National Post*, September, 23, p. A20.

35. Bill Broadway, Broadway, "The Evangelical-Israeli Connection: Scripture Inspires Many Christians to Support Zionism Politically, Financially," *Washington Post*, March 27, 2004, p.B9.

36.Ibid.

37. Randy Boswell, "Izzy Asper: A True Original," *National Post*, October 8, 2003, p. A8; CBC Online, "Biography of Israel Asper," CBC News Web site, October 8, 2003, http://www.cbc.ca/news/background/asper/

38. DeNeen L. Brown, "Canadian Publisher Raises Hackles: Family is Accused of Trying to Restrict Local Newspapers' Autonomy," *Washington Post*, January 27, 2002, p. A25;

Aaron J. Moore, "Ownership: A Chill in Canada," *Columbia Journalism Review*, March/April, (2002), http://archives.cjr.org/year/02/2/moore.asp

39. Haroon Siddiqui, "CanWest Censorship is Shameful," *Toronto Star*, March 10, 2002, p. OP01.

40. Graham Fraser, "Aspers Say They Won't Dictate News Coverage," *Toronto Star*, July 12, 2002, p. A8.

41. Bill Schiller, "Axing of Column Sparks Controversy," *Toronto Star*,

January 12, 2002, p. A27.

42. Ibid.

43. For example, Graham, "Religion on TV News," pp. 4, 5.

44. Fraser Institute, "Religious Character of Canada Not Represented in TV reports," *On Balance* 9, no. 1 (1999), http://oldfraser.lexi.net/publications/onbalance/1996/9-1/

45. S. Robert Lichter, Linda Lichter, and Dan Amundson, *Media Coverage of Religion in America: 1969–1998* (Washington, DC: Center for Media and Public Affairs, 2000), pp. 9–10; Garrett-Medill Center for Religion and the News Media, *Media Coverage of Religion, Spirituality and Values/1999* (Evanston, IL: Garrett Evangelical Theological Seminary, 2000), p. 28; Graham, "Religion on TV News," p. 7.

46. Graham, "Religion on TV News," pp. 9–10.

47. Larry Cornies, "Religion Content in Ontario Daily Newspapers, 1986" in *Essays in Journalism,* ed. Heather Hiscox (London, ON: Graduate School of Journalism, University of Western Ontario, 1988). Available online at the Centre for Faith and Media Document Archive Web site, paragraph 53, http://www.geocities.com/faithmedia/readings/weblarry.html

48. Gertrude Robinson and Armande Saint-Jean, "Canadian Women Journalists: The "Other Half" of the Equation," in *The Global Journalist: News People Around the World,* ed., David H. Weaver (Cresskill, NJ: Hampton Press, 1998) pp. 360-366.

49. Ibid., pp. 361, 362, 363.

50. See Dietram Scheufele, 'Framing as a Theory of Media Effects," *Journal of Communication* 49, no. 1 (1999), pp. 114–116.

51. See Johan Galtung and M. Holmboe Ruge, "The Structure of Foreign News. The Presentation of the Congo, Cuba, and Cyprus Crises in Four Norwegian Newspapers," *Journal of Peace Research* 2 (1965), p. 65, 68, 70.

52. Aileen VanGinkel, *Evangelical Beliefs and Practices: A Summary of the 2003 Ipsos Reid Survey Results* (Markham, ON: Evangelical Fellowship of Canada, 2003), p. 7.

53. Kelley Mark. "Seven: Seven Days with Evangelical Christians," *CBC's The National,* December 19, 2006. Can be viewed online at, http://www.cbc.ca/news/media/seven.html

54. Ian Brown, "Letting Jesus Drive," *Globe and Mail,* February, 26, 2005, p. F1.

Ian Brown, "Supersize Thee," *Globe and Mail,* March 5, 2005, p. F4.

Ian Brown, "Colorado Springs Eternal," *Globe and Mail*, March 19, 2005, p. F1.

Ian Brown, "This Little Light of Mine," *Globe and Mail*, March 26, 2005, p. F6.

55. Gail Reid, Evangelical Fellowship of Canada Communications Director. E-mail message to author, May 10, 2006.

CHAPTER 9

AFFIXING EVANGELICALS' NEGATIVE IMAGE

1. Reginald W. Bibby, *The Boomer Factor* (Toronto, ON: Bastian, 2006), p. 24.

2. David M. Haskell, "News Media Influence on Nonevangelicals' Perceptions of Evangelical Christians: A Case Study," *Journal of Media and Religion* 6, no. 3 (2007), pp. 153–79.

3. Muzafer Sherif and Carolyn W. Sherif, "Attitude as the Individual's Own Categories: The Social Judgement-Involvement Approach to Attitude and Attitude Change," in *Attitude, Ego-Involvement, and Change*, ed., Carolyn W. Sherif and Muzafer Sherif (New York, NY: John Wiley & Sons, 1967) pp. 129–133, 134–135.

4. The first quote is found in Holly Doan's, "Report featuring American Evangelicals and the Issue of Homosexuality," *CTV National News*, June 25, 1999; the second quote is from David Halton's, "Report featuring American Evangelicals and the Issue of Homosexuality," *CBC's The National*, October 16, 1998; the third quote is found in Natalie Van den Bosche's, "Report featuring American Evangelicals and the Issue of Homosexuality," *CTV National News*, August 1, 1999.

5. Mark Schneider, "Report featuring Canadian Evangelicals and the Issue of Homosexuality," *CTV National News*, April 12, 2002.

Chapter 10

FIXING EVANGELICALS' NEGATIVE IMAGE

1. Lydia Miljan and Barry Cooper, *Hidden Agendas: How Journalists Influence the News* (Vancouver, BC: UBC Press, 2003), p.60.

2. Sandie Rinaldo, "Introducing the New CTV Horizon Series of Reports," *CTV National News*, June 14, 2001.

3. Leslie Hughs, "Faith in the Newsroom: Can a Reporter be a Person of Faith and Still be a Good Reporter?" (paper presented at the Faith and Media Conference, Ottawa, Ontario, Canada, June 7–9, 1998).

4. Patrick N. Allitt, "Lecture 20: The Civil Rights movement" (lecture in the series *American Religious History* produced by The Teaching Company, Chantilly, VA, 2001).

5. Marvin Olasky, "Telling the Truth: How to Revitalize Christian Journalism; Chapter One, 'Biblical Ojectivity'," *World Magazine* Web site, 1996, paragraphs 23, 26, http://www.worldmag.com/world/olasky/truthc1.html

6. Ibid.

7. Ibid., paragraph 28.

8. Ibid., paragraph 29.

9. Stephen Hiltgarner and Charles L. Bosk, "The Rise and Fall of Social Problems: A Public Arenas Model," *American Journal of Sociology* 94, no. 1 (1988), pp. 65–66.

10. Regina v. Big M Drug Mart Ltd., [1985] CanLII 69 (Supreme Court of Canada).

11. Richard E. Petty and John T. Cacioppo, Communication and Persuasion: The Central and Peripheral Routes to Attitude Change (New York, NY: Springer-Verlag, 1986), pp. 33–34, 142–146.

12. Ibid., pp. 20–21.

13. Ibid., pp. 31–32, 190–195.

14. A. Chris Downs & Phillip M. Lyons, "Natural Observations of the Links Between Attractiveness and Initial Legal Judgements," *Personality and Social Psychology Bulletin* 17, October (1991), pp. 542–243, 544–546.

15. Sandie Taylor and Megan Butcher, "Extra-legal Defendant Characteristics and Mock Juror Ethnicity Re-Examined" (paper presented at the British

Psychological Society's Annual Conference at University of York, UK, March 21–23, 2007).

16. See Linda A. Jackson; John E. Hunter; Carole N. Hodge, "Physical Attractiveness and Intellectual Competence. A Meta-Analytic Review," *Social Psychology Quarterly*, 58, no. 2 (1995), esp. pp. 116–118.

17. Petty and Cacioppo, *Communication and Persuasion*, pp. 142–143, 158–159.

18. Ibid., pp. 141–165.

19. Ibid., pp. 87–90.

20. Ibid., pp. 111–115.

21. Ibid., pp. 115, 214–215.

22. Ibid., pp. 168–169.

23. See Leon Festinger, *A Theory of Cognitive Dissonance* (Stanford, CA: Stanford University Press, 1957). pp. 3, 13.

24. Petty and Cacioppo, *Communication and Persuasion*, pp. 124, 126–129.

25. Muzafer Sherif and Carolyn W. Sherif, "Attitude as the Individual's Own Categories: The Social Judgement-Involvement Approach to Attitude and Attitude Change," in *Attitude, Ego-Involvement, and Change*, ed., Carolyn W. Sherif and Muzafer Sherif (New York, NY: John Wiley & Sons, 1967) pp. 115–120.

26. Environics, *Canadians' Attitudes Towards Abortion Issues* (Toronto, ON: Environics, 2005).

27. To a large extent this was how evangelical spokespersons approached the media during the national debate over changing the definition of marriage. As noted in the Afterword of this book, despite their efforts to "play by the rules" evangelical arguments were still misrepresented in the popular press. Regardless, I am still convinced that evangelicals have no better option than to use "faith-neutral words to outline compelling arguments replete with examples and objective evidence" when lobbying for public policy.

Afterword

IMPORTANT FINDINGS ABOUT NEWSPAPERS

1. Lydia Miljan and Barry Cooper, *Hidden Agendas: How Journalists Influence the News* (Vancouver, BC: UBC Press, 2003), pp. 56–58, 173.

2. David M. Haskell, "'What we have here is a failure to communicate . . . : Evangelicals, the News Media, and Canada's Same-Sex Marriage Debate" (paper presented at the Sacred and Secular in a Global Canada Conference, University of Western Ontario's Huron College, May 9–12, 2008).

Please note: In addition to newspaper coverage, CTV and Global Television's national television news coverage of the same-sex marriage debate was also examined as part of the "What we have here is a failure to communicate . . ." study. It was shown that reports from national television news followed the same patterns as reports found in the national newspapers. Because the focus of discussion here in the Afterword is newspaper coverage, I felt it was best to isolate and present the results specifically related to print news. As noted in the Introduction, the full article will be available as a chapter in the forthcoming volume *Religion Unbound* edited by Dr. William Acres.

3. According to its literature, the Canada Family Action Coalition (CFAC) is a coalition comprised of different conservative religious groups. However, its public face is evangelical. Its spokespersons are Canada Christian College President, Charles McVety, and Victory Bible College Professor Brian Rushfeldt. Confusingly, both men were also co-founders of a similar organization, Defend Marriage Canada (DMC), a secondary lobbying body that grew out of the Canada Family Action Coalition (CFAC). The CFAC and DMC simultaneously lobbied against changes to the traditional definition of marriage from the summer of 2003 to late 2006. I noted in my study, news reports were inconsistent when describing which organization these men represented— sometimes it was DMC at other times is was the CFAC; sometimes these men were generically described as representing a coalition of traditional Christian believers. Nonetheless, it was always clear in the reports that McVety and Rushfeldt represented a large constituency of evangelical Christians and were speaking from a conservative Protestant perspective.

4. Lorna Dueck, "The Making of a Moral Majority," *Globe and Mail*, November 30, 2005, p. A25.

5. The internet archive retrieval system is commonly referred to as the

"Wayback Machine." It can be found at: http://www.archive.org/index.php

6. A dozen documents were gathered from the Evangelical Fellowship of Canada, 19 from Focus on the family Canada, and over 30 from the Canada Family Action Coalition (Defend Marriage Canada documents were also included in this final group).

7. Obviously, staff at these evangelical organizations did not have to read Chapter 10 of this book to figure out non-religious audiences are best addressed using non-religious arguments.

8. Evangelical Fellowship of Canada, *Marriage Talking Points / Talking Points on Marriage for Pastors* (Markham, ON: Evangelical Fellowship of Canada, 2006), p. 1.

9. Glen T. Stanton, *Defending marriage: Debate-tested Sound Bites* (Vancouver, BC: Focus on the Family Canada, 2005), p. 1. Though originally created for use in the U.S., the FOTF *Debate-Tested Sound Bites* document was used in Canada as well. While FOTF Canada created many of its own documents, some of the persuasive literature the organization used came from its American parent.

10. Defend Marriage Canada/Canada Family Action Coalition, "*Sample Marriage Letter to Member of Parliament (Talking Points for Members of Defend Marriage Coalition),*" Canada Family Action Coalition Web site, October 2006, http://www.familyaction.org/defendmarriage/contactmp.htm

11. Evangelical Fellowship of Canada, *Marriage Talking Points*, p. 2.

12. Defend Marriage Canada/Canada Family Action Coalition, "Targeting those opposed to homosexual marriage," Canada Family Action Coalition Web site, July 20, 2005, http://www.familyaction.org/Articles/marriage.htm/issues/family/marriage/issues/family/marriage/PDFs/PDFs/PDFs/issues/family/marriage/evicted.htm; James Dobson, "Arguments against same-sex marriage: Excerpts from Marriage Under Fire," Focus on the Family Canada Web page collection of the Internet Archive Web site, 2004, http://web.archive.org/web/20051213204148/www.fotf.ca/familyfacts/

13. Miljan and Cooper, Hidden Agendas, pp. 81; 155-166.

14. On raw numbers alone it appears evangelicals received a fairer shake in the *National Post* than they did in the *Globe and Mail*. It must be noted that as a CanWest media outlet the *Post*, like Global TV, is owned an operated by the Asper family. Earlier in this book suggestions were given as to why the media outlets owned by the Asper family tend to be more "evangelical-friendly" than other news bureaus (see the section *Do Some Networks Like Evangelicals More than Others?* Chapter 9).

15. Michael Valpy, "Christianity Hangs in Balance, Leading Theologian Warns; Churches Fear Being Marginalized by State," *Globe and Mail*, October 4, 2004, p. A4.

16. Carly Weeks. "Church Leaders Urge Tories to Reinstate Traditional Marriage," *National Post*, November 10, 2006, p. A6.

17. Jack Aubry, "Bush Advisor Jeered Over Same-Sex Issue," *National Post*, August 9, 2004, p. A6.

18. Ibid.

19. Elizabeth Nickson, "Christians Will Win the Culture War," *National Post*, March 5, 2004, p. A16.

20. Bruce Clemenger, EFC President, telephone conversation and e-mail exchange with author, May 6, 2008; Janet Epp-Buckingham, personal meeting with author [Huron College, London, Ontario], May 12, 2008. 21. Miljan and Cooper, *Hidden Agendas*, pp. 81, 155–166.

22. Kevin Newman, "Report on Same-Sex Marriage Legislation," *Global National*, February 1, 2005; Elizabeth Thompson and Anne Dawson, "Church Told to Butt Out: Same-sex Debate No Place for Religion: Pettigrew," *National Post*: January 28, 2005, p. A1.

For each script that you analyze, you must complete a code sheet. Each code sheet has numerous sections or categories that must be filled in. This guidebook is to be used in conjunction with your code sheet; it explains each of the coding categories.

Story Number: Each news script is assigned a number in its top right hand corner. The numbers are sequential.

Coder Initials: the initials of the first and last name are to be printed.

Date Report Aired: the date is to be found near the lead of each story.

Network: the network affiliation is found near the top of the first page of the news script.

FORMAT OF NEWS REPORT

For the purpose of this study, news reports will be coded according to one of four general formats. They are:

1. Anchor Read—these are shorter stories that are read live by the anchor during the newscast to the viewing audience (only the anchor lines are seen and heard).

2. Anchor Read to a Clip—similar to the Anchor read in that the story is read live by the anchor. However, at one point in the story (it can be right at the beginning, in the middle, or at the end) the anchor's lines are interrupted/replaced by pre-recorded interview clip from someone else. The 'clip' is generally a 10 to 15 second quote from someone who was interviewed in the field/on the scene.

3. Reporter's Pre-recorded Package—these are reporter-based stories introduced by the anchor (when he/she reads the lead to the story) but 'told' by the reporter. They are generally

the longest type of news story. They feature narration by the reporter and clips (quotes) from several different sources. A reporter's pre-recorded report is easily identified because the anchor always names the reporter who is "bringing us the story."

4. Live Interview/Live Commentary—the live interview is easily identifiable because it appears in question and answer format. Generally, it involves the anchor asking questions of an in-studio guest or of someone linked to the news station electronically. The live commentary involves a single speaker, most often the anchor or someone else from the network, delivering a prepared speech on an issue.

TOTAL WORD COUNT

At a TV station news reports that are broadcast are measured according to running time—that is, how long a single news report is on the air from start to finish. However, because this study is examine scripts of TV news reports the number of words in each news script will be measured. The total word count is generally tabulated by the network and is placed near the top of each script. Where the total word count is not recorded by the network on the script by the network the coder is to manually count the number of words in the script.

MAIN FOCUS/TOPIC OF THE NEWS REPORT

Television news reports generally have a predominant focus. In simple terms, the main focus or topic of a news piece details who was involved and what they were doing. For this coding category a list of topics is provided for you. After reading the news story select the most applicable topic from the list. What follows are more detailed explanations of the kinds of stories that fit with each of the summaries on the list.

Evangelicals involved in religious observance/theological discussion: Use if the focus is purely upon religious practice, belief, or doctrine. Specifically, stories may about special Church services (including Christmas concerts and the like), sermons or seminars by Church leaders, lectures given by key note speakers at the church, polls and surveys of religious belief and practices. These stories involve evangelicals talking amongst themselves.

Evangelicals involved in internal church business/church governance: Stories will focus on non-theological discussions and decisions made by a church or denomination. New building construction, new hymn books adopted, hiring of a new minister, or two churches or denominations amalgamating are all possible topics.

Evangelicals involved in charity work/volunteer work/mission work: Stories will focus on helping others locally or abroad to live a better material life.

Evangelicals involved in proselytizing/ "witnessing": Stories will focus on evangelicals trying to influence the religious lives/religious beliefs of people locally and abroad. Stories may be about large concerts, crusades, programs or other events that are held with the specific goal of teaching non-Christians/non-evangelicals about Jesus and Christianity. Stories may also be about individual evangelicals talking to one or two people about Jesus and Christianity.

Evangelicals involved in social actions/protest (but not in the courts, not related to education and not with an overtly political focus): These stories may be about marches, petitions, sit-ins, letter writing campaigns or other actions meant to elicit change in society. These stories are about evangelicals out of the church and into the public sphere but the actions, as mentioned, do not involve the courts, education or specific political parties or politicians—other categories better suit stories of that nature.

Evangelicals involved in political action/issues (but not related to education and not enacted through the courts): These stories clearly show evangelicals involved in the political process or political discussion at the local, provincial or federal level. These stories will involve direct references to politics, political process, and politicians. Stories may be about evangelicals trying to influence political parties, politicians, political policy or governmental practices and procedures; or they may be about evangelical political candidates. A story will not be coded as evangelicals involved in politics if it relates to education or court action—there are more specific categories for stories of that nature.

Evangelicals involved in legal actions/issues (but not related to criminal activity and not related to education): These stories focus on evangelicals using the courts to elicit change or to stop change. They may be using the courts to stop or challenge decisions made by government or regulatory bodies, businesses, or community organizations. If the court action is related to educational matters do not code the story as evangelicals involved in courts, go to the education category instead. If the court action is related to an evangelical having committed a crime, go to the crime story category.

Evangelicals involved in educational actions/issues: These stories focus on evangelicals and their specific interactions with public schools both elementary and secondary, private schools both elementary and secondary, and universities and colleges both public and private. Stories may be about evangelicals trying to implement or change curriculum, implement or change school practices, implement or change selection processes involving students or staff.

Evangelicals involved in criminal or immoral actions/issues: These stories focus on criminal or immoral actions that have been committed by evangelicals. Stories may be about evangelicals perpetrating sexual or physical abuse or engaged in sexual or financial impropriety.

The life/exploits/thoughts of a famous/important evangelicals (i.e., TV evangelist or entertainers/big business owners): These stories focus on biographical information about famous evangelicals. ThGloat is to say, the personality, lifestyle and history of the person is highlighted over any overtly Christian message they may be relaying. If an evangelical is famous due to political activity, do not code in this category, go to politics category.

Other (please indicate):

If the story defies all other categories write what you believe the topic is in the space provided.

THEOLOGICAL REFERENCES USED IN THE NEWS REPORT

When theology or statements of religious belief are made they must be coded and the source of the statement—be it an evangelical, non-evangelical, or the reporter—must be identified.

Specifically, if a scripture verse(s) is quoted (or paraphrased) by a source or by a reporter it is counted as a theological reference. A theological reference is also to be counted if the quote of a source or reporter includes one of the following syntactic structures: "I/we/they believe . . ." (in reference to religion); "God/Jesus/Christ says . . ."; "the Bible/scripture says . . .". To capture the nature of the theological reference the sentence or two in which it appears must be transcribed verbatim on the code sheet.

When a section of the news report mentions several different theological points/beliefs in an unbroken sequence it is to be counted as just one theological reference. For a second theological reference to be counted, the new reference must be separated from the first reference by non-theological information.

To determine the religious leanings or affiliation of the source—evangelical or non-evangelical—take note of how they are described in the body of the report. If a source is shown actively supporting evangelical religious beliefs and causes, is called an evangelical (or a similar religious descriptor), and/or is said to belong to an evangelical group circle "evangelical" on the code sheet. Conversely, sources should be coded as non-evangelical if they show no signs of evangelical belief or behaviour, are described in terms unrelated to evangelical faith, and/or are said to belong to a non-evangelical organization (for example academic institutions, businesses, government agencies, community service organizations).

FRAMES USED IN THE NEWS REPORT

This section asks: "how were evangelicals depicted in this news report and what did the journalist in this news story choose to highlight or accentuate about evangelicals?" You have been provided with a list of twenty-four frames presented in 12 pairs as opposites. These frames suggest the most probable ways that the evangelicals in the story could have been depicted. Your task is to determine when any one of these listed frames is used in a news story. When found, you are to measure the negative, positive or neutral quality of the frame. To facilitate measurement, on your code sheet each pair of frames is placed on an ordinal scale. The frame from the pair that expressed the negative quality (e.g., intolerant) is stationed on the left of the scale where it was subdivided into its very negative and somewhat negative manifestations (e.g., very intolerant; somewhat intolerant). Similarly, the frame that expresses the positive quality is stationed on the right side of the scale and subdivided into its somewhat positive and very positive manifestations (e.g. somewhat tolerant; very tolerant). A rating of balanced is positioned at mid-scale.

Each news report may frame evangelicals in several different ways; therefore, you may have to code for many different frames. If no evidence of a frame is found then you should circle "did not mention." If the presence of a frame is detected but it appears equally in its negative and positive manifestations then code that frame as neutral or balanced.

When a frame has been identified and its intensity has been measured and marked on the ordinal scale, you must next supply textual evidence from the news report to support the coding decision that you made. That is to say, you must prove that the frame is present in the text by transcribing the phrase(s) or sentence(s) that lead you to make your coding decision. These phrases or sentences are to be written in the space provided to the right of the ordinal scale on the code sheet.

Throughout this process of analysis, do not conclude that a news report is "guilty" of employing a negative frame simply because it showed an evangelical saying or doing something negative; remember, evangelicals, like all humans, can and do perform ignoble acts and to report an ignoble act *as it happened* does not constitute negative framing. It was only when the text of a report contains manifest signs that the ideas and actions of the evangelicals have been subjected to interpretation according to someone else's biases and worldview that you are to rate a frame as other than balanced.

Below are definitions explaining what each frame entails, use these as a guide:

Intolerant/Tolerant: For evidence of this frame look for evangelicals being portrayed as able to sympathize (or not) with beliefs or values contrary to their own. The frame of "Very intolerant" will be identified if the evangelical is explicitly (with hostility) referred to or portrayed as very closed minded, condemning and/or disrespectful toward others' views. "Somewhat intolerant" will be selected if the close-mindedness or disrespect toward others' is suggested less dramatically perhaps in a matter-of-fact way. "Somewhat tolerant" will be selected if the evangelical is shown or described as resolutely holding one belief or value while neither slighting nor supporting the opposing view. Code "Very tolerant" when the evangelical is being portrayed as holding a differing view, but open-minded/non-condemning and/or respectful toward the opposing viewpoint/person/group. The tolerance scale is not meant to measure the level of *disagreement* with other viewpoints, but the ability or inability to accept such differences in a respectful/rational manner (it measures one's ability to "agree to disagree").

Unintelligent/Intelligent: For evidence of this frame look for evangelicals being portrayed in terms of their intellectual ability or education level. "Very unintelligent" may be explicitly stated or implied by citing low educational achievement or by referencing such terms as "backward", "naïve", "uninformed", or by ridiculing religious beliefs or values as irrational. "Somewhat unintelligent" would be a milder form of the above, or it could be suggested when evangelical beliefs are contrasted against more scientific or liberal beliefs and the former are made out to be less credible than the latter. "Somewhat intelligent" would portray evangelicals as rational, knowledgeable, or credible, whereas "Very intelligent" has the news report directly complimenting their intellectual achievements or capabilities by citing high educational achievement or by referencing terms such as "very bright" or "has a keen mind."

Neglectful/Responsible: For evidence of this frame look for evangelicals being portrayed in terms of their obligations or duties to themselves, their jobs, their families, and society. "Very neglectful" may involve failure to admit a major mistake, failure to perform duties that, if not done, could endanger themselves or others. "Somewhat neglectful" may portray evangelicals shifting blame, being lazy in community affairs, or unwilling to perform tasks necessary for society. "Somewhat responsible" involves portrayal of evangelicals doing their duty, owning up to their positions and the consequences of them, implicitly showing them to be trustworthy. "Very responsible" is when the story explicitly portrays evangelicals as being trustworthy, conscientious, dependable, or mature and performing their required duties with gusto and excellence.

Pushy with social views/Respectful advocating social views: This frame does not involve proselytizing (religious conversion) but does involve trying to change society or social policy. For evidence of this frame look for evangelicals involved in activities (e.g. marches, petitions, protests) with the goal of advancing their own social views and values. (Note: If the evangelicals are *reacting* to the social movements/activities of other groups it may be more accurate to employ the intolerance/tolerance frame.) "Very pushy with social view" would depict or describe evangelicals as militant, 'mobbish' and coercive when trying to elicit social change; they would be portrayed as openly ridiculing the social values of others. "Somewhat pushy with social views" would portray evangelicals as impolite and too forceful when trying to elicit social change: rude but not dangerous. "Somewhat respectful advocating social views" would depict or describe evangelicals as a legitimate minority with the democratic right to have their opinions heard. "Very respectful advocating their social views" would portray evangelicals as a calm and thoughtful minority (good people) with the democratic right to have their opinions heard. Furthermore, the causes/ideals would be depicted as worthwhile and beneficial to society.

Threatening Politically/Reassuring Politically: For evidence of this frame look for evangelicals involved in politics or politicians who are evangelicals. "Very politically threatening" would involve explicit references to evangelicals' political activities as a "bad thing" or "scary"; they would be clearly portrayed as "outsiders" not intended for the political arena. "Somewhat politically threatening" would involve portrayals similar to those above though less explicit; the portrayal would subtly imply that evangelicals did not belong in politics. "Somewhat reassuring politically" would portray evangelicals as a legitimate force, or one among equals, on the Canadian political scene. "Very reassuring politically" would portray evangelicals as having solid political ideas and policies; furthermore, they would be depicted or described as a good choice for elected office.

Criminally-Minded/Law Abiding: For evidence of this frame look for evangelicals involved in courts, criminal activity or legal issues. "Very criminally minded" depicts or describes evangelicals as breaking laws without remorse or knowingly bending laws without remorse. This may be a refusal to go to court or to comply with court orders, or it may involve extreme examples of criminal activity. The evangelicals are not described or depicted as morally justified for their actions. "Somewhat criminally minded" will show evangelicals breaking or bending the law but with remorse. It might also portray evangelicals as rationalizing their behaviour using weak or inadequate reasons. "Somewhat law abiding" portrays evangelicals as following the laws and upholding legal or ethical standards of the land in a fashion no better or worse than the rest of the population. Or, it can depict evangelicals as breaking or bending the law but with good reason. "Very law abiding" shows clear examples of evangelicals adhering to a strict definition of the law and ethics, more so than the average person, and at times to their own detriment.

Superstitious/Spiritual: For evidence of this frame look for evangelicals involved in or talking about the supernatural. Specifically, look for ecstatic or boisterous worship, prayer, or in acts of the miraculous (e.g., spontaneous healings, speaking in tongues, prophecy, or being "slain in the spirit"). "Very superstitious" portrays evangelicals explicitly as "unscientific" or "irrational" or as "being duped" for their beliefs or participation in the miraculous; references will be made that belittle evangelicals' beliefs in supernatural phenomenon. "Somewhat superstitious" portrays evangelicals as having "unproven" beliefs; skepticism will be present in the news report but it will not be malicious; evangelicals are shown as slightly odd but not hurting anyone. "Somewhat spiritual" portrays evangelicals involved in supernatural phenomenon as "interesting" and "enlightened". "Very spiritual" portrays evangelicals involved in the miraculous as possessing something that is unique and precious; they are held up as models that others should follow; they are shown as having some inner power that others might envy.

Insincere/Sincere: For evidence of this frame first look for evangelicals involved in preaching, decorous or controlled worship, proselytizing, charity work or community outreach and then look for implicit and explicit references as to the motivation behind their words and actions. "Very insincere" would portray evangelicals as blatantly hypocritical or deceptive in these activities. It would show them as having ulterior motives or a hidden agenda for the things they do. It would portray them as acting solely for the good of themselves. They might be depicted as "performers" only pretending to believe/live the values or ideals that they are advocating. "Somewhat insincere" would portray evangelicals as overly showy/ostentatious, lacking humility, and possibly a little hypocritical or deceptive. They may be shown as the major beneficiaries of their actions. "Somewhat sincere" portrays evangelicals being true to their word, their values and beliefs but perhaps being slightly self-righteous because of their strong moral stand or good works. Their actions would be shown as meant to benefit others. "Very sincere" portrays evangelicals as being true to their word, their values and beliefs in a humble fashion; they will also be shown as having a resolve to endure hardships rather than give up or compromise their values and beliefs. They are willing to make personal sacrifices in an attempt to benefit others.

Vengeful/Forgiving: Look for news stories in which evangelicals have been wronged or in which they perceive that they have been wronged. This is not a measure of how evangelicals treat groups that are opposed to their views—that is the tolerance measure above. "Very vengeful" will portray evangelicals as outraged and calling for swift and extreme penalties to be applied to the person/group that has wronged them; the evangelicals will refer to the offending group in disparaging terms. "Somewhat vengeful" portrays evangelicals as demanding the offending party be punished. "Somewhat forgiving" portrays evangelicals as compassionate to the offending party but still interested in seeing justice done. "Very forgiving" emphasizes evangelicals wanting to forgive the offending party with no call for retribution.

Un-Canadian/Canadian: Look for direct examples of evangelicals being compared to, or rated against, others in Canadian society. "Very Un-Canadian" would portray evangelicals as dangerously different from the rest of society; terms such as "too American" or "like Americans" or "Un-Canadian" may be explicitly cited. "Somewhat Un-Canadian" would portray evangelicals as different from the rest of society but not so much a danger as an oddity or annoyance. "Somewhat Canadian" would portray evangelicals as a unique group in Canadian society with differences that should be respected. "Very Canadian" would portray evangelicals as a legitimate and important group in Canada whose members make valuable contributions to society.

Deserving of Media and Societal Bias/Undeserving of Media and Societal Bias: Look for stories that specifically mention societal or media bias in favour of or against evangelicals. Stories rated "Very right to critical" will state unequivocally that the negative treatment evangelicals are subjected to in the media/society is brought on entirely through their own actions. Stories gauged as "Somewhat right to be critical" will suggest that the negative treatment evangelicals endure is, most of the time, due to their own behaviours. Stories rated "Somewhat unfair to be critical" will put forth the idea that evangelicals have odd beliefs and values but they should not be subjected to negative treatment because of those beliefs and values. Stories rated "Very unfair to be critical" will strongly put forth the idea that evangelicals' beliefs and values are positive, beneficial, and worthwhile and to treat them negatively for holding those beliefs and values is scandalous.

Outdated Values and Beliefs/Contemporary Values and Beliefs: Look for stories that refer to evangelicals' values and beliefs with regard to their current relevance. Stories that rate "Very outdated values and beliefs" will specifically refer to evangelicals' values and beliefs as old fashioned, irrelevant, no longer of use and should be discarded because they are holding society back. "Somewhat outdated" will suggest that evangelicals' beliefs and values are old fashioned and ridiculous but of little harm to society. "Somewhat contemporary" will imply or suggest that evangelical beliefs and values are valid and beneficial to today's society. "Very contemporary" will explicitly cite specific evangelical beliefs and values and explain why they are valid and beneficial to today's modern society.

Frame Analysis of Canadian National Television News Coverage of Evangelical Christians

Story Number: _____   **Coder Initials:** _____   **Date Report Aired:** _ _ / _ _ / _ _   **Network (circle one):** CBC   CTV   GLOBAL

Format of Report: Anchor Read   Anchor Read to Clip   Reporter's Package   Live   **(circle one)**

Main focus/Topic of the News Report (check only one):

___ Evangelicals involved in religious observance/theological discussion

___ Evangelicals involved in internal church business/church governance (not involving doctrine or theology)

___ Evangelicals involved in charity work/volunteer work/mission work

___ Evangelicals involved in proselytizing/ "witnessing"

___ Evangelicals involved in social actions/protest (but not in the courts, not related to education and not with an overtly political focus)

___ Evangelicals involved in political action/issues (but not related to education and not enacted through the courts)

___ Evangelicals involved in legal actions/issues (but not related to criminal activity and not related to education)

___ Evangelicals involved in educational actions/issues

___ Evangelicals involved in criminal or immoral actions/issues

___ The life/exploits/thoughts of a famous evangelical (e.g., TV evangelist, entertainer or big business owner)

___ Other (please indicate):_____

Theological Reference (as designated by statements like "God/Jesus says…" "Scripture states…" "We/I/They believe…" or specific Bible quotes)

Reference #1 (Please Transcribe)

Source of Reference (circle one): evangelical interviewee   non-evangelical interviewee   journalist

Reference #2 (Please Transcribe)

Source of Reference (circle one): evangelical interviewee   non-evangelical interviewee   journalist

Reference #3 (Please Transcribe)

Source of Reference (circle one): evangelical interviewee   non-evangelical interviewee   journalist

Reference #4 (Please Transcribe)

Source of Reference (circle one): evangelical interviewee   non-evangelical interviewee   journalist
...continue on back if necessary)

Frames Used in the News Report (for EACH dimension listed below circle the answer that best reflects how the news report framed evangelicals)

						Sentence/phrase that suggests the presence of this frame
Very intolerant	Somewhat intolerant	Balanced	Somewhat tolerant	Very tolerant	DID NOT MENTION	
Very unintelligent	Somewhat unintelligent	Balanced	Somewhat intelligent	Very intelligent	DID NOT MENTION	
Very neglectful	Somewhat neglectful	Balanced	Somewhat responsible	Very responsible	DID NOT MENTION	
Very pushy with social views	Somewhat pushy with social views	Balanced	Somewhat respectful advocating social views	Very respectful advocating social views	DID NOT MENTION	
Very threatening politically	Somewhat threatening politically	Balanced	Somewhat reassuring politically	Very reassuring politically	DID NOT MENTION	
Very criminally-minded/immoral	Somewhat criminally-minded/immoral	Balanced	Somewhat law-abiding/moral	Very law-abiding/moral	DID NOT MENTION	
Very superstitious	Somewhat superstitious	Balanced	Somewhat spiritual	Very spiritual	DID NOT MENTION	
Very insincere	Somewhat insincere	Balanced	Somewhat sincere	Very sincere	DID NOT MENTION	
Very vengeful	Somewhat vengeful	Balanced	Somewhat forgiving	Very forgiving	DID NOT MENTION	
Very Un-Canadian	Somewhat Un-Canadian	Balanced	Somewhat Canadian	Very Canadian	DID NOT MENTION	
Very right to criticize evg. for non-mainstream values/beliefs	Somewhat right to criticize evg. for non-mainstream values/beliefs	Balanced	Somewhat unfair to criticize evg. for non-mainstream values/beliefs	Very unfair to criticize evg. for non-mainstream values/beliefs	DID NOT MENTION	
Very outdated values/beliefs	Somewhat outdated values/beliefs	Balanced	Somewhat Contemporary values/beliefs	Very Contemporary values/beliefs	DID NOT MENTION	

CPSIA information can be obtained
at www.ICGtesting.com
Printed in the USA
LVOW08s1539090117
520312LV00003B/438/P